LIBRARIES

CONNECT

COMMUNITIES

PUBLIC LIBRARY FUNDING &
TECHNOLOGY ACCESS STUDY
2006 - 2007

AMERICAN LIBRARY ASSOCIATION
AND
INFORMATION INSTITUTE,
COLLEGE OF INFORMATION,
FLORIDA STATE UNIVERSITY

AMERICAN LIBRARY ASSOCIATION
2007

Copyright © 2007 by the American Library Association. All rights reserved except for those which may be granted by Sections 107 and 108 of the Copyright Revision Act of 1976.

ISBN-10: 0-8389-8436-3
ISBN-13: 978-0-8389-8436-9

Printed in the United States.

Contents

Figures	v
Contributors	vii
Acknowledgments	ix
Executive Brief: The State of Technology and Funding in U.S. Public Libraries in 2007	1
Compiled by: Larra Clark, Denise M. Davis	
The Library Funding Landscape	11
Author: Denise M. Davis	
Challenges for the Future and A Call to Action	21
Authors: John Carlo Bertot, Denise M. Davis, Charles R. McClure	
Additional Resources	27
Compiled by: Larra Clark	
Section 1: Findings from Public Libraries and the Internet 2006-07 survey	28
Authors: John Carlo Bertot, Charles R. McClure, Susan C. Thomas, Kristin M. Barton, Jessica McGilvray, Denise M. Davis	
Introduction	
Methodology	
Selected key findings and implications	
Additional views of the data	
National branch findings	
National system findings	
State summaries	
Section 2: Findings from Chief Officers of State Library Agencies Qualitative Questionnaire	124
Author: Joe Ryan	
Executive summary	
Introduction	
Findings	
Section 3: Findings from Focus Groups and Site Visits	144
Authors: Larra Clark, Peggy Barber, Linda K. Wallace	
Introduction	
Methodology	
Executive summary	
Delaware case study	
Maryland case study	
Nevada case study	
Utah case study	
Appendices	186
A. Public Libraries and the Internet 2006-07 survey	
B. Chief Officers of State Library Agencies' questionnaire	
C. Focus group questions	
D. Focus group follow-up questions	

Contents

Appendices
- E. Site visit questions
- F. Delaware focus group participants and site visit locations
- G. Maryland focus group participants and site visit locations
- H. Nevada focus group participants and site visit locations
- I. Utah focus group participants and site visit locations

Figures

A	Percentage Public Library Expenditures by Type and Metropolitan Status	13
B	Percentage Technology-Related Expenditures by Metropolitan Status and Fiscal Year	14
C-F	Technology-Related Expenditures by Funding Source	15-17
G	Operating Revenue by Source, Fiscal Years 1990-2004	23
GIS-1.	Average Number of Public Access Workstations by State	36
GIS-2.	Wireless Internet Access by State	37
GIS-3.	Public Library Bandwidth by State	37
1	Public Library Outlets	38
2	Public Library Outlets Connected to the Internet	38
3	Connected Public Library Outlets Providing Public Access to the Internet	39
4	Average Number of Hours Open per Outlet	39
5	Public Library Outlets Change in Hours Open	40
6	Public Library Outlets Closed	40
7	Average Number of Public Library Outlets Public Access Internet Workstations	41
8	Average Age of Graphical Public Access Internet Workstations	41
9	Public Library Outlets Public Access Internet Workstations Addition Schedule	42
10	Public Library Outlets Public Access Internet Workstations Replacement Schedule	42
11	Public Library Outlets Public Access Internet Workstations Upgrade Schedule	43
12	Public Library Outlet's Ability to Follow Its Upgrade/Replacement Schedule	43
13	Factors Influencing Addition of Public Access Internet Workstations	44
14	Factors Influencing Replacement of Public Access Internet Workstations	44
15	Sufficiency of Public Access Internet Workstations	45
16	Public Access Wireless Internet Connectivity in Public Library Outlets	45
17	Public Access Wireless Internet Connectivity Using Laptops in Public Library Outlets	46
18	Public Access Wireless Internet Connectivity Outside of Public Library Outlets	46
19	Public Library Outlets Maximum Speed of Public Access Internet Services	47
20	Public Library Outlets Type of Public Access Internet Service	48
21	Public Library Outlets Shared Wireless-Workstation Bandwidth	48
22	Public Library Outlets Public Access Internet Connection Adequacy	49
23	Possibility of Increasing Adequacy of Public Library Outlets Public Access Internet Connection	49
24	Public Access Internet Services Critical to the Role of Public Library Outlets	50
25	Public Library Outlets Information Technology Training for Patrons	51
26	Factors Affecting Public Library Outlets' Ability to Provide Public Access Internet Connection	52
27	Public Library System Public Access Internet Services	53
28	Disaster/Emergency Roles and Services of the Public Library Systems	54
29	E-Government Roles and Services of the Public Library Systems	54
30	Public Library Systems' Disaster/Emergency Plan	55
31	Public Library Systems as the Only Provider of Free Public Internet Access	56
32	Percentage Public Library Systems that Applied for an E-rate Discount	56

33	Percentage Public Library Systems' Receiving E-rate Discount	56
34	Public Library System Reasons for Not Applying for E-rate Discounts	57
35	FY 2006 State Funded Technology Expenditures for the Public Library Systems	58
36	FY 2007 State Funded Technology Expenditures for Public Library Systems	59
37	FY 2006 Public Library System Technology-Related Expenditures	60
38	FY 2007 Public Library System Technology-Related Expenditures	61
39	FY 2006 Public Library System Total Operating Expenditures	61
40	FY 2007 Public Library System Total Operating Expenditures	62
41	FY 2006 Rural Public Library System Total Operating Expenditures	63
42	FY 2007 Rural Public Library System Total Operating Expenditures	63
43	FY 2006 Suburban Public Library System Total Operating Expenditures	63
44	FY 2007 Suburban Public Library System Total Operating Expenditures	64
45	FY 2006 Urban Public Library System Total Operating Expenditures	64
46	FY 2007 Urban Public Library System Total Operating Expenditures	65
47	FY 2006 Low Poverty Public Library System Total Operating Expenditures	65
48	FY 2007 Low Poverty Public Library Systems Total Operating Expenditures	65
49	FY 2006 Medium Poverty Public Library System Total Operating Expenditures	66
50	FY 2007 Medium Poverty Public Library System Total Operating Expenditures	66
51	FY 2006 High Poverty Public Library System Total Operating Expenditures	67
52	FY 2007 High Poverty Public Library System Total Operating Expenditures	67
53	FY 2006 Public Library System Total Technology-Related Operating Expenditures	68
54	FY 2007 Public Library System Total Technology-Related Operating Expenditures	68
55	FY 2006 Rural Public Library Systems Total Technology-Related Operating Expenditures	69
56	FY 2007 Rural Public Library System Total Technology-Related Operating Expenditures	69
57	FY 2006 Suburban Public Library System Total Technology-Related Operating Expenditures	70
58	FY 2007 Suburban Public Library System Total Technology-Related Operating Expenditures	70
59	FY 2006 Urban Public Library System Total Technology-Related Operating Expenditures	71
60	FY 2007 Urban Public Library System Total Technology-Related Operating Expenditures	71
61	FY 2006 Low Poverty Public Library System Total Technology-Related Operating Expenditures	72
62	FY 2007 Low Poverty Public Library System Total Technology-Related Operating Expenditures	72
63	FY 2006 Medium Poverty Public Library System Total Technology-Related Operating Expenditures	73
64	FY 2007 Medium Poverty Public Library System Total Technology-Related Operating Expenditures	73
65	FY 2006 High Poverty Public Library System Total Technology-Related Operating Expenditures	74
66	FY 2007 High Poverty Public Library System Total Technology-Related Operating Expenditures	74
67	Percentage of public libraries with broadband connectivity by state	128
68	How libraries achieve broadband connectivity by state	128
69	Major barriers to public library broadband connectivity by state	129
70	Number of "vulnerably networked public libraries" by state	131
71	Checklist for the identification of "vulnerably networked public libraries"	132
72	Characteristics of "unexpectedly" successfully networked public libraries	139

Report Contributors

Peggy Barber
Peggy Barber is co-founder and partner of Library Communication Strategies, a consulting firm for libraries. She was formerly Associate Executive Director for Communication for the American Library Association (ALA), where she established the ALA Public Information Office, Public Programs Office and the ALA Graphics program, including the widely known "READ" poster series. She has chaired the National Coalition for Literacy and now serves on the Board of Friends of Libraries USA. She served as coordinator for the Orange County Cooperative Library System and as a reference librarian for the Bay Area Reference Center, San Francisco Public Library, before joining ALA. http://www.librarycomm.com/

Kristin M. Barton
Dr. Barton is an Assistant Professor at Dalton State College in Dalton, Georgia. He completed his Ph.D. in mass communication at Florida State in 2007. Dr. Barton's research includes quantitative analyses of media effects and qualitative analyses of popular culture in contemporary film. He has been using the SPSS statistical package since 2000 in conjunction with his research.

John Carlo Bertot
John Carlo Bertot is Professor and Associate Director of the Information Use Management and Policy Institute. His research interests are in the areas of public library use of, and involvement with, the Internet; telecommunications and information policy development with an emphasis on electronic network-based issues; organization and management of electronic network-based information; and development and implementation of electronic network performance measures. He serves as editor of Government Information Quarterly, and co-editor of Library Quarterly. He also serves as chair of the ALA Library Research Round Table (LRRT), chair of the ISO 11620 Library Performance Indicator international standard, and is a member of the Florida Library Association's Legislative Committee.

Larra Clark
Larra Clark is project manager for the ALA Office for Research and Statistics. She joined the office in late January 2007 after working more than six years in the ALA Public Information Office as the manager of media relations. Ms. Clark completed her Master's in Library Science through the distance education program at the University of Illinois at Urbana-Champaign in December 2006. Previously, she worked in nonprofit public affairs, media relations and print journalism in Chicago and Arizona.

Denise M. Davis
Denise M. Davis, director of the ALA Office for Research & Statistics, is overall project coordinator for the *Public Library Funding and Technology Access* study. Ms. Davis has managed multi-year research projects and currently is principal investigator on a two-year study of library networks, cooperatives, and consortia. Several other research initiatives are underway within this office, and additional information on those activities can be found at http://www.ala.org/ala/ors/.

Charles R. McClure
Charles R. McClure is the Francis Eppes Professor of Information Studies and the Director of the Information Institute (a research center) at Florida State University. Prior to his current position, he was a Distinguished Professor at the School of Information Studies, Syracuse University. He has written extensively on topics related to planning and evaluation of library and information services, as well as federal information policies. He also has received funding for a range of grants and research projects from the U.S. Institute of Museum and Library Services, the Bill & Melinda Gates Foundation, the National Science Foundation, and others. www.ii.fsu.edu/~cmcclure/

Jessica McGilvray
Jessica McGilvray is a Graduate Research Associate at the Information Use Management & Policy Institute. She is pursuing a master's degree in Library and Information Studies at Florida State University, and her main area of interest lies in the relationship between government and public libraries. She is co-author of the *E-Government and Public Libraries: Current Status, Meeting Report, Findings, and Next Steps* (Tallahassee, FL: Florida State University, Information Use Management and Policy Institute, 2007).

Joe Ryan
Joe Ryan is President of Ryan Information Management (RIM). RIM is a publisher, consultant and researcher to libraries of all types and all places. Ryan is also Senior Research Associate with the Florida State University School of Information Studies Information Use Management and Policy Institute. Current projects include developing valuing public library and successfully networked public library modules as part of a web-based Evaluation Decision Making System (EDMS). jzryan@earthlink.net

Susan Thomas
Susan Thomas has a Master's in Library Science and has 16 of years of work experience with Florida State University. At the Information Use Management and Policy Institute she has been responsible for development and submission of research proposals, management of Institute contracts and budgets, coordination of research projects, and management of project deadlines, deliverables and invoicing. She has taken a leading role in the planning, preparation and processes of the PL Internet survey mail out, and responding to and tracking of questions via phone and email. She also assists with report compilation and editing.

Linda Wallace
Linda Wallace is co-founder and partner of Library Communication Strategies. She was formerly director of the ALA Public Information Office, where she developed and implemented creative strategies for National Library Week, Library Card Sign-Up Month, Teen Read Week and other public awareness campaigns. Wallace is the author of *Libraries, Mission and Marketing: Writing Mission Statements That Work* published by ALA Editions (2004), and has written and edited many other ALA publications. A journalism graduate of Ohio University (Athens), Wallace worked as a newspaper reporter before becoming community relations coordinator for the Mideastern Michigan Library Cooperative.

Acknowledgments

Large-scale national surveys and site visits such as this involve substantial effort and support from many individuals and groups. While we cannot easily mention each individual or community, we would like to highlight the efforts of those who provided substantial assistance.

The study team wishes to express their gratitude to the Bill & Melinda Gates Foundation and the American Library Association (ALA), whose support and participation have made this study and the previous 2006 study possible. Also, we thank ALA and the Gates Foundation for their assistance in securing a high survey response rate.

The study team would like to recognize the significant efforts of the state librarians, the state data coordinators, and other state library staff members. As with the 2006 study, the amount of time, energy, and support the state library community invested in this study contributed directly to the survey's response rate – we cannot thank them enough for all of their efforts.

We also extend a debt of gratitude to all the public librarians who completed the survey and participated in the focus groups and site visits. Without your interest and participation, we simply would not have any data. The time you take to provide the data in this report offers valuable information for national, state, and local policymakers, library advocates, researchers, practitioners, government and private funding organizations, and others to understand the impact, issues, and needs of libraries providing public access computing. The data also provide public librarians with the opportunity to advocate the importance of their library for the communities that they serve.

We are also in debt to the study's Advisory Committee. These individuals assisted us in a number of key areas, including issue identification, question development, survey pre-testing, survey Web site development, and providing perspectives on study findings. Our thanks to Stacey Aldrich (Omaha Public Library), Nancy Ashmore (Prairie du Chien Memorial Library), Robert Bocher (Department of Public Instruction, Wisconsin State Library), Linda Crowe (Peninsula Library System), Wanda V. Dole (University of Arkansas at Little Rock, CORS representative), John D. "Danny" Hales, Jr. (Suwannee River Regional Library), Christopher Jowaisas (Texas State Library), Sarah Ann Long (North Suburban Library System), Charlie Parker (Tampa Bay Library Consortium), Rivkah K. Sass (Omaha Public Library) and Patricia Wallace (Enoch Pratt Free Library).

The study team thanks Letitia Earvin for her ongoing work on behalf of this study and other ALA Office for Research & Statistics projects; Sara T. Behrman for her skillful and comprehensive edits; Brian Benson for designing the project logo, book cover and other materials for this project; Chris Mefford, Allison Davis and George Eberhart for thoughtful and timely feedback on report drafts; and ALA Publishing staff for their guidance and support throughout the production process.

Finally, we thank all members of the Information Institute staff for their help and dedication throughout this entire process; in particular we would like to recognize Carla B. Wright. We also wish to acknowledge the outstanding technical support and work done by Paragon New Media in Tallahassee, Florida, for developing and maintaining the survey Web site.

Executive Brief
The State of Technology and Funding
in U.S. Public Libraries in 2007

EXECUTIVE SUMMARY

Libraries have always been about the business of connecting communities of people with the information they want and need in order to learn, explore, create and build success. Computers and the Internet have been a growing part of fulfilling this mission over the past dozen years.

Funded by the Bill & Melinda Gates Foundation and the American Library Association (ALA), the accompanying comprehensive *Public Library Funding & Technology Access Study* is part of a sustained effort to provide current information that describes access to computers and the Internet in U.S. public libraries.

The study presents national and state data gathered through three integrated approaches: a national survey that collected information about public library Internet connectivity, use, services, funding and sustainability issues (see page 28); a questionnaire sent to the Chief Officers of State Library Agencies (see page 124); and focus groups and site visits held in four states: Delaware, Maryland, Nevada and Utah (see page 144).

Three significant themes emerged from the study research:

- **Technology is bringing more – not less – public library use**
Providing education resources and services for job seekers are the Internet services most critical to the role of public libraries (see figure 24). Seventy-three percent of libraries report they are the only source of free public access to computers and the Internet in their communities (see Figure 31).

- **Library infrastructure (space, bandwidth and staffing) is being pushed to capacity**
An increased number of visitors to libraries coupled with increasingly complex technology products and services challenge libraries with facilities that were built before the advent of networked services and budgets and staff sizes that have not grown even with the addition of new services (see Figures 13, 14 and Section Three).

- **Libraries need more technology planning and dedicated technology support**
Providing technology access does not represent a one-time investment of funds or staff training. More than a quarter of libraries do not have upgrade or replacement schedules for their computers (see Figure 12), and state libraries identified an inability to plan and budget for IT upgrades, replacement and maintenance as a significant challenge for public libraries with vulnerable technology services.

This report – along with more than a decade of research from the *Public Libraries and the Internet* studies (www.ii.fsu.edu/plinternet) – demonstrates that libraries have moved rapidly into Internet-based services that their communities want and need. Ongoing attention and investments must be made to ensure that these essential services provided by libraries are sustained.

STUDY METHODOLOGY

There are multiple dimensions to consider when looking at public access computing in public libraries. These include: (1) the technology infrastructure (network, desktop, wireless, other) which libraries design and implement; (2) the human infrastructure involved in supporting the technology; (3) the services and resources made available to patrons as a result; and (4) the funding mechanisms used to support public access computing services and infrastructures.

Since the mid-1990s, the ways in which public libraries sustain public access computing services using fiscal and human resources has been of concern to the library and policy community. Complicating this issue of sustainability is the even longer-term concern regarding the status of public library funding in general. Until now, there has been little evidence gathered regarding how libraries are sustaining expenditures related to public access computing. In particular, there is little understanding about the relationship between funding and various levels of services, including how funding impacts innovation, sustainability, maintenance, staffing, and other key variables.

To begin answering these questions, the three-part study methodology used in this comprehensive research effort was implemented. The first was to continue the research initiated by Drs. John Bertot and Charles R. McClure in 1994 *with Public Libraries and the Internet Survey*. This year, a Web-based survey approach was used, and each library also received an invitation mailing with a print survey. The survey collected connectivity and service data at the branch level, and budget and broad service data at the system level. The fall 2006 survey relied upon the most recent (2002) National Center for Education Statistics public library geocoded dataset as a sample frame, which has 8,921 systems comprised of 16,457 outlets (central libraries and branches). To achieve an adequate response to the survey and ensure the ability to generate national and state level data, the study used a "sample with replacement" strategy. Responses totaled 4,027 with an overall response rate of 57.7 percent of libraries sampled.

Concurrent with this quantitative data collection, an opportunistic iterative learning strategy was employed to explore trends, issues and solutions. This was accomplished using two qualitative methods – a *survey of Chief Officers of State Library Agencies* (COSLA) to understand state trends, and *focus groups and site visits* to understand "on-the-ground" trends.

A 12-question survey was sent by e-mail to all COSLA members, focusing on the issues faced by public libraries developing and sustaining networked services. Conducted by Joe Ryan (Ryan Information Management) in December 2006, the questions were designed to align with characteristics identified by McClure and Ryan in their 2005-2006 research around successfully networked public libraries (http://www.ala.org/ala/washoff/contactwo/oitp/2006_plinternet.pdf). Forty-three states responded to the COSLA questionnaire.

Using focus groups and site visits allowed us to drill further into the public access computing services issues facing public libraries. Four states were identified based on three criteria: eligibility to participate in year one of the Bill & Melinda Gates Foundation Opportunity Online grant program; responses to the 2006 and 2007 Internet connectivity survey; and state library recommendations. Questions were asked in three key areas: use of public access computing and related services; technology infrastructure (including staff and funding); and challenges for sustaining these services into the future. These focus groups and site visits took place in Delaware, Maryland, Nevada and Utah between February and April 2007, conducted by Larra Clark (ALA), and Peggy Barber and Linda Wallace (Library Communications Strategies, Inc.).

KEY FINDINGS

Three significant themes emerged from the various research methods:

- Technology has brought more – not less – library use;
- Library infrastructure (space, bandwidth and staffing) is being pushed to capacity; and
- There is a growing need for technology planning and dedicated technology support.

Technology Has Brought More – Not Less – Library Use

While technology is being woven more and more into people's everyday lives, about one-third of Americans still do not own desktop computers[1] or have Internet access at home. At the same time, more people are visiting their local public libraries – 1.3 billion visits in fiscal year 2004,[2] up from 821.6 million a decade earlier (more than 4.6 percent annual growth).

Seventy-three percent of libraries report they are the only source of free public access to computers and the Internet in their communities.

The continuing importance of the physical building is sometimes forgotten when talking about the increase in access to online sources. The public library offers more than just access to the hardware – computers, printers, scanners – it offers trained staff to help library users gain technology skills and navigate the extensive material available online. More than 76 percent of libraries offer some information technology training, which encourages and motivates technology use. The library building also is a community meeting place open to everyone, regardless of income, age or background.

A broad range of services are provided by public libraries through their public computing resources. Providing educational resources across the spectrum of learners leads the list of public Internet services that library staff considers most critical to the role of the public library branch in its local community:

- Provide education resources and databases for K-12 students (67.7 percent);
- Provide services for job seekers (44 percent);
- Provide computer and Internet skills training (29.8 percent);
- Provide education resources and databases for adults/continuing education students (27.5 percent); and
- Provide education resources and databases for students in higher education (21.4 percent).

---

[1] Pew Internet & American Life Project. "A Typology of Information and Communication Technology Users," May 2007. http://www.pewinternet.org/pdfs/PIP_ICT_Typology.pdf
[2] National Center for Education Statistics. Public Libraries in the United States: Fiscal Year 2004. (NCES 2006-349). Washington, DC: NCES, 2006. http://www.nces.ed.gov/pubs2006/2006349.pdf

Of the specific Internet services libraries offer (e.g., digital reference, licensed databases, e-books), more than 68 percent of libraries reported offering homework resources – serving the educational needs of more than 36 million school-age children – up 7.3 percent from last year.

The vital role libraries play for job seekers was particularly pronounced in site visits to dozens of public libraries. An emerging aspect of this use is the apparent increase in the number of businesses that require applicants to apply online. From grocery stores to state governments to casinos, library staff reported that many more library users are coming to the library – often for the first time – to apply for jobs.

Library Infrastructure Is Being Pushed to Capacity

The 2006 *Public Libraries and the Internet* survey posed a question that came to the forefront in this year's research: Can libraries continue to add services and resources which require substantial retraining and retooling of librarians and library technology infrastructure? The 2007 study found that many libraries have reached or are nearing their maximum capacity for space, bandwidth, and the additional burden placed on staff support for technology.

Many library buildings predate the Internet – and even TV, in the case of historic Carnegie buildings. As a result, these buildings are ill-equipped to accommodate the space and electrical needs of more than a few workstations. Seventy-six percent of public libraries reported that space limitations are the top factor affecting their ability to add computers. Related to this, 31 percent of libraries reported this year that the availability of electrical outlets, cabling or other infrastructure issues limited additional computers. *"As we design new buildings, there's going to be more of an issue to power them (laptops) all over the library,"* said one Utah library director.

Funding is the second greatest factor limiting the ability of libraries to add computers. While operating budgets largely have remained flat for the past several years, costs of providing library services of all types have increased. Add to this that seven states and the District of Columbia reported library capital expenditures (i.e., for new construction or renovations) of less than $2 million total in 2004, the most recent national statistics available. Most capital expenditures are under $10,000 – not enough to pay for major electrical improvements to libraries, for example.

Another consistent capacity concern was the need for more electronic data transfer infrastructure, or simply greater bandwidth at branches. While bandwidth is essentially unchanged since the 2006 survey, state libraries and library staff report significant increases in broadband demand. Fifty-two percent of libraries report their connectivity speed is insufficient some or all of the time, an increase of about 6 percent from only one year ago. One library reported blocking access to the graphics- and media-heavy "March Madness" college basketball Web site after its use brought down the entire library's network.

Finally, as library patrons become more active and sophisticated technology users, the demand for faster and better service is growing. Patrons are bringing MP3 players, digital cameras, USB drives and laptop computers to the library and often looking to the library for assistance configuring their laptops or downloading and emailing photos, for instance. Keeping current with both the technology and how to use that technology is an ongoing challenge for all libraries, but is perhaps the most difficult for smaller and rural libraries with the most limited staff and fewest hours open. About 35 percent of U.S. public libraries have fewer than two full-time equivalent staff members (FTE),[3] making travel and time off for staff training very difficult.

There Is a Growing Need for Technology Planning and Dedicated Technology Support

Providing technology access does not represent a one-time investment of funds or staff training. While virtually every library now offers public computers and free Internet access to their patrons, many libraries struggle to evaluate, plan and expand technology in their communities. Just over 25 percent of libraries reported they have no technology replacement plan, and 12.9 percent of libraries reported they didn't know the maximum speed of their Internet connection.

State library staff also identified an inability to plan and budget for IT upgrades, replacement and maintenance as a significant challenge for public libraries with vulnerable technology services.

"You almost need two levels of IT staff. How do we push to the next level while keeping things running on the floor?" asked one library director.

A lack of local expertise by library staff was the third most common barrier to broadband connectivity reported (40 percent) by state library agencies surveyed this year. This expertise includes the ability to assess the library's telecommunications needs; identify commercial providers; negotiate rates; identify opportunities for reduced rate connections and complete the application process; develop technology plans; and develop, maintain and upgrade library infrastructure. Ensuring every library user not only has access to a computer and the Internet, but also the skills and support to successfully use emerging technologies depends on continuing – and increasing – investments in staff training and specialized IT support for libraries.

SNAPSHOT OF FINDINGS FROM THE PUBLIC LIBRARIES AND THE INTERNET SURVEY

Connectivity and Access

Since the first study of public libraries and the Internet in 1994,[4] the significant research question has shifted from "How many U.S. public libraries are online?" to "How are libraries expanding and sustaining the computer and Internet services they make freely available in almost every community in this nation?"

Virtually every public library (99.1 percent) now offers free public access to the Internet (see Figure 3 in Section 1). On average, there are 10.7 computers in U.S. public library branches (Figure 7), a number that has remained nearly constant for libraries of all sizes since 2002. In the next year, 17.2 percent of library outlets plan to upgrade their computer workstations (Figure 9), and 25 percent plan to replace computers (Figure 10).

---

[3] National Center for Education Statistics. Public Libraries in the United States: Fiscal Year 2004. (NCES 2006-349). Washington, DC: NCES, 2006. http://www.nces.ed.gov/pubs2006/2006349.pdf
[4] Information about the reports from the 1994-2006 studies is available at: http://www.ii.fsu.edu/plinternet.

Libraries also are expanding access by providing wireless Internet connectivity. Wireless access is now available in 54.2 percent of outlets (Figure 16), up from 36.7 percent only last year and 17.9 percent of outlets in 2004. Urban libraries are 30 percent more likely to offer wireless access than rural libraries. Focus groups and site visits also reinforced the importance of integrating "anywhere" access to increase access to library resources.

Even with this expansion, demand is still outpacing supply in many libraries. Nearly 80 percent of libraries report there are fewer public Internet computers than patrons who wish to use them at different times throughout a typical day (Figure 15). Space limitations (76 percent) and cost factors (73 percent) are the leading factors influencing library decisions about adding computers (Figure 13).

Internet Services

About 62 percent of libraries now have connection speeds of 768kbps or more (Figure 19), compared with 48 percent in 2004. This is an important improvement considering the data also document a broad range of Internet-based services provided by public libraries (Figure 27). Significant numbers of U.S. public libraries offer online resources as follows:

- 85.6 percent of libraries offer licensed databases;
- 68.1 percent offer homework resources;
- 57.7 percent offer digital/virtual reference;
- 38.3 percent offer audio content (podcasts, audiobooks, etc.); and
- 38.3 percent offer e-books.

The number of libraries reporting providing these services increased since 2006 by between 0.4 to 7.2 percent.[5] Many states or state libraries purchase or subsidize at least a basic package of licensed databases – and sometimes virtual reference services and downloadable media, as well – and make these available to all of the libraries in the state. As a result, library users in even the smallest communities have free access not only to the Internet, but also to expensive and specialized resources like those listed above through their local libraries. Databases may include resources as varied as full-text publications, investment information, encyclopedias and other reference works, genealogy resources, health research and automotive repair manuals.

Nationwide, urban libraries were more likely to offer these Internet services. This was particularly pronounced with e-books (67.2 percent of urban libraries compared with 30 percent of rural libraries) and audio content like podcasts and audiobooks (51.4 percent compared with 29.7 percent).

Questions about e-government roles and services highlighted the importance of library staff, as well as library hardware. Fifty-five percent of libraries reported that staff provide assistance to patrons applying for or seeking access to e-government services (Figure 29). Another 12.8 percent of libraries are partnering with government agencies, non-profits and others to provide e-government services.

---

[5] Bertot, John and Charles McClure. *Public Libraries and the Internet 2006: Study Results and Findings.* http://www.ii.fsu.edu/projectFiles/plinternet/2006/2006_plinternet.pdf

Funding

For the first time, the study asked libraries to identify revenue and expenditures for technology by a broad range of categories by fiscal year – staff salaries, hardware, software and telecommunications.

Total technology expenditures reported by state for fiscal year 2006 ranged from a low of $5,181 to just over $1.4 million, with a national average of $166,181. Libraries reported the greatest technology-related expenditure in FY 2006 was on staff ($55,126), followed by licensed resources ($39,788) and telecommunications services ($21,224). The proportion of expenditures is consistent with overall spending by public libraries.

High-poverty public libraries (often located in urban areas) report spending more on public computing software, instructional technology, and licensed resources than any other type of system. Urban and medium-poverty library systems reported spending the most on wireless access ($5,497 and $8,606, respectively) as compared to the average ($1,377). This, too, aligns with other data reported regarding the slower adoption of wireless in rural communities.

The largest single source for technology-related expenditures comes from the local/county sources. With rare exception, federal funds were most likely to be applied to telecommunications expenses across all public libraries. A large proportion of funds from donations and grants were allocated to hardware expenditures, telling us that libraries may not be in a position to rely on local tax support to fund technology, but are relying on external fundraising to provide what have become basic library services.

Further details about technology-related expenditures were complicated by a roughly 50 percent drop off in question completion on these items compared with the rest of the national survey. Follow-up discussions with librarians indicated a range of reasons for this, including the lack of a separate technology budget; lack of knowledge regarding technology expenditures; inability to report as asked because of the library's or city/county budgeting process; and because this section of the survey was too time-consuming to complete. Despite this complication, the data are still valuable to those interested in gaining a better understanding of patterns of spending in these broad technology categories.

SNAPSHOT OF FINDINGS FROM THE CHIEF OFFICERS OF STATE LIBRARY AGENCIES SURVEY

Providing public technology access presents both challenges and opportunities for public libraries, urban and rural. Forty-three states responded to the questionnaire to Chief Officers of State Library Agencies (COSLA), representing 86 percent of all states. When asked to comment on the status of technology access and funding for the public libraries in their state, especially with regard to broadband connections, areas of network vulnerability, challenges, unexpected successes, and ways in which external agents might be able to improve current conditions, the Chief Officers of State Library Agencies responded as follows:

Connectivity

Twenty-eight states (65 percent) reported that over 90 percent of their public libraries currently have broadband connectivity (defined as a connection that is direct, "always on," and not a dial-up connection). All but one reported that more than 50 percent of their public libraries currently have broadband connectivity.

Public libraries are using a variety of means to obtain the connections to the broadband capacity they need, and often use more than one approach. The most common ways that public libraries achieve broadband connectivity are through:

- Local telecommunications companies (77 percent);
- Local city/county government (65 percent); and
- Local school districts (63 percent).

Major Barriers

Twenty-four states (56 percent) identified high cost as the principal major barrier to broadband connectivity. Twenty-one (49 percent) reported that the capacity for connectivity did not exist in all parts of their state. Eighteen respondents (42 percent) reported few or no barriers to their state's public library broadband connectivity. Sixteen (37 percent) reported the lack of local library staff expertise as a major barrier to implementing or sustaining broadband connectivity. Other major barriers reported are slow and unreliable connections.

Assistance Needed

Chief Officers also identified the types of assistance that external partners (including the state library, ALA, external funders and others) might provide to public libraries to demonstrably improve (within a 3-5 year timeframe) and sustain their networked resources and services. Three priorities emerged:

- Obtain enough broadband to meet public library demand at an affordable price;
- Provide adequate IT to make efficient/effective use of broadband connection and meet users' needs for other IT-based services; and
- Provide library networked services of interest to their communities.

SNAPSHOT OF FINDINGS FROM THE FOCUS GROUPS AND SITE VISITS

Funding

In general, library funding is stable but flat, and library directors are not optimistic about future increases. Libraries have always had to compete for public dollars, but the competition is becoming more intense, particularly in states with population growth and stretched public infrastructure. In some of the smaller communities, library directors said their funding was fine, but then described the reality of trying to do more with less.

Directors in Maryland and Delaware reported recent funding successes at the state level. Maryland libraries will see annual increases in state funding through 2010, and Delaware has dedicated matching funding for technology replacement in libraries.

While many libraries have integrated technology costs into their general operating budgets and created line items for equipment, electronic collections and telecommunications costs, some libraries reported that their greatest funding successes were in securing grant funding for new computers – most often from the Library Services and Technology Act (LSTA) and/or the Bill & Melinda Gates Foundation. One director reported: *"We wouldn't have a single computer without LSTA."* Friends groups also are an important fundraising source for general library funding.

Internet Services

Among the services reported to be the most used were:

- Email;
- Job-related searching, applying and resume writing;
- Social networking (including MySpace, YouTube);
- E-commerce (e.g. paying bills, printing boarding passes, investing);
- Research (e.g. genealogy, homework, etc.);
- E-government (e.g. tax forms, immigration services); and
- Online games (e.g. Runescape)

The vital role libraries play for job seekers was particularly pronounced in site visits to dozens of public libraries. For instance, staff in several Las Vegas-area libraries, reported their libraries were inundated when a new casino opened within the last year and required *all* applicants to apply online. Not only did job seekers need to fill out the online application, they also needed to establish an email account and check back frequently to see if they were a candidate for employment. In addition to low technology skills, many of these new library patrons had low literacy rates and/or spoke English as a second language. Not surprisingly, the impact on staff was significant in helping these users: *"Online job applications are a killer."* Nevada and Delaware also recently put their state government jobs online and are encouraging job applicants to go to their local libraries and apply online.

One single mom in Maryland looking for a job put it this way: *"You have people who can't afford computers. People need to find jobs, get on their feet."*

Staffing

High on almost every focus group participant's wish list is at least one – or additional – dedicated information technology staff. Many library staff, particularly in rural libraries, learned computers skills on the job or in training offered at the state or county level rather than bringing these skills when hired.

Larger libraries with dedicated staff may still have only one IT employee. *"We have well over 100 computers and just the one guy,"* reported a Maryland library director. While many local libraries reported receiving some support from city or county IT departments, there also was sometimes difficulty balancing the government agency security/firewall concerns with public access needs. A lack of dedicated and skilled library IT staff affects not only day-to-day maintenance and troubleshooting, but, perhaps more importantly, the ability for libraries to plan effectively for future technology innovations.

Advocacy

Library directors reflect a wide-ranging level of skills in advocating support for their libraries. In general, they said it is easier to win support for new buildings than it is for ongoing expenses such as staff or technology. While some directors indicated they make special efforts to build community partnerships and relationships with funders, others, especially in small libraries, indicated they feel they lack the time and resources needed to be effective.

The Library Funding Landscape

INTRODUCTION

For the first time, the 2007 *Public Library Funding & Technology Access Study* asked libraries about funding of public access computing services. Libraries were asked to report what services were paid by state agencies on their behalf, as well as what they spent and from what sources the funding was derived (local, state, federal, fines/fees, grants, etc.). This level of finance detail does not exist in other national library data collection initiatives, and represents the most current fiscal year actual and projected available on a national basis.

These data, however, were gathered in a context provided by annual surveys by the National Center for Education Statistics (NCES) and a 2006 report by the ALA on funding issues in U.S. public libraries.

The ALA study determined that libraries experienced significant reductions in fiscal years 2003, 2004, and 2005.[6] During these three years, public library services continued and, in some instances, increased despite flat or reduced operating budgets. A vast majority of public libraries had stagnated or reduced buying power as a result of level funding coupled with increasing staff and utility costs.

The 2006 report also revealed that libraries serving more than 500,000 and fewer than 25,000 people saw the greatest midyear funding cuts. About 80 libraries serve communities over 500,000 and more than 7,200 libraries serve communities under 25,000.

The study also found that libraries in the West and Midwest sustained greater cuts than their counterparts in the South and East. Little relief was anticipated for our smallest public libraries in the West and Midwest – 48 percent experienced reductions in fiscal year 2003, 35.8 percent in fiscal year 2004, and 34.5 percent in fiscal year 2005. Nearly 20 percent of Northeast libraries indicated budget reductions in fiscal year 2004, up from 12 percent in fiscal year 2003.

Looking ahead to fiscal year 2006, 58.2 percent of public libraries anticipated funding to remain about the same, and about 32.4 percent anticipated some improvement in local tax revenue. Approximately 9.4 percent of libraries anticipated more reductions.

FUNDING LIBRARY PUBLIC ACCESS COMPUTING SERVICES

This year's *Public Library Funding & Technology Access* study picked up from and went further than the 2006 ALA study. Providing this detailed fiscal data was no easy task for public libraries, and the drop off in responses from the connectivity portion of the study to the funding portion was telling.

---

[6] Davis, Denise M. *Funding Issues in U.S. Public Libraries, Fiscal Years 2003-2006*. March 2006
http://www.ala.org/ala/ors/reports/FundingIssuesinUSPLs.pdf

As a result, there are caveats to reviewing and using these data that must be understood. First, this was the first year libraries were asked for any detailed operating budget or expenditure data about technology-related expenditures. Given this, any amount of detailed reporting was a challenge. In this first attempt, most libraries were able to report current total fiscal year expenditures for traditional broad categories – staffing, collections and "other." It was far more difficult for libraries to report detail on technology-related expenditures and to parse those expenditures by funding sources. The increased difficulty in reporting detailed revenue and expenditures occurred for a few reasons that can be summarized into three key areas: local fiscal reporting requirements, library legal basis (e.g., city/county, municipal government, library district, etc.), and time.

Another caveat comes with comparison of these very timely fiscal data and those reported through longitudinal national library data collection efforts, specifically those of NCES. Understanding previous revenue and expenditure trends is important in grounding the fiscal data collected in this study and national averages from NCES annual public library reports are used whenever appropriate.

Operating Expenditures

Distributions for overall expenditures (e.g., staff salaries, collections and other expenditures) by revenue source reported by libraries for fiscal years 2006 and 2007 align somewhat with national averages – more so with fiscal year 2007 estimates than with actual fiscal year 2006. When scrutinized by metropolitan status, expenditure distributions by type align most closely for rural libraries; suburban and urban libraries fiscal year 2006 reporting was skewed significantly to staff expenditures and far less to collection and other expenditures. This may be explained by unencumbered collection expenditures for these larger libraries, where end of fiscal year collection purchases are not uncommon. This was not the case when estimating for fiscal year 2007, where estimates aligned almost exactly with national trend data.

These data also offer insight into how other sources of revenue are used to support library operations. Libraries applied fines/fees and donations to "other" expenditures by nearly a two-to-one ratio. In estimating for fiscal year 2007, libraries reported a significant increase in fines/fees being applied to "other" expenditures. If this projection holds true, it suggests that libraries may not be in a position to rely on local tax support to fund technology, but are relying on fines, fees and fundraising to provide what have become basic library services.

Overall expenditures by revenue source also skewed for fiscal year 2006 toward local funding sources and noticeably away from state or federal revenue. Again, this is less the case with fiscal year 2007 estimates and may be explained by libraries not having fully reconciled current fiscal year expenditures. The study team will look closely at financial data reported in the coming study to see if similar anomalies appear when actual fiscal year 2007 data are reported compared with estimates provided in the previous year.

Figure A: Percentage Public Library Expenditures by Type and Metropolitan Status

		Staff	Collections	Other
NCES FY 2004	All	65.8%	13.2%	21.0%
	Rural	60.3%	15.6%	24.1%
	Suburban	66.8%	13.2%	20.1%
	Urban	65.6%	13.0%	21.4%
PLFTAS FY 2006	All	82.7%	6.2%	11.0%
	Rural	60.2%	14.6%	25.2%
	Suburban	86.3%	5.2%	8.6%
	Urban	82.7%	5.9%	11.4%
PLFTAS FY 2007	All	61.0%	14.3%	24.7%
	Rural	60.5%	14.9%	24.6%
	Suburban	65.7%	14.2%	20.1%
	Urban	57.8%	13.4%	28.7%

Note: NCES data are reported in National Center for Education Statistics. *Public Libraries in the United States: Fiscal Year 2004*; PLFTAS are reported in *2007 Public Library Funding & Technology Access Study*

Nationally, rural libraries report spending about 60 percent on staff, just less than 16 percent on collections, and about 24 percent on other expenditures. The data reported in this study align almost exactly for both fiscal years reported – 60 percent on staff, 14.6 percent on collections, and just more than 25 percent on other expenditures.

Suburban libraries historically have spent slightly more than 66 percent on staff, 13 percent on collections and slightly more than 20 percent on "other" expenditures. Distributions reported in this study for fiscal year 2006 were skewed heavily to staffing and away from collections and other expenditures. Fiscal year 2007 estimates, however, were very closely aligned with national data. Although categories of expenditures aligned, estimates by funding source were skewed from national trends in fiscal year 2006. Local funding was reported at 10 percentage points higher than national trends. Expenditures by funding source aligned more closely with national trends for fiscal year 2007 estimates, with slightly more expected to come from local sources and less from other sources, such as fines, fees, donations and grants.

Urban libraries historically spend about 65 percent on staff, 13 percent on collections, and 21 percent on other expenditures. They also spend approximately 81 percent from local sources, 9 percent from state, 0.5 percent from federal, and about 9 percent from "other" sources of funding. Figures reported for both fiscal years were skewed away from national trends in all categories except federal funding, and the most significant skew was in local/county funding sources. Urban libraries reported expenditures from local sources at 89 percent in fiscal year 2006, and an estimated 85 percent in fiscal year 2007. Researchers in this study will be looking very closely at future responses from urban libraries compared with national reporting patterns to determine if any significant shifts are occurring nationally. As a result of this anomaly, data reported by urban libraries in this study should be used with caution.

Technology-Related Expenditures by Revenue Source

Libraries were asked to report, to the best of their ability, technology-related expenditures by sources of library operating revenue. This is complicated because so much of library operating revenue comes from local sources, and because libraries aggregate expenditures by type rather than by source of revenue. The reason for asking expenditure detail by funding source was to determine how much of "other expenditures" (those other than staff and collections) are paid from local, state, federal or other sources of library operating revenue. It has long been assumed that "other expenditures" was the catch-all for technology-related expenditures. Also, this study attempted to collect detail of staff assigned to technology-related services.

Careful attention must be paid when examining or reusing these responses because of the overall low response to the technology expenditures questions. For instance, response to the fiscal year 2006 broad finance questions ranged between 2,423 and 6,230, and responses to the technology finance questions ranged between 1,858 and 4,053, representing a decline in responses of between 23-35 percent within the finance questions. With this caution, the data reported are useful because they have never before been reported at this level of detail.

Figure B: Percentage Technology-Related Expenditures by Metropolitan Status and Fiscal Year

		Staff	Hardware	Software	Telecommunications
FY 2006	All	49.5%	24.5%	11%	14.8%
	Rural	48.0%	26.0%	11%	14.0%
	Suburban	52.0%	24.0%	13%	11.0%
	Urban	43.0%	27.0%	10%	20.0%
FY 2007	All	47.5%	21.0%	14%	17.6%
	Rural	49.0%	24.0%	13%	14.0%
	Suburban	51.0%	18.0%	19%	12.0%
	Urban	39.0%	24.0%	11%	26.0%

Libraries reported spending nearly 50 percent on technology staff, about 25 percent on hardware, 11 percent on software, and about 15 percent on telecommunications for technology-related expenditures in fiscal year 2006. Estimates for fiscal year 2007 were only slightly different, with more expenditures projected to go to software and telecommunications than for staff and hardware. Interestingly, distributions by funding source for technology-related expenditures closely matched national averages of local and state funding, but exceeded national averages for federal and expenditures from "other" sources. For fiscal year 2006 technology-related expenditures, libraries reported funding from local sources at about 77 percent, 8.6 percent from state, 2.6 percent from federal, and 10.8 percent from other revenue sources. By comparison, national fiscal year 2004 estimates of library operating revenue by sources were 81.5 percent local, 10 percent state, .5 percent federal, and 8 percent other.[7]

This study also was able to gather detail of the "other" revenue sources applied to technology-related expenditures. Libraries estimated about 1 percent of revenue come from fines/fees, 4.3

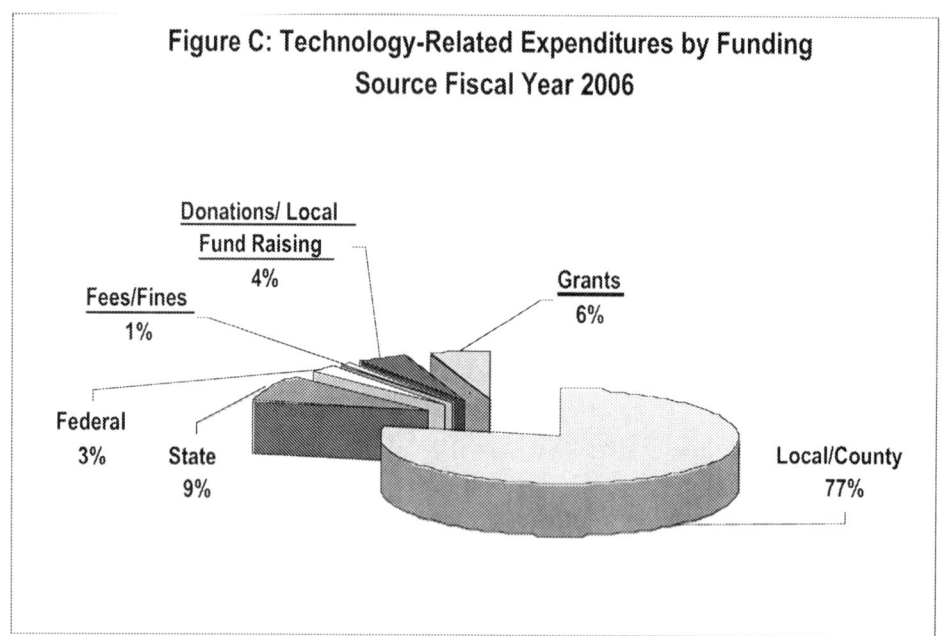

percent from donations, and 5.5 percent from grants of all types (local, state, or national programs) in fiscal year 2006, about as much as comes from state and federal support. Fiscal year 2007 expenditure estimates by funding source were similarly distributed, although fines/fees and other donation estimates were slightly lower than actual expenditures reported in fiscal year 2006. What is unfortunate about these estimates is that they support the hypothesis that non-tax revenue sources are paying for a portion of basic technology-related library services.

Technology-related expenditures by revenue source were further stratified by metropolitan status and poverty. As with data reported historically by public libraries in the NCES annual studies, distributions shifted for all funding categories when viewed by metropolitan status. Therefore, the distribution of technology-related expenditures indicates that libraries are spending about the same proportion of operating revenue for these services regardless of metropolitan status. Figures 53-65 provide complete data reported for fiscal years 2006 and 2007.

---

[7] National Center for Education Statistics. Public Libraries in the United States: Fiscal Year 2004. (NCES 2006-349). Washington, DC: NCES, 2006. http://www.nces.ed.gov/pubs2006/2006349.pdf

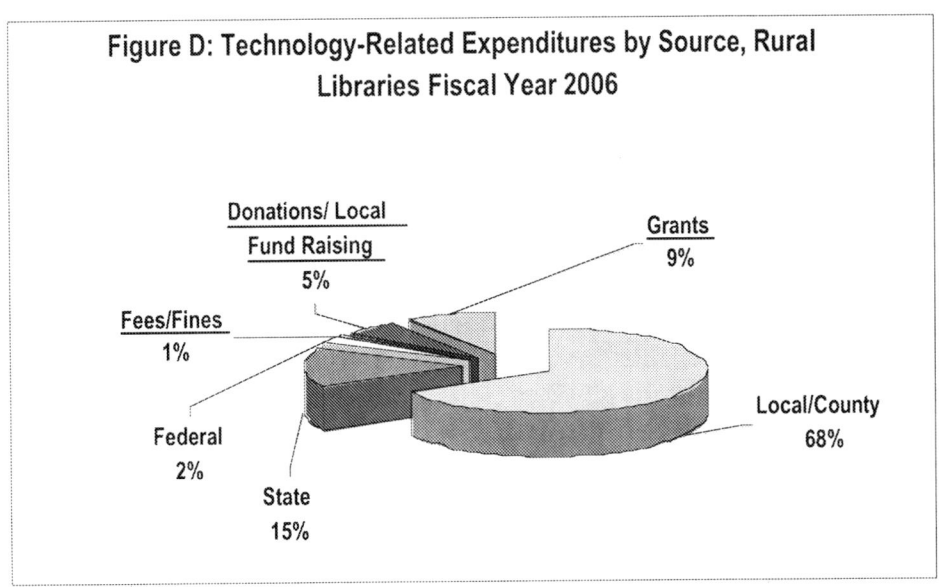

About 67 percent of rural library funding comes from local sources, almost 23 percent less than was reported by all libraries in fiscal year 2006. Fifteen percent was spent from state sources (about 7 percent more than reported by all libraries); slightly more than 2 percent from federal funding; and 15.5 percent from "other" funding sources (about 5 percent more than the average) for this period. This disproportionate funding, however, is supported by historical national averages of operating expenditures reported by rural libraries as compared with suburban and urban libraries. Rural libraries also reported relying heavily on grants and donations, 9 percent and 5 percent, respectively.

In fiscal year 2006, rural libraries devoted about 48 percent of their technology budgets for staff, 26 percent for hardware, 11 percent for software, and about 14 percent for telecommunications expenditures. Knowing the funding challenges faced by rural libraries, this information further highlights the need for stronger local tax support for basic library services in these communities.

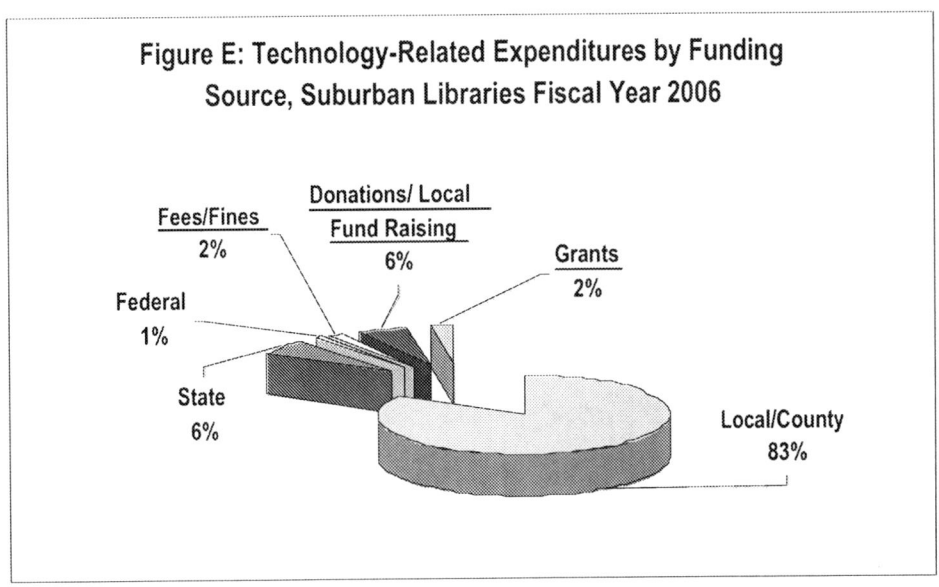

Compared with the overall expenditure distributions, suburban libraries spend slightly more on staff and hardware, and about the same on software and telecommunications as all other libraries. When considered by revenue source, in fiscal year 2006 suburban libraries spend about 84

percent from local/county, 6 percent from state source, one-seventh-of-one percent from federal sources, and nearly 10 percent from other sources of revenue. There was little difference between fiscal year 2006 technology-related expenditures and those projected for fiscal year 2007. The expenditures by funding source also align closely with those historically reported by suburban libraries, with only slight variation in state support. Overall, suburban libraries report about 10 percent of operating revenue coming from state sources, but only about 6 percent of state funds are used for technology-related expenditures. Suburban libraries reported using state funding more often for staff than "other" expenditures, almost two-to-one. Not surprisingly, suburban libraries pay less than rural libraries for telecommunications and use nearly 60 percent less in state support for those expenditures than do rural libraries. Telecommunications costs in suburban communities are primarily supported from local funding sources.

Suburban libraries reported spending about 52 percent of their technology budgets on staff, about 24 percent on hardware, 13 percent on software, and 11 percent on telecommunications.

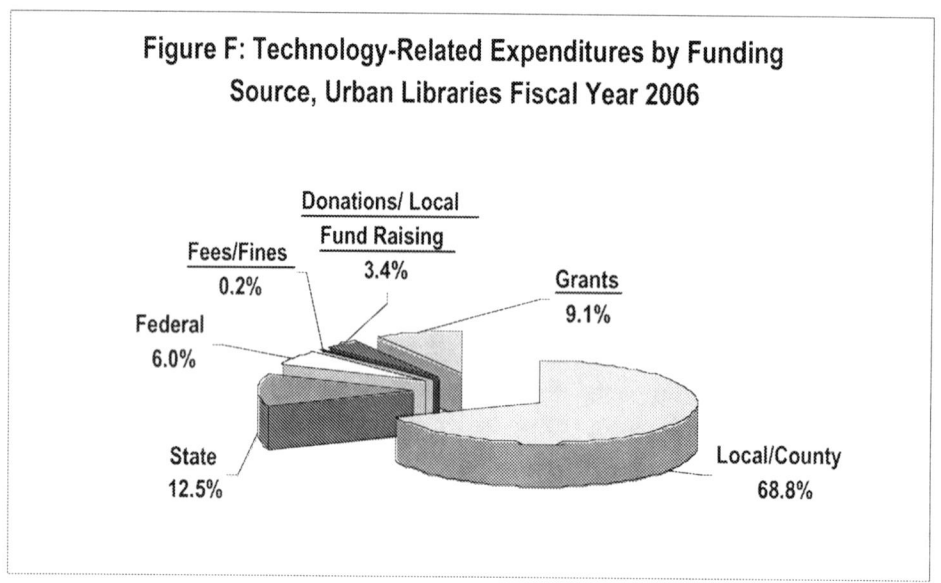

Not unlike rural libraries, urban libraries also see less support for technology expenditures from local and state funding. Urban libraries reported that in fiscal year 2006 about 69 percent of technology-related expenditures came from local funding, 12 percent from state sources, 6 percent from federal, and nearly 13 percent from other sources. Similar distributions are anticipated for fiscal year 2007, with slightly more funding coming from local sources than in 2006. Also like rural libraries, urban libraries benefited from grants – about 9 percent of revenue came from grants and was spent on staff and hardware.

Not surprisingly, urban libraries reported a larger proportion of expenditures going to telecommunications than did rural and suburban libraries. Increased expenditures for urban libraries represent more capacity for more users (higher connection speeds for more computer workstations). The converse is true for rural libraries, which pay more for fewer users because of their geographic isolation. Urban libraries also reported greater state support than did other libraries, about $136,000 compared with $17,000 to suburban and $7,000 to rural libraries. This may be explained in part by state aid programs based on population.

Urban libraries reported spending about 43 percent of its technology budget on staff, 27 percent on hardware, 10 percent on software, and 20 percent on telecommunications in fiscal year 2006. Estimates for fiscal year 2007 are only slightly different, with estimates on staff expenditures being about 4 percent less and costs for telecommunications being about 6 percent more.

CHALLENGES REPORTING DETAILED DATA

For the most part, libraries were able to report operating budget information about technology-related services, as well as current fiscal year and projected next fiscal year estimates. Some drops in reporting specific expenditures, such as hardware and software, did occur. This can be explained in a few ways: the first is the library did not incur nor anticipate such expenditures; the second is that they could not provide the level of detail for the purchase because of local accounting procedures or insufficient time to determine the expenditures (Figures 37-38).

Local fiscal reporting requirements was the single most common reason libraries were challenged in reporting detailed budget or expenditure data for technology related expenses. Local accounting practices may prevent libraries from understanding detail of both operating revenue and from what sources expenditures are made. In many cases it was reported that the operating revenue was aggregated into a single operating budget – most typically local/county - and libraries were unable to get reports with the level of detail requested from this study.

Knowing where operating revenue originate also impacted the library's ability to accurately report whether the state paid for technology based services directly. As Figures 35 and 36 in the study findings shows, more than 50 percent of libraries were unable to report if the state library or another state agency paid directly for a range of technology services. In only one instance, licensed resources (such as full text periodical databases), were libraries more likely to know if the state provided these services. This is explained by the fact that some states pay directly on behalf of the library so no revenue actually flows to the library operating budget. Library's inability to report whether the state support technology-related expenditures raises concerns, especially when the study also found a number of statewide telecommunication networks in place. Libraries lack of awareness of state support for these services is an area of concern for the researchers of this study.

Reporting fiscal information was somewhat easier for independent libraries that managed its budget directly, and for libraries with in-house fiscal officers. However, it is common that the legal basis of the library is a part of local government thereby putting its financial records administration outside of the library. Without ready access to recent fiscal year reports, libraries were less likely to provide detail on revenue by source or expenditures by type. Regardless of legal basis, libraries could readily provide the aggregated revenue and expense figures for the current fiscal year, but had difficulty providing anticipated operating budget figures.

The third reason noted by libraries was time. Spending time tracking down fiscal information from people outside the library was considered too time consuming for respondents. Library response rates dropped by more as much as 35 percent when finance questions delved more deeply than the broad staff, collections and other expenditure categories (Figures 53-66).

Considering the three most prevalent causes for the drop in response to the finance questions section of the study, one must still ask "How well are libraries able to plan for technology related expenditures when they cannot report what they are spending?"

CONCLUSIONS

Libraries rely as much on other sources of revenue as they do state and federal to pay for technology-related expenditures
One of the most significant findings was how much libraries are relying on fines, fees, donations and grants to support technology-related expenditures. Although local/county funding sources were the greatest source of revenue (about 78% in fiscal year 2006), many libraries reported spending almost as much from "other" revenue sources as they did state and federal support (about 10.8 percent and 11.6 percent, respectively). In fact, libraries reported applying "other" revenue sources to the purchase of hardware. Whereas about 19 percent of local funding went to pay for hardware, nearly 56 percent of "other" funding did. Without these "other" sources of revenue, libraries would be unable to upgrade or replace existing computers as needed, impacting technology planning and replacement schedules.

Expenditures continue to shift from collections to staff and "other" expenditure categories
As was discovered in the 2006 ALA funding study, libraries have patterns of shifting expenses away from collections to cover increased expenditures in staffing, utilities, library programs, and technology. Once shifted, it is difficult to regain that revenue. In this study, libraries repeatedly reported that costs of hardware and telecommunications prevented them from adding more computers and offering faster connection speeds. improving technology-related services. Recognizing the inflexibility of some infrastructure operating expenses – staffing and utilities – it is not surprising that libraries rely heavily on "other" sources of revenue to pay for technology-related services. When infrastructure expenditures increase unexpectedly, as did utility costs across the nation, libraries responded by reducing collection, technology, and other expenditures. This reality further impacts libraries ability to adequately plan for improvements to technology-related services.

Technology budget planning requires detailed expenditure data
Until this study, libraries have not been asked to report detailed technology-related expenditures beyond their local governance groups (e.g., city managers, library trustees, etc.). For the first time we can begin to understand how libraries pay for technology-related services, and begin demonstrating to libraries the value and significance of capturing this level of detail both for planning and advocacy purposes. Further, without dedicated IT support, significant pieces of information required for planning may be missing. Expert IT staff and detailed budget and expenditure information are needed for effective planning for technology-related services. Libraries more and more are relying on technology to support information access in their communities, and are being relied upon by the community to be the primary access point for these services. Without detailed expenditure information and expert IT advice libraries cannot effectively plan, nor can the communities in which they operate.

Challenges for the Future and A Call to Action

CHALLENGES FOR THE FUTURE

As this report demonstrates, libraries have moved rapidly into Internet-based services, have in many respects reached capacity both with regard to availability of computers for the public and infrastructure to support them, and rely heavily on local funding to support these services. As we look to improving access in the future, we must acknowledge that significant support is necessary to help librarians maintain and grow services.

The authors of this report offer the following observations and recommendations to improve the environment for libraries and enhance free public access to computers and the Internet in their communities. Many of these recommendations have been made before in earlier *Public Libraries and the Internet* studies, but there has been little movement in these areas. It is our hope this call to action will help to begin or advance dialog at all levels.

Making Buildings Work for Public Access Computing Services
Libraries struggle to build sufficient infrastructure for providing free access to technology services. Retrofitting old buildings to accommodate new technology is expensive and in some cases may be impossible without major renovations or a new building. It may be easier to upgrade electrical and telecommunications infrastructure in newer library buildings, but the space may not be available to add more computers. One Utah library is addressing this by providing laptop computers to its patrons, but nationally only 7 percent of libraries are purchasing laptops instead of desktop computers. Further, NCES public library data demonstrates the dearth of capital revenue to support even minor renovations. Often fewer than 50 percent of libraries in any state benefit from capital revenue and, of those that do receive funding, a majority receive less than $50,000 to make improvements.

Hiring or "Growing their Own" IT Staff
Dedicated IT staff is essential to supporting library technology, and keeping library staff trained to use the myriad of resources available is critical. The study reports that local funding is the primary source of fiscal support for IT staff and staff training. Sadly, many libraries reported having inadequate or no dedicated IT staff. For many libraries, staffing is small and there are too few to attend off-site IT or Internet training. Another concern anecdotally reported in the focus groups and site visits was the pending retirements of library workers. In two studies conducted by the ALA (2002 and 2004), similar to many professions, retirements will significantly impact libraries in the next 10 years.[8]

Responding to the Ongoing Demand for Books and Traditional Library Services
More and more people are visiting the library, and they are demanding the traditional services (books, audio, video, etc.), as well as the technology. Household surveys reinforce that people

---

[8] American Library Association. Library Retirements: What We Can Expect.
http://www.ala.org/ala/ors/reports/LISGradsPositionsAndRetirements_rev1.pdf

read, and they use their local libraries to find and borrow books.[9] NCES public library data show that annual circulation totals increase between 2 and 3.5 percent each year, translating into more than 45 million additional circulations each year.

Library use is up, as well, increasing an average of 3 percent each year (about 38 million visits). This is not just adult use. In fact, teens also are strong library users. A recent study conducted for ALA of teen use of libraries indicated 78 percent used the public library to borrow books and other materials for personal use, and 67 percent borrowed books and other materials for school assignments in the last year.[10]

CALL TO ACTION

Investments must be made to ensure that basic community services provided by libraries are sustained. Public libraries have moved strategically into providing innovative services while maintaining those services highly valued by their communities. Keeping up with rapidly changing technologies while maintaining existing and sometimes older technologies, and providing longstanding services such as summer reading programs and homework assistance, have stretched libraries' budgets.

How can community stakeholders, government agencies and other library partners support libraries as they transform their services to better serve communities?

There are five related areas that demand attention from the public library community, national and state library associations, national and state library agencies and organizations, regional library consortia and networks, library and information science schools and funders:

Funding

Reliable and sustainable funding is essential for libraries to provide the services patrons so clearly value, and demand.

- Technology and technology-related services have become basic services in public libraries. Yet they are too often funded as "extras" or non-essential services. While libraries get more than half of their technology funding from local taxes, they also rely too heavily on fundraising and grants (10.8 percent). In fact, money raised in this manner nearly equals what comes from state and federal sources.

- Libraries should receive adequate funding so they do not have to compromise their collections. In the decade 1994-2004, more of the responsibility for funding public libraries shifted away from state and federal government to the local level in all but a handful of states. Since 2000, library operating budgets have experienced very little growth. Libraries dealt with this by redistributing expenditures away from collections to staff to cover contractual salary increases and retirement plans (1.5 percent increase), and to pay for services and technology (only a 0.8 percent increase). Libraries in our smallest communities were most seriously impacted.

---

[9] American Library Association. @ your library: Attitudes Toward Public Libraries Survey 2006. http://www.ala.org/ala/ors/reports/2006KRCReport.pdf
[10] ALA. Youth Use of Public and School Libraries (2007). http://www.ala.org/ala/yalsa/HarrisYouthPoll.pdf.

Figure G: Operating Revenue by Source, Fiscal Years 1990-2004

Fiscal Year	Operating Revenue by Source (in thousands)				Percent of Revenue by Source			
	Federal	State	Local	Other	Federal	State	Local	Other
1990	$56,176	$604,975	$3,275,507	$384,591	1.3	14	75.8	8.9
1991	$55,919	$610,451	$3,578,827	$419,393	1.2	13.1	76.8	9
1992	$49,974	$599,691	$3,927,973	$419,783	1	12	78.6	8.4
1993	$55,759	$633,625	$3,669,666	$425,796	1.1	12.5	78	8.4
1994	$57,861	$646,991	$4,113,388	$441,847	1.1	12.3	78.2	8.4
1995	$55,940	$671,288	$4,380,156	$486,684	1	12	78.3	8.7
1996	$59,050	$720,406	$4,611,779	$43,932	1	12.2	78.1	8.7
1997	$56,405	$758,337	$4,863,384	$582,854	0.9	12.1	77.6	9.3
1998	$53,903	$848,965	$5,228,548	$606,404	0.8	12.6	77.6	9
1999	$42,858	$907,162	$5,550,117	$642,871	0.6	12.7	77.7	9
2000	$53,919	$985,954	$5,938,834	$724,060	0.7	12.8	77.1	9.4
2001	$49,336	$1,044,273	$6,356,084	$772,926	0.6	12.7	77.3	9.4
2002	$51,552	$1,005,258	$6,796,228	$747,499	0.6	11.7	79.1	8.7
2003	$43,564	$949,686	$6,970,170	$749,293	0.5	10.9	80.0	8.6
2004	$46,951	$909,042	$7,440,083	$733,513	0.5	10	81.5	8

All data from NCES *Public Libraries in the United States* annual reports

- There appears to be less federal and state money available to help local libraries pay for hardware, software and technology improvements. This is due, in part, to state libraries and state governments using state and federal (LSTA) funds to pay for database licensing, digital virtual reference and other services, and because federal filtering requirements (CIPA) limit how federal dollars may be applied. This trend has the biggest negative impact in small communities, and state libraries should explore and address this inequity.

Training and Planning

The 2007 study clearly indicates the need for public librarians to obtain a range of additional training and knowledge. The most important areas for training include:

- *Management of information technology.* Public librarians need to better understand how to plan for and evaluate information technology and networked services. There is inadequate knowledge of what constitutes "sufficient and adequate" bandwidth given the library's existing network services and current and future user demand for these services.

As a result, there is inadequate planning of networked services and even less ongoing and formal evaluation to determine the effectiveness and impact of public library information technology deployment and networked services. A particular evaluation need is the ability of libraries to demonstrate the value that library technology adds to the communities that libraries serve.

- *Deployment of information technology.* Given the various issues related to limited physical facilities (as discussed above), librarians need to learn how to better deploy, arrange, maintain, and maximize the space and facilities currently available for public access computing. Because the majority of libraries will not receive significant renovation or new capital expenditure money in the near future, how to best take advantage of existing physical facilities with least cost and effort is essential.

- *Information technology and network finances.* The limited response to questions on the survey related to information technology expenditures and the numerous responses of "don't know" suggest that there is a critical need for public librarians to maintain better records and better understand the types of information technology expenditures, what exactly is being spent on what types of information technology and networked services, and the costs and impacts of competing forms of hardware, software, and telecommunications.

- *New models for information technology management.* There are a number of innovative approaches for how libraries are re-thinking how information technology and networked services can be organized through new models. Some libraries receive such services directly from the state library, some have developed consortia for sharing information technology costs and maintenance, others outsource information technology management and maintenance and so forth. Librarians need to be aware of new and evolving models and be able to make informed decisions about how they might work best in their particular situation.

- *The ability to communicate the need for and the impact of library services.* The 2007 study confirms findings from previous years that librarians need to do a better job of "telling their story" on the importance and impact of public access computing to their community. This includes a range of advocacy efforts such as partnering with key groups in the community, working the political environment better, and marketing/promoting the impact of public access computing. Qualitative and quantitative data should be used to accomplish these objectives.

Internet Services

The study demonstrated that public libraries are expanding and evolving services to meet public demand and needs. Public libraries, for example:

- Offer a range of training programs, including computer skills, Internet searching and database use, e-mail instruction and information literacy;
- Assist students and parents with school assignments;
- Provide education support for adult learners;

- Provide disaster services and support to victims of natural disasters;
- Provide support for a range of e-government services such as application filing, disaster relief application, income tax filing, and many others; and
- Provide employment support through workshops and enabling the public to submit employment applications electronically – a practice increasingly required by employers.

This list of services and resources is not exhaustive, but rather demonstrates the range and breadth of public access services that libraries provide to the communities that they serve. Because many of these services are available to the public remotely through the library's Web site, the library serves as an Internet provider in both the physical and digital environments.

Public libraries offer these services by and large, however, without any clear mandate from any authoritative agencies. Rather, public libraries offer these services and resources because library staff saw a need in their communities. For example:

- Federal, state, and local governments increasingly mandate the use of e-government approaches for government-citizen interaction and yet provide no place or support for users to actually engage in those services. Thus, those individuals without the knowledge or capacity to engage in e-government head to the public library for both assistance and access to technology.
- During the hurricanes of 2004 and 2005, residents in the Gulf states flocked to their public libraries for assistance in filing disaster relief applications and locating family members – something neither Federal Emergency Management Agency (FEMA) nor state equivalents were equipped or prepared to do.
- Students often use the public library after school hours to research and complete a range of school projects and assignments. These require the libraries to develop collections, license resources, establish tutoring services, etc., to assist students with these efforts. And yet, public libraries are not included in the education system and budgets.

The public library community should engage in discussions with state and local government agencies, including education departments and e-government agencies, to bring public libraries to the table and discuss the role of public libraries in the support of education and government services and resources. For too long public libraries, in their service to their communities, have provided support to educational and government programs out of their own resources, and the strain is beginning to show. The outcome of this discussion should be the identification of specific roles that public libraries can provide, support mechanisms for public libraries to successfully provide these services, staff training requirements, and other public library needs.

Facilities

Anyone who visits public libraries is immediately struck by the diversity in design, functionality, and architecture of the buildings, reflecting the communities they serve. The building design, however, also can be a substantial challenge to public libraries since many libraries are quite old and were never designed for functionality in a networked environment. The increased integration of technology into library service places a range of stresses on buildings – physical space for workstations and other equipment and specialized furniture, power, server rooms, and cabling, for example. Patron needs also present challenges, particularly the need for power so that they may plug in their laptops or other devices, as well as conducive spaces to work.

The shift from the federal Library Services and Construction Act to the Library Services for Technology Act in the 1990s marked a clear move away from federal support of library construction and renovation projects to technology-based projects and services. Current efforts undertaken by the Chief Officers of State Library Agencies (COSLA) to review state construction support is a good first step in benchmarking library construction and understanding the impact of this change in funding strategy.

Results of this research should be carefully reviewed by national and state library associations and the IMLS to meet the physical facility needs of public libraries as they increasingly operate in the networked environment.

Information Policy

Public libraries operate in a complex information policy environment shaped by federal, state and local governments. Government policymakers have not often given adequate policy attention to the role of public libraries in today's society, the types of laws and regulations that would best support public libraries, and how governments can better partner with public libraries as a means to benefit the population at large.

There is a need to address a number of public policy issues related to public libraries, including:

- What are the responsibilities of federal, state, and local governments in supporting public libraries and the various services public libraries provide?
- What roles and responsibilities should public libraries provide to assist residents to be successful in today's and tomorrow's society?
- To what degree are librarians adequately prepared to offer these roles and activities successfully?
- How can federal and state government best support library building and technology infrastructure to meet the increasing load of public access computer and Internet services and resources?
- What are the roles for public libraries as the United States develops a national telecommunications policy? What responsibilities do federal, state, and local governments have to provide adequate bandwidth in support of public library services?
- Are adequate resources available to public libraries to accomplish these roles and activities?
- How successful are public libraries in meeting public access computing, networked services, and e-government roles and responsibilities?

These specific questions can foster national, state and local discussions intended to reevaluate public libraries' roles in the areas of public access computing, networked services, financial support for public libraries, and e-government.

Taking action will require library organizations and agencies at the state and national levels to understand and address the topics and issues the authors have identified in this section. In addition, these key organizations and agencies can establish policy discussions with members of

Congress and the current Administration regarding these and related federal information policy topics. The ALA Office for Information Technology Policy is well-suited to coordinate this effort. Ultimately, strategically positioning libraries in a national and statewide dialog to extend libraries' impact and effectiveness strengthens the country as a whole.

Additional Resources

This study, of course, does not exist in a vacuum. Not only do the *Public Libraries and the Internet* studies ground this data, but report contributors also pulled on other data sources and were informed by other research done in the library field. Cited sources are listed in footnotes throughout the report, but the authors also would like to draw attention here to several sources that contribute to understanding the value of library services in general and/or the challenges and opportunities afforded by expanded technology resources in our libraries.

Americans for Libraries Council. *Worth Their Weight: An Assessment of the Evolving Field of Library Valuation.* May 2007.
http://www.lff.org/documents/WorthTheirWeight_000.pdf

Davis, Denise M. *Funding Issues in U.S. Public Libraries, Fiscal Years 2003-2006.* March 2006
http://www.ala.org/ala/ors/reports/FundingIssuesinUSPLs.pdf

Florida State University,. School of Information Studies, Information Use Management and Policy Institute. *Economic Benefits and Impacts from Public Libraries in the State of Florida.* September 2004. http://dlis.dos.state.fl.us/bld/finalreport/

MaintainIT Project. http://maintainitproject.org/

McClure, Charles R., Jessica McGilvray, Kristin Barton, and John Carlo Bertot. *E-Government and Public Libraries: Current Status, Meeting Report, Findings, and Next Steps.* (2007)
http://www.ii.fsu.edu/announcements/e-gov2006/egov_report.pdf

Morrill Solutions for the Wisconsin Public Library Consortium. *The Wisconsin Library User (and Non-User) II: Outcomes of a Second Statewide Survey (2003-2007 comparisons).* June 2007. http://www.wplc.info/current/Wisconsin_Library_User_2003-2007.pdf

Urban Libraries Council. *Making Cities Stronger: Public Library Contributions to Local Economic Development.* January 2007.
http://www.urbanlibraries.org/files/making_cities_stronger.pdf

Weingarten, Rick, Nancy Bolt, Mark Bard, John Windhausen. *American Library Association Office for Information Technology Policy Public Library Connectivity Project: Findings and Recommendations.* July 2007.
http://www.ala.org/ala/washoff/contactwo/oitp/papersa/public_version_final.pdf

Section I:
Findings from the Public Libraries and the Internet 2006-2007 Survey

INTRODUCTION

This report to the American Library Association (ALA) presents the national and state data from the *2007 Public Libraries and Internet* survey. The 2007 survey (see Appendix A) continues the research of previous surveys conducted by John Carlo Bertot and Charles R. McClure, with others, since 1994.[11] The 2007 study data expanded on findings from the 2006 survey, but also explored new areas such as library technology budgets, e-government roles of public libraries, and issues associated with maintaining, upgrading, and replacing a range of public access technologies.

The data collected by this annual survey can provide national and state policymakers, library advocates, practitioners, researchers, government and private funding organizations, and a range of other stakeholders, with a better understanding of the issues and needs of libraries associated with providing Internet-based services and resources. Equally important, the data can also assist public librarians to better plan for and deliver Internet-based services and resources to their users.

The 2007 survey is part of a larger study funded by the ALA to gain a better understanding of public library technology access and funding, which includes the national survey, case site visits to public libraries in selected states, and a survey of state librarians. The overall study's primary focus was to obtain comprehensive data related to these topics and explore the issues that public libraries encounter when planning for, implementing, and operating their public access technology components (e.g., workstations, bandwidth, services, and resources).

Objectives of Study
The main objectives for this survey were to provide data that would determine the extent to which public libraries:

- Provide and sustain public access Internet services and resources that meet community public access needs;
- Install, maintain, and upgrade the technology infrastructure required to provide public access Internet services and resources;
- Serve as a public Internet access venue of first choice within the libraries' communities for content, resources, services, and technology infrastructure (e.g., workstations and bandwidth), rather than the access point of last resort/only option;
- Serve as key technology and Internet-based resource/service training centers for the communities that the libraries serve;
- Serve as agents of e-government; and
- Fund their information technology investments.

---

[11] Reports from the 1994-2006 studies are available at: http://www.ii.fsu.edu/plinternet.

The findings detailed in this report address these objectives as well as a range of related topics and issues.

METHODOLOGY

The 2007 study employed a web-based survey approach to gather data, with a mailed survey participation-invitation letter from the ALA sent to the directors of libraries in the sample. The letter introduced the study, provided information regarding the study sponsors and the research team, explained the study purpose and goals, provided instructions on how to access and complete the electronic survey, and provided contact information to answer any questions that participants might have.

The study obtained data that enabled analysis by the following categories:
- Metropolitan status[12] (e.g., urban, suburban, and rural);
- Poverty[13] (less than 20 percent [low], 20 percent-40 percent [medium], and greater than 40 percent [high]);
- State (the 50 states plus the District of Columbia); and
- National.

Given the quality of the data, findings could be generalized to each of these four categories. Finally, the survey explored topics that pertained to both public library system and outlet (branch) level data. Thus, the sample required for this study was complex.

The study team used the 2002 public library dataset available from the NCES as a sample frame, which was the most recent file at the time the geocoding process began. The study team employed the services of the GeoLib database (http://www.geolib.org/PLGDB.cfm) to geocode the NCES public library universe file in order to calculate the poverty rates for public library outlets. Given the timeframe of the study, GeoLib was able to geocode 16,457 library outlets.[14] From these totals, the researchers used SPSS Complex Samples software to draw the sample for the study. The sample needed to provide the study team with the ability to analyze survey data at the state and national levels along the poverty and metropolitan status strata discussed above. The study team drew a sample with replacement of 6,979 outlets. Finally, the sample drawn used a 95% confidence interval for data analysis purposes.

---

[12] Metropolitan status was determined using the official designations employed by the Census Bureau, the Office of Management and Budget, and other government agencies. These designations are used in the study because they are the official definition employed by NCES, which allows for the mapping of public library outlets in the study.

[13] In previous studies, the authors have used the less than 20%, 20%-40%, and greater than 40% poverty breakdowns. Though previous studies by the authors have employed these percentages, the data from this study can be analyzed at different levels of granularity, if desired. The poverty of the population a library outlet serves is calculated using a combination of geocoded library facilities and census data. More information on this technique is available through the authors as well as by reviewing the 1998 and 2000 public library Internet studies:
Bertot, J. C., and McClure, C. R. (2000). *Public Libraries and the Internet 2000: Summary Findings and Data Tables*. Washington, D.C.: National Commission on Libraries and Information Science. Available at: http://www.nclis.gov/statsurv/2000plo.pdf; Bertot, J. C., and McClure, C. R. (1998). *Moving Toward More Effective Public Internet Access: The 1998 National Survey of Public Library Outlet Internet Connectivity*. Washington, D.C.: National Commission on Libraries and Information Science. Available at: http://www.nclis.gov/statsurv/1998plo.pdf

[14] Geocoding is the process by which all public library buildings are mapped to determine their physical location. Census data are then overlaid to determine the poverty of the population served by the library.

The study team developed the questions on the survey through an iterative and collaborative effort involving the researchers, representatives of the funding agencies, and members of the Study Advisory Committee. The study team pre-tested the initial surveys with the project's advisory committee, public librarians, and the state data coordinators of the state library agencies and revised the survey based on their comments and suggestions.

The survey asked respondents to answer questions about specific library branches and about the library system to which each respondent branch belonged. The 2007 *Public Libraries and the Internet* survey sampled 6,979 public libraries based on three library demographics—metropolitan status (roughly equating to their designation of urban, suburban, or rural libraries), poverty level of their service population (as derived through census data), and state in which they resided. Respondents answered the survey between November 2006 and February 2007. After a number of follow-up reminders and other strategies the survey received a total of 4,027 responses for a response rate of 57.7 percent. Figure 1 below shows that the responses were representative of the population, and thus demonstrated the quality of the data.

Outlet (Branch) Versus Systems

The survey deployed a two-stage approach that included questions regarding sampled outlets (branches) and questions regarding an entire library system. For roughly 85% of public libraries, there is no distinction between a branch and system, as these are single facility systems (i.e., one branch, one system). The remaining roughly 15 percent of public libraries, however, do have multiple branches. There was a need to separate branch and system-level questions, as some of the survey questions were point-of-service delivery questions (e.g., number of workstations, bandwidth, and training) whereas others were administrative in nature (e.g., e-rate applications, operating budgets, and technology budgets).

Questions 1 through 12 of the survey explored branch level issues (e.g., Internet connectivity, speed of connection, workstations, etc.). Questions 13 through 21 posed questions regarding the entire library system (e.g., E-rate applications, funding for information technology, patron and staff information technology training, etc.). Upon completion of questions 1 though 12 for all sampled branches, respondents were then taken to the system level questions. Given that the actual respondent for the system level data might be different than for the branch level data, users were permitted to leave and reenter the web-based survey for completion. See Appendix 1 for a print version of the survey. The analysis of system and branch level data required different approaches, considerations, and weighting schemes for national and state analysis.

Data Analysis

The survey uses weighted analysis to generate national and state estimates. As such, the analysis uses the actual responses from the 4,027 library outlets from which a completed survey was received to estimate to all geocoded outlets. For example, Anchor Point Public Library in Anchor Point, Alaska, is coded as a rural library outlet with less than 20 percent poverty. Anchor Point Public Library's responses (and all others designated rural with less than 20 percent poverty) are weighted by 3.6 to generate an estimate for all rural outlets with less than 20 percent poverty.

The same process is used for analyzing and estimating state level data. The key difference is that the weighting process is limited to the poverty and metropolitan status library designations for the state.

The data reported have a margin of error of 5 percent.

SELECTED KEY FINDINGS AND IMPLICATIONS

The below presents selected key findings and their implications from the national survey. These are not meant to be exhaustive, but rather, serve to highlight a range of findings and implications that the survey identified.

Public Access Connectivity and Infrastructure

The study found that public libraries face a number of issues and challenges as providers of free public access Internet and computing services. In this capacity as community-based public access venues, libraries and employ a range of strategies to maintain, upgrade, and make available their public access infrastructure. The findings indicate that, while public libraries provide substantial public access services and resources, their ability to do so is not limitless and, in some cases, may be reaching a saturation point.

Libraries as Community Access Computing and Internet Access Points

Public libraries continue to provide important public access computing and Internet access in their communities:

- 99.7 percent of public library branches are connected to the Internet;
- 99.1 percent of public library branches offer public Internet access;
- 54.2 percent of public library branches offer wireless Internet access, up from 36.7 percent in 2006;
- 100 percent of urban library branches are connected to the Internet; and
- Public library branches have an average of 10.7 public access workstations, with rural libraries having an average of 7.1 workstations and high poverty libraries having 25.4 workstations.

Together these findings demonstrate the extent to which public libraries serve their communities through Internet connectivity.

The Addition, Upgrade, and Replacement Challenge

The survey data indicate (see Figures 7 through 14) that the average number of public access workstations is 10.7, a figure that has not changed significantly since the 2002 *Public Libraries and the Internet* study (the average number in 2002 was 10.8; the average number in 2004 was 10.4; the average number in 2006 was 10.7). Moreover, Figures 9 through 11 demonstrate that libraries are by and large not adding workstations (58 percent of libraries have no plans to add workstations in the coming year, and another 29 percent are "considering" adding but don't know how many). Nor are libraries upgrading existing workstations; rather, they are essentially pursuing a workstation replacement strategy (nearly 50 percent, see Figure 10).

Combined with the survey data on wireless Internet access in which respondents indicated that 51.9 percent of libraries are providing wireless access to expand service rather than adding workstations (see Figure 17), it is clear that public libraries are neither adding nor upgrading workstations. Instead, they are replacing what workstations they have to the extent possible and expanding public access by allowing patrons to bring in their own technology.

Reasons that respondents cited for the inability to add workstations (see Figure 13) include space (76.1 percent), cost (72.6 percent), and infrastructure (e.g., cabling, electrical outlets; 31.2 percent). Reasons cited for the inability to replace public access workstations include cost (84.1 percent), maintenance (maintenance (37.8 percent), and staff (28.1 percent) (see Figure 14). Thus the challenges faced by libraries in enhancing their public access workstation infrastructure include a range of cost, building, and personnel issues.

Quality of Public Access

A key issue woven through the survey's findings is that, while public libraries provide a substantial *amount* of public access Internet and computing service, the overall physical infrastructure they are able to provide may be lacking in *quality*. Take the below data points as examples:

- Bandwidth has essentially remained unchanged since the 2006 survey. For example, 62.1 percent of public libraries report connection speeds of greater than 769kbps, as compared to 63.3 percent in 2006 (see Figure 19).
- Overall, 16.6 percent of respondents reported that their connection is the maximum speed that they can acquire, 18.1 percent cannot afford to increase their bandwidth, and 19.3 percent indicated that they could increase their bandwidth but had no plans to do so. Thus, over 50 percent of libraries indicate that they will not be increasing their bandwidth for a range of reasons – affordability, ability, or availability (see Figure 23).
- At the same time, roughly 52 percent of respondents reported that their connectivity speed is insufficient some or all of the time (see Figure 22). This is up about 6 percent from 2006.
- Nearly 80 percent of respondents report that they have insufficient workstations some (58.8 percent) or all (18.7 percent) of the time (see Figure 15). These figures are fairly consistent with the 2006 survey findings, in which 13.7 percent of respondents reported insufficient workstations all of the time and 71.7 percent of respondents reported insufficient workstations some of the time (see Figure 32 in the 2006 report).
- Just below 50 percent of public libraries report that their wireless connections share the same bandwidth as their public access workstations (see Figure 21).

Together, these data point to a public library public access infrastructure that is increasingly unable to keep up with the demands of the Web 2.0 environment[15] – an environment that requires increasingly sophisticated workstations, substantial bandwidth, and a range of resources that libraries are beginning to indicate that they may not be able to support.

---

[15] Originally a phrase coined by O'Reilly Media, Web 2.0 in general refers to Web-based technologies which promote and facilitate interaction and collaboration among and between a range of user groups. These technologies require libraries to provide an increasingly complex range of computing and bandwidth technologies.

The Infrastructure Challenge
The 2007 survey asked a range of questions that assessed the ability of public library infrastructure to provide public access Internet and computing services. The questions were exploratory and provided initial views of library capabilities. Essentially, respondents reported that they face a range of challenges that are best summarized as follows (see Figures 13 through 15 and 17):

- Building. Library buildings are out of space and cannot support more workstations; they are insufficiently wired to support more cable drops; and they are insufficiently wired for the power requirements of workstations and patron-provided laptops.
- Cost. Respondents indicated that funding workstation replacements, upgrades, bandwidth enhancements, and a range of other services related to public Internet access and computing was a major issue.
- Staff. Respondents indicated that staff skills and time were factors in their decisions to upgrade their public access infrastructure. Lacking dedicated IT staff proved a particular burden to many public libraries.

Together, these data point to what may be the beginning of a trend: public libraries have essentially added as much public access infrastructure possible with their current buildings. Moreover, they have a range of challenges in moving the public access technologies forward with their current funding and staffing levels and skills.

Extensive Range of Library Services Provided
The data document a very broad range of Internet-based services provided by public libraries. The range, depth, and extent of Internet and public access services that public libraries provide is extensive. In reviewing the types of Internet services libraries provide that public libraries consider to be critical (Figure 24), the overall growth in Public Access Internet Services (Figure 27), the types of technology training provided (Figure 25) and expanding services such as E-government (Figure 29), it is clear that public libraries offer their communities a significant amount of service. And for many communities, the public library is the only organization in that community that can provide these services. As Figure 31 indicates, 73.1 percent of respondents indicate that their public library is the only provider of free public Internet access in the library's community.

The Federal government provides only very limited direct technology support to public libraries (Figures 51-58), yet the argument could be made that the many Internet-based services libraries provide – and especially E-government services – directly support numerous Federal programs and services. With public libraries moving into the provision of disaster and emergency planning services (Figure 28), many of which support the Federal government, a reconsideration of the nature and extent of Federal technology support to public libraries may be needed.

The challenge for public librarians is the degree to which they can maintain and/or expand upon these services in the future. With the rapid development of new services and applications that the web environment produces and the move to Web 2.0 applications, librarians will be challenged to both provide quality bandwidth, information technology infrastructure as well as new services.

Funding Technology and Public Access Services
The survey asked libraries to identify their technology budget expenditures by a broad range of categories by fiscal year – staff salaries, hardware, software, and telecommunications. Respondents by and large were unable to provide answers to these questions, as there was a roughly 50 percent drop off in question completion on these items (see Figures 51 through 66). Discussions with librarians completing the survey indicated a range of reasons for their inability to answer the technology budget questions accurately. These include the following:

- Lack of a technology budget. A number of respondents, particularly those from smaller rural libraries, stated that their libraries do not have a separate technology budget and that all funds are expended from a general operating budget. In short, there is only ad hoc technology budgeting in these libraries.
- Lack of knowledge regarding technology expenditures. Some respondents indicated that their libraries have a general technology budget, but that they do not formally track their technology expenditures.
- Inability to report as asked. For some respondents whose libraries do have technology budgets, they were unable to report the technology expenditures as requested due to their library's internal or city/county budgeting processes.
- Time factor. Some respondents simply indicated that they were unwilling to take the time to complete the budget questions, as the questions were time consuming.

With this limited knowledge of expenditures related to Internet services and infrastructure, planning for future Internet services and infrastructure becomes problematic. In addition, this limited knowledge of expenditures related to Internet services and infrastructure also limits how well the librarians can evaluate the purchase and use of this technology. Thus, if the public library community wishes to improve its overall management (planning and evaluation) of technology in the library, better control over technology-related expenditures is necessary.

Moving Connectivity and Public Access Forward
Public libraries continue to prepare for future of their public access services, resources, and infrastructure. In doing so, however, public libraries face a number of challenges.

Enhancing Public Access Infrastructure
Public libraries plan to add, replace, or upgrade workstations and make other enhancements to their public access computing and Internet access services:

- 17.2 percent of public library branches plan to add more workstations within the next year, while 21.7 percent of branches are considering doing so;
- 50.1 percent of public library branches plan to replace some workstations within the next year. Of the 50.1 percent of libraries, 25.0 percent have plans to replace a definite number of workstations, with an average replacement of 6.2 workstations;
- A total of 28.9 percent of public library branches plan to upgrade some workstations within the next year. Of the 28.9 percent, 7.1 percent have plans to upgrade a definite number of workstations, with an average upgrade of 6.6 workstations; and
- 17.4 percent plan to add wireless access within the next year, which means that over 71 percent of public libraries would then offer wireless access.

These data demonstrate the continual cycle of upgrades and enhancements that connectivity and public access computers require.

Challenges Remain

Challenges remain as public libraries continue to improve their public access computing and Internet access services:

- 52.3 percent of public library branches indicate that their connection speeds are inadequate to meet user demands some or all of the time;
- Only 21.9 percent of public library branches indicate that the number of workstations they currently have is adequate to meet patron demands at all times;
- 57.8 percent of public library branches have no plans to add workstations in the next year;
- Space (76.1 percent), cost factors (72.6 percent), and availability of electrical outlets, cabling, or other infrastructure (31.2 percent) most commonly influence decisions to add public access Internet workstations;
- Rural public libraries tend to have the fewest hours open, fewest public access workstations, fewest workstations to be added, replaced, or upgraded, and are less likely to offer public access Internet workstations; and
- Lack of space for workstations and/or necessary equipment (48.2 percent) and no access to adequate telecommunications services (27.1 percent) most commonly influence public library branches' ability to provide public Internet access to patrons.

The data show, therefore, that although public libraries provide a wide range of Internet-based services and resources, along with a robust public access computing infrastructure, public libraries are under pressure to meet all the demands that public access computing requires, face a range of limitations, and may even be at capacity or unable to overcome some barriers (e.g., space and other physical plant limitations).

Importance of Public Library-Provided Internet Access

Taking a broad view of the survey findings clearly demonstrates, for a range of reasons, the importance of public library provided Internet access. The range of services provided by the public library in the Web-based environment includes support of education (K-12 and beyond); E-government services; electronic reference services; access to an astounding amount of books, reports, articles and other material; communication with others around the country and the world; and numerous indicators of how this public access improves the users' overall quality of life (see also Figure 27 and 28).

Two additional factors indicating the importance of public library provided access are first, that that nation-wide, 73 percent of libraries responded that they are the only free public access to the Internet in their community (Figures 31 and 93) and second, that the demand to use the public access workstation is consistently greater than the workstations available (Figures 15 and 70). In short, the impacts and benefits resulting from public library free public access to the Internet is significant – and were it not for public libraries many residents of the country would have significantly reduced Internet-based services or no access/services at all.

ADDITIONAL VIEWS OF THE DATA

In addition to the national and state-level cross-tabulation and frequency data analysis, the study team engaged in geographic information system (GIS)-based analysis of selected survey data. The goals of this analysis were to:

- Conduct preliminary experimental data analysis at the state level to represent national trends;
- Demonstrate the potential of GIS-based analysis;
- Provide alternate views of the survey data; and
- Graphically represent additional analysis.

Below are selected graphical representations of public access workstation, bandwidth, and wireless connectivity.

As Figure GIS-1 demonstrates, the Southwestern, Southeastern, selected Midwestern, and Mid-Atlantic States, as well as California, tend to have the highest average number of public access workstations available for patron use. Figure GIS-2 shows that wireless access is most prevalent in Texas, selected Midwestern states, and the Northeast.

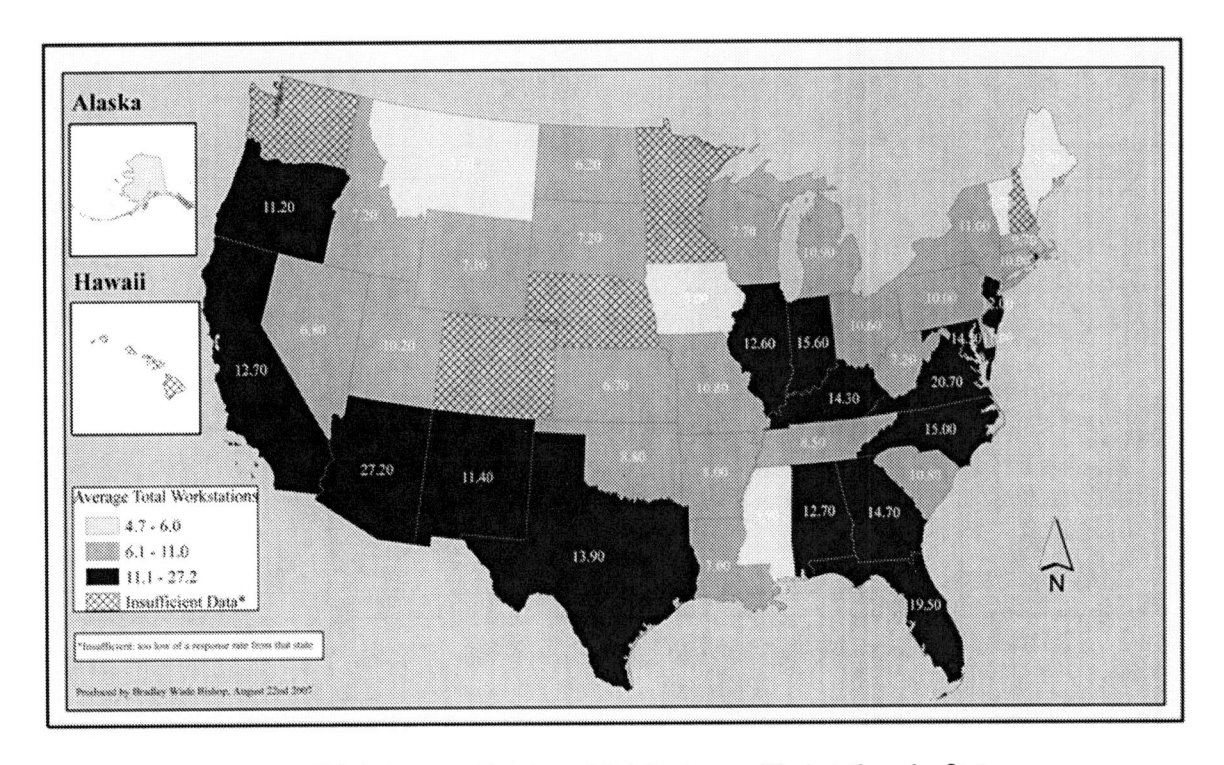

Figure GIS-1. Average Number of Public Access Workstations by State

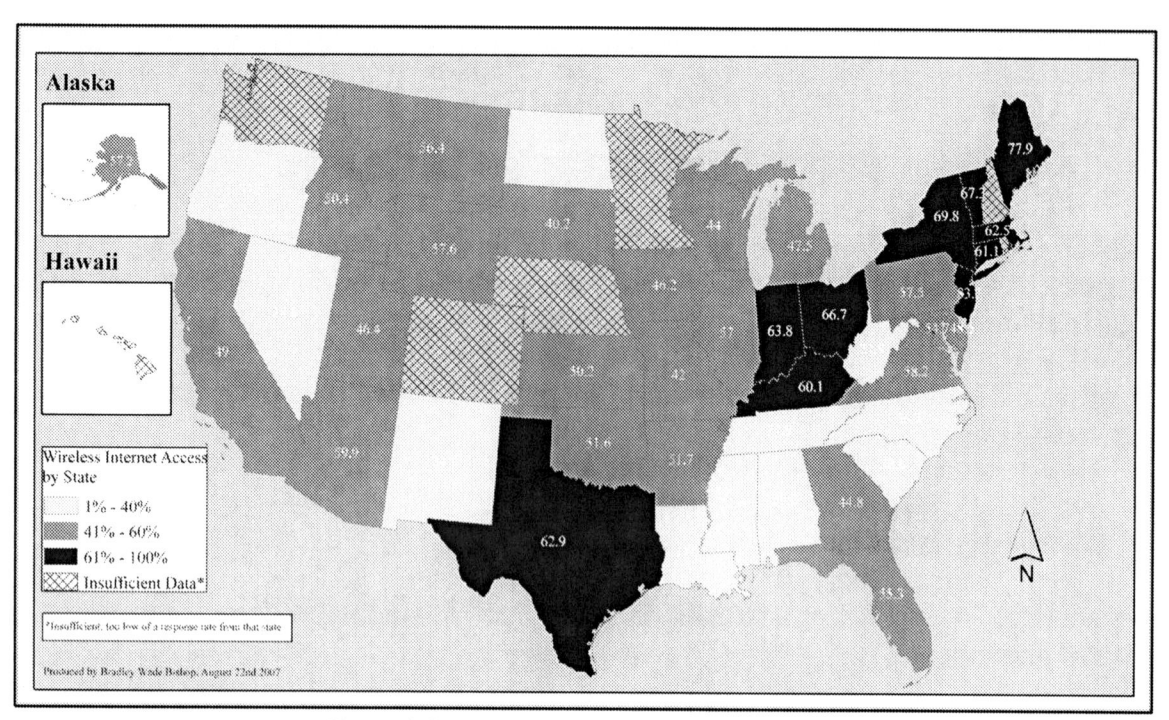

Figure GIS-2. Wireless Internet Access by State

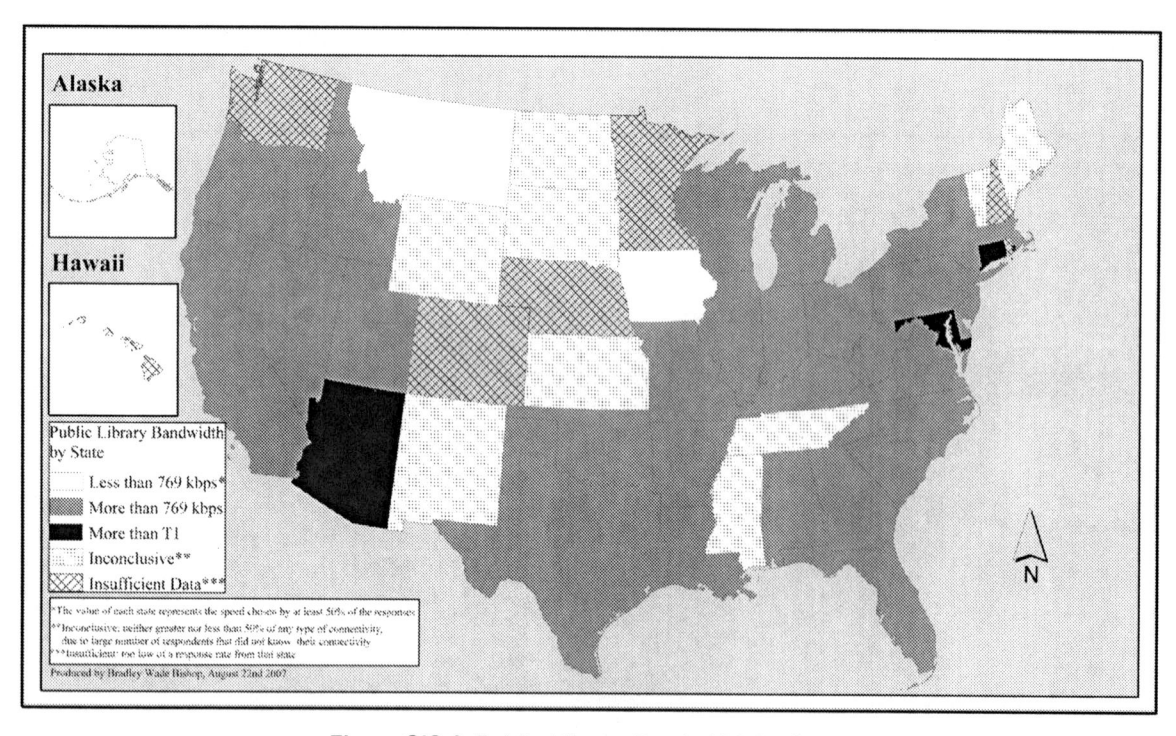

Figure GIS-3. Public Library Bandwidth by State

Figure GIS-3 offers a view on public library bandwidth. By looking at public library bandwidth below 769kbps, greater than 769kbps but less that 1.5MBPS (T1), and 1.5MBPS (T1) or greater, it is clear that few states have 50% or more of their public libraries with connections of a T1 or greater. Indeed, Arizona, Maryland, and Connecticut are the only states in which 50% or more of their public libraries have T1 or better connectivity. The data also show that the rural states by and large, though not in all cases, have low connectivity speeds.

There are a range of additional figures that could be generated from the survey data. The above are merely some selected findings for illustrative purposes. And yet, they demonstrate that the data can show different trends when represented through GIS analysis.

Data tables and findings

The next sections present the national survey's findings and data tables. The national branch findings are presented first, followed by the national system findings.

As Figure 1 shows, the overall distribution of the survey is representative of the total population

Figure 1: Public Library Outlets

	Poverty Level							Overall	
	Low (Less than 20%)		Medium (20%-40%)		High (More than 40%)			
	Responding Facilities As a Proportion of All Respondents	Responding Facilities As a Proportion of National Population	Responding Facilities As a Proportion of All Respondents	Responding Facilities As a Proportion of National Population	Responding Facilities As a Proportion of All Respondents	Responding Facilities As a Proportion of National Population	Responding Facilities As a Proportion of All Respondents	Responding Facilities As a Proportion of National Population
Metropolitan Status								
Urban	6.1% (247 of 4,027)	10.0% (1,650 of 16,457)	4.1% (164 of 4,027)	6.6% (1,092 of 16,457)	0.9% (38 of 4,027)	0.9% (148 of 16,457)	11.1% (449 of 4,027)	17.6% (2,890 of 16,457)
Suburban	31.5% (1,207 of 4,027)	30.2% (4,967 of 16,457)	1.7% (68 of 4,027)	2.1% (342 of 16,457)	0.05% (2 of 4,027)	0.4% (7 of 16,457)	33.3% (1,340 of 4,027)	32.3% (5,316 of 16,457)
Rural	49.5% (1,995 of 4,027)	43.6% (7,182 of 16,457)	5.9% (236 of 4,027)	6.3% (1,040 of 16,457)	0.2% (7 of 4,027)	0.2% (29 of 16,457)	55.6% (2,238 of 4,027)	50.1% (8,251 of 16,457)
Overall	87.2% (3,512 of 4,027)	83.8% (13,799 of 16,457)	11.6% (468 of 4,027)	15.0% (2,474 of 16,457)	1.2% (47 of 4,027)	1.1% (184 of 16,457)	100.0% (4,027 of 4,027)	100.0% (16,457 of 16,457)

Based on geocoding of 16,457 outlets.
Overall Response Rate = 57.7%

Figure 2: Public Library Outlets Connected to the Internet

Metropolitan Status	Poverty Level				Overall
	Low	Medium	High	
Urban	100.0% (n=1,570)	100.0% (n=1,039)	100.0% (n=136)	100.0% (n=2,745)
Suburban	99.8% (n=4,821)	100.0% (n=327)	100.0% (n=7)	99.8% (n=5,155)
Rural	99.7% (n=7,052)	98.2% (n=988)	85.7% (n=25)	99.5% (n=8,065)
Overall	99.8% (n=13,443)	99.3% (n=2,354)	97.6% (n=168)	99.7% (n=15,965)

Weighted missing values, n=38

The connectivity rate of public libraries over that past several years has effectively reached its saturation point, as only a small percentage of libraries remain without an Internet connection (see Figure 2). The connectivity rate over that past several years has included 98.7 percent in 2002, 99.6 percent in 2004, to 98.9 percent in 2006. All of these numbers are within the margin of error (+/- 5 percent) of one another, illustrating the level of consistency across public library outlets in terms of Internet connectivity. Considering the margin of error, virtually every public library outlet in the United States has access to the Internet.

As Figure 2 also shows, urban libraries reported 100 percent connectivity across all poverty levels, with the lowest connectivity (85.7 percent) reported by rural libraries in high-poverty communities.

Figure 3: Connected Public Library Outlets Providing Public Access to the Internet				
	Poverty Level			
Metropolitan Status	Low	Medium	High	Overall
Urban	99.6% (n=1,563)	99.4% (n=1,032)	97.1% (n=132)	99.4% (n=2,728)
Suburban	99.3% (n=4,798)	100.0% (n=327)	100.0% (n=7)	99.3% (n=5,132)
Rural	99.1% (n=7,009)	98.2% (n=988)	85.7% (n=25)	98.9% (n=8,022)
Overall	99.2% (n=13,370)	99.0% (n=2,347)	95.3% (n=164)	99.1% (n=15,881)
Weighted missing values, n=34				

As Figure 3 indicates, a vast majority of public library outlets provide public Internet access. When compared with Figure 2, Figure 3 shows that of the 15,965 public library outlets with Internet connections, only 84 libraries do not provide access to the public – approximately .5 percent. However, high poverty rural outlets showed a decline of 14.3 percent in providing public internet access from a reported 100 percent in 2006. The number of library outlets with public Internet access has increased since the 2006 study, when only 98.4 percent outlets provided public access to the Internet.

Figure 4: Average Number of Hours Open per Outlet				
	Poverty Level			
Metropolitan Status	Low	Medium	High	Overall
Urban	53.0 (n=1,570)	56.1 (n=1,039)	54.4 (n=136)	54.2 (n=2,745)
Suburban	52.1 (n=4,848)	46.4 (n=327)	30.5 (n=7)	51.7 (n=5,182)
Rural	38.3 (n=7,088)	37.0 (n=1,010)	36.6 (n=29)	38.1 (n=8,127)
Overall	45.0 (n=13,507)	47.0 (n=2,376)	50.4 (n=172)	45.2 (n=16,055)

The average number of hours that public library outlets are open has continued to increase slightly since 2004. In Figure 4, the average number of hours open per outlet was 45.2. In 2004, the average number was 44.5 and 44.8 in 2006. Not surprisingly, urban library outlets have the highest average hours open (54.2), while rural outlets have the lowest average (38.1). Urban outlets in medium poverty areas show the biggest increase (4.1) in hours open. It should be noted that rural outlets had the lowest average in 2006 as well (38.7), and that rural, low poverty, and high poverty outlets have all reported decreased average hours open since 2006.

Figure 5: Public Library Outlets Change in Hours Open							
	Metropolitan Status			Poverty Level			
Hours Open	Urban	Suburban	Rural	Low	Medium	High	Overall
Hours increased since last fiscal year	13.5% (n=371)	11.5% (n=595)	10.3 (n=834)	11.3% (n=1,531)	10.8% (n=257)	7.1% (n=12)	11.2% (n=1,800)
Hours decreased since last fiscal year	2.6% (n=71)	3.7% (n=190)	3.2% (n=260)	3.4% (n=461)	2.4% (n=57)	2.3% (n=4)	3.2% (n=521)
Hours stayed the same as last fiscal year	83.9% (n=2,303)	84.8% (n=4,393)	86.5% (n=7,033)	85.3% (n=11,511)	86.8% (n=2,062)	90.7% (n=156)	85.5% (n=13,730)
Number of hours increased	6.2 (n=371)	5.5 (n=568)	4.7 (n=834)	5.4 (n=1,503)	4.8 (n=257)	3.0 (n=12)	5.3 (n=1,773)
Number of hours decreased	6.6 (n=71)	6.7 (n=190)	5.6 (n=260)	6.4 (n=461)	4.3 (n=57)	8.0 (n=4)	6.1 (n=521)

Figure 5 illustrates the stability of the hours that public library outlets are open. For 85.5 percent of libraries, hours open remained unchanged from the previous year. The hours open increased in 11.2 percent of outlets with the average increase at 5.3 hours from the previous year. The remaining 3.2 percent of libraries reported decreased hours open, with an average decrease from the previous year of 6.1 hours. Urban outlets were most likely to increase their hours open, and suburban and high poverty outlets were most likely to decrease their hours open.

Figure 6: Public Library Outlets Closed							
	Metropolitan Status			Poverty Level			
Reasons Closed	Urban	Suburban	Rural	Low	Medium	High	Overall
Closed temporarily due to renovations	7.3% (n=11)	14.8% (n=20)	--	9.0% (n=26)	--	33.3% (n=4)	7.5% (n=30)
Closed temporarily due to storm or other damage	4.6% (n=7)	20.3% (n=27)	2.9% (n=4)	5.3% (n=15)	21.9% (n=22)	--	9.2% (n=37)
Closed temporarily due to budgetary reasons	2.7% (n=4)	5.9% (n=8)	2.9% (n=4)	3.9% (n=11)	--	33.3% (n=4)	3.8% (n=15)
Closed permanently due to budgetary reasons	39.4% (n=57)	14.8% (n=20)	28% (n=35)	21.0% (n=61)	46.9% (n=47)	33.3% (n=4)	27.8% (n=112)
Closed for other reasons	46.0% (n=67)	41.3% (n=55)	57.6% (n=72)	55.7% (n=162)	31.2% (n=31)	--	48.0% (n=193)
Percent of branches that closed	5.0% (n=145)	2.5% (n=132)	1.5% (n=124)	2.1% (n=291)	4.0% (n=99)	6.3% (n=12)	2.4% (n=402)
Key: -- : No data to report							

Figure 6 shows the reasons public library outlets reported for both temporary and permanent closures in 2006-2007. Budgetary reasons were the largest single factor influencing permanent outlet closings (27.8 percent) and this affected medium poverty outlets more frequently than low or high poverty outlets. High poverty outlets were the most likely to be closed temporarily due either to renovations or for budgetary reasons. Suburban and medium poverty outlets were four-times more likely to close due to storm or other damage than were urban libraries, and nearly eight times more likely to close than rural libraries. High poverty area outlets experienced the greatest percentage of closing at 6.3 percent, and rural outlets had the lowest percentage of closings at 1.5 percent.

Figure 7: Average Number of Public Library Outlets Public Access Internet Workstations				
Metropolitan Status	Poverty Level			Overall
	Low	Medium	High	
Urban	14.1 (n=1,416)	23.5 (n=872)	30.3 (n=113)	18.3 (n=2,401)
Suburban	13.0 (n=4,414)	8.8 (n=302)	4.0 (n=7)	12.7 (n=4,723)
Rural	7.0 (n=6,779)	7.4 (n=944)	9.2 (n=25)	7.1 (n=7,747)
Overall	9.9 (n=12,609)	14.3 (n=2,118)	25.4 (n=145)	10.7 (n=14,872)

Figure 7 indicates that the overall average of public access Internet workstations in each library outlet at 10.7. This average has remained relatively steady over the past several years, averaging 10.7 in 2006, 10.4 in 2004, and 10.8 in 2002. High poverty urban libraries offer the highest average number of workstations at 30.3. The lowest number of workstations per library outlet generally is reported in rural libraries, though high poverty suburban libraries offer the lowest average number of workstations at 4.0 (down from 5.0 in the 2006 study). Regardless of poverty level, urban libraries offer the greatest average number of public access workstations at a rate of 2.4 times that of rural libraries and 1.4 times that of suburban libraries.

Figure 8: Average Age of Graphical Public Access Internet Workstations							
Average Age	Metropolitan Status			Poverty Level			Overall
	Urban	Suburban	Rural	Low	Medium	High	
Less than 1 year old	9.8 (n=930)	6.6 (n=1,776)	3.7 (n=3,398)	5.1 (n=5,013)	7.2 (n=1,024)	8.3 (n=67)	5.4 (n=6,104)
1-2 years old	10.5 (n=964)	6.8 (n=2,220)	3.5 (n=3,022)	5.3 (n=5,228)	7.3 (n=904)	23.0 (n=74)	5.8 (n=6,206)
2-3 years old	11.1 (n=873)	7.1 (n=2,083)	3.5 (n=3,083)	5.4 (n=5,249)	8.6 (n=727)	12.5 (n=62)	5.8 (n=6,038)
3-4 years old	11.2 (n=710)	6.8 (n=1,460)	3.3 (n=2,929)	4.9 (n=4,508)	9.5 (n=536)	7.7 (n=55)	5.4 (n=5,099)
Greater than 4 years old	8.7 (n=813)	5.6 (n=1,487)	3.5 (n=3,192)	4.6 (n=4,723)	6.8 (n=715)	3.9 (n=54)	4.8 (n=5,492)

Figure 8 shows the average number of public access Internet workstations by age. The highest number of workstations (5.8) clusters in the age ranges of 1-2 and 2-3 years old, while the fewest number of workstations (4.8) were greater than 4 years old. Urban libraries have the greatest number of workstations in all age range categories. High poverty libraries also have the greatest number of newer workstations (e.g., less than one year old, 1-2 years old and 2-3 years old) yet these libraries did report an average decline of 9.1 workstations less than 1 year-old.

Figure 9: Public Library Outlets Public Access Internet Workstations Addition Schedule

Workstation Addition Schedule	Metropolitan Status			Poverty Level			Overall
	Urban	Suburban	Rural	Low	Medium	High	
The library plans to add workstations within the next year	20.2% (n=539)	18.0% (n=909)	15.7 (n=1,247)	16.8% (n=2,223)	18.6% (n=430)	27.1% (n=42)	17.2% (n=2,695)
The library is considering adding more workstations or laptops within the next year, but does not know how many at this time	23.1% (n=629)	24.2% (n=1,242)	19.7% (n=1,580)	22.4% (n=2,991)	18.1% (n=424)	21.3% (n=35)	21.7% (n=3,450)
The library has no plans to add workstations within the next year	52.0% (n=1,419)	54.0% (n=2,769)	62.1% (n=4,980)	57.4% (n=7,664)	60.4% (n=1,417)	52.8% (n=87)	57.8% (n=9,168)
The library has plans to reduce the number of workstations	*	*	*	*	*	--	*
The average number of workstations that the library plans to add within the next year	7.2 (n=539)	5.4 (n=909)	3.3 (n=1,247)	4.4 (n=2,223)	5.4 (n=430)	16.8 (n=42)	4.8 (n=2695)

Weighted missing values, n=8
Key: -- : No data to report
      * : Insufficient data to report

Figure 9 shows the status of adding public access Internet workstations in public library outlets. In the next year, 17.2 percent of outlets are planning to add more workstations, while a further 21.7 percent of outlets are considering doing so. High poverty outlets are the most likely to add workstations. Of those planning on adding workstations in the next year, high poverty outlets plan to add the highest average number of workstations (16.8), which is more than double the second highest average (urban outlets with an average number of 7.2) and well above the overall average (4.8).

Over half of public library outlets (57.8 percent) have no plans to add or remove workstations in the next year. Rural outlets are 10 percent more likely to have no plans to change the number of workstations than are urban and suburban libraries. An additional 14.3 percent of medium poverty outlets reported having no plans to add workstations within the next year as compared with 46.3 percent reported in 2006.

Figure 10: Public Library Outlet Public Access Internet Workstations Replacement Schedule

Workstation Replacement Schedule	Metropolitan Status			Poverty Level			Overall
	Urban	Suburban	Rural	Low	Medium	High	
The library plans to replace workstations within the next year	24.8% (n=676)	26.4% (n=1,353)	24.2% (n=1,941)	24.9% (n=3,330)	25.3% (n=593)	28.1% (n=46)	25.0% (n=3,969)
The library plans to replace some workstations within the next year, but does not know how many at this time	33.2% (n=906)	26.6% (n=1,363)	21.3% (n=1,712)	25.3% (n=3,376)	24.1% (n=566)	23.7% (n=39)	25.1% (n=3,981)
The library has no plans to replace workstations within the next year	37.1% (n=1011)	43.8% (n=2,242)	51.2% (n=4,104)	46.5% (n=6,211)	45.8% (n=1074)	43.4% (n=71)	46.3% (n=7,357)
The number of workstations that the library plans to replace within the next year	12.2 (n=676)	7.3 (n=1,353)	3.4 (n=1,941)	5.6 (n=3,330)	8.7 (n=593)	16.4 (n=46)	6.2 (n=3,969)

Figure 10 shows the status of the replacement schedules for public access Internet workstations in public library outlets. Within the next year, 50.1 percent of outlets are planning to replace some workstations. Of these libraries, 25 percent plan to replace workstations at an average of 6.2 workstations per library outlet. High poverty outlets have plans to replace the greatest average number of workstations. Interestingly, not only are a majority of public libraries not adding public access workstations (Figure 9), 46.3 percent of outlets have no plans to replace workstations. Not surprisingly, rural outlets are least likely to replace workstations, in fact showing the fewest number (3.4) of planned workstation replacements.

Figure 11: Public Library Outlet Public Access Internet Workstations Upgrade Schedule

Workstation Upgrade Schedule	Metropolitan Status			Poverty Level			Overall
	Urban	Suburban	Rural	Low	Medium	High	
The library plans to upgrade workstations within the next year	2.8% (n=77)	6.7% (n=344)	8.8% (n=708)	7.5% (n=1,009)	4.8% (n=112)	4.9% (n=8)	7.1% (n=1,129)
The library plans to upgrade some workstations within the next year, but does not know how many at this time	21.5% (n=588)	22.3% (n=1,143)	21.6% (n=1,734)	22.2% (n=2,968)	20.0% (n=470)	16.6% (n=27)	21.8% (n=3,465)
The library has no plans to upgrade workstations within the next year	64.4% (n=1,758)	63.9% (n=3,280)	65.9% (n=5,284)	64.5% (n=8,624)	67.3% (n=1,580)	71.4% (n=117)	65.0% (n=10,322)
The number of workstations that the library plans to upgrade within the next year	20.5 (n=77)	7.8 (n=344)	4.4 (n=708)	6.1 (n=1,009)	11.0 (n=112)	5.9 (n=8)	6.6 (n=1,129)

Figure 11 reveals the number of outlets that have plans to upgrade public access Internet workstations. In the next year, 28.9 percent of library outlets are planning on upgrading at least some of their existing workstations. Of these libraries, 7.1 percent plan to upgrade a definite number of workstations, with an average of 6.6 upgraded workstations. Urban outlets have the highest average number of workstations for which upgrades are planned. Sixty-five percent of library outlets have no plans to upgrade workstations within the next year, with high poverty outlets being the least likely to upgrade (71.4 percent). Rural outlets (8.8 percent) were the most likely to upgrade workstations.

Figure 12: Public Library's Ability to Follow Its Upgrade/Replacement Schedule for Public Access Internet Workstations

Ability of Library to Follow Its Schedule	Metropolitan Status			Poverty Level			Overall
	Urban	Suburban	Rural	Low	Medium	High	
Yes	68.5% (n=1,868)	60.0% (n=3,079)	45.3% (n=3,634)	53.7% (n=7,175)	54.9% (n=1,289)	71.2% (n=117)	54.0% (n=8,581)
No	15.4% (n=420)	11.3% (n=580)	13.2% (n=1,055)	12.5% (n=1,670)	15.4% (n=361)	14.4% (n=24)	12.9% (n=2,054)
The library has no workstation replacement or addition schedule	9.8% (n=266)	21.2% (n=1,088)	33.6% (n=2,693)	26.4% (n=3,531)	21.2% (n=497)	11.9% (n=19)	25.5% (n=4,047)
Not applicable	2.9% (n=80)	3.7% (n=192)	4.1% (n=332)	3.7% (n=498)	4.5% (n=106)	*	3.8% (n=604)
Key: * : Insufficient data to report							

Figure 12 reveals the number of outlets that are able to follow upgrade and replacement schedules for public access Internet workstations. A majority of outlets (54 percent) are able to

43

follow upgrade/replacement schedules, and 12.9 percent are not. Approximately one-quarter of outlets (25.5 percent) lack an upgrade/replacement schedule. High poverty and urban outlets are most likely to be able to follow their schedules. Suburban and rural outlets are significantly less likely than urban libraries to have upgrade/replacement schedules in place.

Figure 13: Factors Influencing Addition of Public Access Internet Workstations							
	Metropolitan Status			**Poverty Level**			
Factors Influencing Workstation Addition Decisions	Urban	Suburban	Rural	Low	Medium	High	Overall
Space limitations	77.5% (n=2,115)	76.9% (n=3,941)	75.2% (n=6,031)	76.3% (n=10,197)	75.7% (n=1,777)	68.7% (n=113)	76.1% (n=12,087)
Cost factors	71.1% (n=1,940)	66.9% (n=3,428)	76.8% (n=6,159)	72.7% (n=9,720)	71.7% (n=1,682)	76.6% (n=126)	72.6% (n=11,527)
Maintenance, upgrade, and general upkeep	22.0% (n=601)	21.5% (n=1,102)	30.9% (n=2,475)	26.6% (n=3,555)	25.2% (n=592)	19.1% (n=31)	26.3% (n=4,178)
Staff time	17.9% (n=489)	16.3% (n=837)	15.3% (n=1,231)	15.1% (n=2,015)	21.2% (n=497)	26.4% (n=43)	16.1% (n=2,556)
Inadequate bandwidth to support additional workstations	18.4% (n=502)	17.0% (n=872)	8.5% (n=685)	12.3% (n=1,640)	16.0% (n=377)	25.6% (n=42)	13.0% (n=2,058)
Availability of electrical outlets, cabling, or other infrastructure	37.3% (n=1,018)	34.0% (n=1,743)	27.3% (n=2,189)	30.4% (n=4,063)	35.1% (n=824)	38.4% (n=63)	31.2% (n=4,950)
The current number of workstations meets the needs of our patrons	6.0% (n=164)	12.3% (n=628)	17.7% (n=1,417)	14.7% (n=1,971)	9.8% (n=231)	4.9% (n=8)	13.9% (n=2,210)
Other	2.7% (n=75)	2.9% (n=147)	2.4% (n=190)	2.7% (n=356)	1.8% (n=43)	6.9% (n=11)	2.6% (n=411)
Will not total to 100%, as respondents could select more than one option. Weighted missing values, n=8							

Figure 13 reports the factors that influence decisions to add public access Internet workstations. Space limitations (76.1 percent) and cost (72.6 percent) were by far the most common factors reported by public libraries. Space was most likely to be a factor in urban outlets, while cost was most likely to be a factor in rural outlets. The next most frequent factor – availability of electrical outlets, cabling, and other infrastructure – was selected by only 31.2 percent of outlets. A much smaller number of outlets reported sufficient workstations to meet patron need than in the 2006 study, 13.9 percent in 2007 versus 20.7 percent in 2006. Nevertheless, an additional 12.4 percent of high poverty outlets reported that the current number of workstations is meeting patron needs, as compared with 4.9 percent in 2006.

Figure 14: Factors Influencing Replacement of Public Access Internet Workstations							
	Metropolitan Status			**Poverty Level**			
Factors Influencing Workstation Replacement Decision	Urban	Suburban	Rural	Low	Medium	High	Overall
Cost factors	81.3% (n=2,217)	79.7% (n=4,083)	87.9% (n=7,052)	85.2% (n=11,388)	78.2% (n=1,835)	79.0% (n=130)	84.1% (n=13,353)
Maintenance, upgrade, and general upkeep	29.0% (n=790)	34.2% (n=1,754)	43.0% (n=3,449)	37.9% (n=5,068)	37.2% (n=874)	31.1% (n=51)	37.8% (n=5,993)
Availability of staff	33.4% (n=911)	27.6% (n=1,414)	26.6% (n=2,133)	27.5% (n=3,677)	30.8% (n=722)	35.9% (n=59)	28.1% (n=4,458)
Other	13.0% (n=356)	15.7% (n=805)	11.6% (n=930)	12.7% (n=1,701)	15.6% (n=367)	13.7% (n=23)	13.2% (n=2,090)
Will not total to 100%, as respondents could select more than one option. Weighted missing values, n=8							

Figure 14 presents the factors influencing replacement of public access Internet workstations. Cost (84.1 percent) was the most significant factor influencing workstation replacement by more than two-to-one for all factors measured. In addition to cost, maintenance, upgrade, and general upkeep were the most likely factors influencing rural and suburban outlets' decisions to replace workstations. Libraries serving urban and high poverty communities were more likely to report availability of staff as an influencing factor in replacing public access Internet workstations.

Figure 15: Sufficiency of Public Access Internet Workstations							
	Metropolitan Status			Poverty Level			
Sufficiency of Public Access Workstations	Urban	Suburban	Rural	Low	Medium	High	Overall
There are consistently fewer public Internet workstations than patrons who wish to use them throughout a typical day	36.4% (n=992)	16.9% (n=867)	13.9% (n=1,117)	17.7% (n=2,372)	24.1% (n=565)	24.0% (n=39)	18.7% (n=2,976)
There are fewer public Internet workstations than patrons who wish to use them at different times throughout a typical day	54.4% (n=1,485)	63.3% (n=3,248)	57.4% (n=4,605)	59.5% (n=7,959)	54.9% (n=1,289)	54.5% (n=89)	58.8% (n=9,337)
There are always sufficient public Internet workstations available for patrons who wish to use them during a typical day	8.5% (n=231)	19.3% (n=993)	28.2% (n=2,259)	22.3% (n=2,983)	19.8% (n=465)	21.5% (n=35)	21.9% (n=3,483)

As Figure 15 indicates, 21.9 percent of public library outlets reported having sufficient workstations to meet patron needs at all times. A majority (58.8 percent) of public library outlets reported too few workstations for patron use at various times throughout the day and 18.7 percent reported consistently fewer workstations than needed. Poverty was less an indicator of sufficiency than was metropolitan status. Urban library outlets were the most likely (90.8 percent) to report having consistently fewer workstations than needed, while rural outlets were most likely (28.2 percent) to report sufficient workstations to meet patron need. However, 57.4 percent of rural outlets reported not having enough workstations to handle patron needs at different times throughout the day.

Figure 16: Public Access Wireless Internet Connectivity in Public Library Outlets							
	Metropolitan Status			Poverty Level			
Availability of Public Access Wireless Internet Services	Urban	Suburban	Rural	Low	Medium	High	Overall
Currently available	66.8% (n=1,822)	60.7% (n=3,112)	45.8% (n=3,676)	55.6% (n=7,425)	47.0% (n=1,102)	50.1% (n=82)	54.2% (n=8,610)
Not currently available, but there are plans to make it available within the next year	18.8% (n=513)	17.3% (n=889)	17.0% (n=1,364)	17.0% (n=2,271)	19.3% (n=452)	25.8% (n=42)	17.4% (n=2,765)
Not currently available and no plans to make it available within the next year	12.5% (n=340)	20.0% (n=1,024)	35.2% (n=2,825)	25.6% (n=3,423)	31.1% (n=730)	21.6% (n=35)	26.4% (n=4,188)
Weighted missing values, n=8							

The number of public library outlets offering wireless Internet access has steadily increased since first measured in 2004. Wireless access was available in 17.9 percent of outlets in 2004 and 36.7 percent in 2006. Figure 16 shows that in 2007 wireless access was available in 54.2 percent of outlets. Furthermore, 17.4 percent of outlets that do not currently have wireless access plan to add it in the next year. Thus, if libraries follow through with their plans to add wireless access, 71.6 percent of public library outlets in the U.S. will have it within a year. There was a notable increase, with the exception of high poverty outlets, in the percentage of outlets now having wireless access available.

In 2007, wireless access was most likely to be available in urban, suburban, and low poverty outlets. High poverty outlets are the most likely to have plans to add wireless access in the next year. Rural outlets and medium poverty outlets are least likely to have wireless access or plans to add it in the next year.

Figure 17: Public Access Wireless Internet Connectivity Using Laptops in Public Library Outlets

Availability of Public Access Wireless Internet Services Through the Use of Laptops	Metropolitan Status			Poverty Level			Overall
	Urban	Suburban	Rural	Low	Medium	High	
Purchasing laptops for in-library patron use instead of Internet workstations	11.5% (n=315)	7.5% (n=385)	5.1% (n=405)	7.0% (n=935)	6.9% (n=163)	4.7% (n=8)	7.0% (n=1,106)
Not adding more Internet workstations or laptops, but provide wireless access for patrons with personal laptops	59.3% (n=1,618)	57.5% (n=2,948)	45.8% (n=3,678)	52.7% (n=7,044)	47.8% (n=1,121)	47.7% (n=78)	51.9% (n=8,244)

As part of the libraries' wireless Internet access strategies, Figure 17 illustrates how outlets are planning on using wireless Internet access to keep up with patron demands. Seven percent of outlets report plans to purchase wireless laptops for patron use instead of workstations, with urban outlets being the most likely to do so. Additionally, 51.9 percent of outlets provide (or soon will provide) wireless access for patrons with personal laptops. Urban outlets are the most likely to incorporate wireless access followed closely by suburban libraries.

Figure 18: Public Access Wireless Internet Connectivity Outside of Public Library Outlets

Availability of Public Access Wireless Internet Services Outside the Public Library	Metropolitan Status			Poverty Level			Overall
	Urban	Suburban	Rural	Low	Medium	High	
Currently available	3.1% (n=84)	1.8% (n=90)	4.3% (n=347)	3.5% (n=470)	1.8% (n=42)	4.9% (n=8)	3.3% (n=521)
Currently available outside and in areas in the community through partnerships	4.3% (n=117)	2.1% (n=107)	1.1% (n=92)	2.0% (n=271)	1.7% (n=40)	2.4% (n=4)	2.0% (n=316)
Currently available through a bookmobile with wireless access	1.0% (n=27)	*	*	*	*	--	*
Not currently available, but there are plans to make it available within the next year	12.3% (n=336)	8.2% (n=422)	8.0% (n=642)	8.6% (n=1,152)	9.9% (n=232)	9.5% (n=16)	8.8% (n=1,400)
Not currently available and there are no plans to make it available within the next year	62.3% (n=1,698)	75.2% (n=3,851)	73.1% (n=5,868)	72.0% (n=9,619)	71.8% (n=1,684)	69.4% (n=114)	71.9% (n=11,417)
Other	13.4% (n=365)	8.6% (n=442)	8.6% (n=693)	9.3% (n=1,237)	10.4% (n=244)	11.4% (n=19)	9.4% (n=1,500)
Key: * : Insufficient data to report --: No data to report								

Figure 18 shows the availability of library wireless Internet access outside the library building. By far, most outlets (71.9 percent) do not provide wireless access outside of the library and have no plans to do so. Only 3.3 percent of outlets provide wireless access outside the library, while another 2 percent provide access to the community through partnerships with others. Urban library outlets were the only to report wireless access provided through bookmobiles, and were the mostly likely to indicate plans to provide wireless Internet access outside the library within the next year.

Figure 19: Public Library Outlets Maximum Speed of Public Access Internet Services								
	Metropolitan Status			Poverty Level				
Maximum Speed	Urban	Suburban	Rural	Low	Medium	High	Overall
Less than 56kbps	*	*	1.4% (n=112)	*	*	--	*
56kbps - 128kbps	1.4% (n=37)	4.1% (n=209)	10.0% (n=799)	6.3% (n=845)	8.2% (n=193)	4.9% (n=8)	6.6% (n=1,045)
129kbps - 256kbps	2.0% (n=53)	3.6% (n=186)	9.3% (n=748)	6.4% (n=856)	5.4% (n=127)	2.5% (n=4)	6.2% (n=987)
257kbps - 768kbps	2.2% (n=60)	6.9% (n=352)	13.4% (n=1,076)	10.0% (n=1,341)	6.1% (n=143)	2.5% (n=4)	9.4% (n=1,488)
769kbps - 1.5mbps	40.5% (n=1,105)	38.4% (n=1,969)	26.8% (n=2,149)	31.9% (n=4,262)	38.1% (n=895)	40.1% (n=66)	32.9% (n=5,223)
1.6mbps - 5.0mbps	21.7% (n=591)	15.2% (n=777)	9.9% (n=791)	13.8% (n=1,841)	12.5% (n=294)	14.2% (n=23)	13.6% (n=2,158)
6.0mbps - 10mbps	13.1% (n=357)	8.0% (n=408)	4.3% (n=349)	6.5% (n=869)	9.5% (n=222)	14.2% (n=23)	7.0% (n=1,114)
Greater than 10mbps	13.1% (n=358)	8.6% (n=442)	7.1% (n=571)	8.4% (n=1,128)	9.1% (n=213)	19.0% (n=31)	8.6% (n=1,372)
Don't Know	3.9% (n=107)	12.7% (n=652)	16.0% (n=1,282)	14.0% (n=1,869)	7.3% (n=172)	--	12.9% (n=2,014)
Weighted missing values, n=8 Key: -- : No data to report * : Insufficient data to report								

As Figure 19 demonstrates, 32.9 percent of library outlets have connection speeds of 769kbps-1.5mbps. Further, 29.2 percent of library outlets have connection speeds of greater than 1.5mbps. Only 22.2 percent of library outlets reported a maximum connection speed of 768kbps or less. Urban outlets were the most likely to have the fastest connections, with 13.1 percent reporting 10mbps or greater. Access at the lower categories of connection speed has decreased since the 2006 data was collected. Connection speeds at 56kbps or less are all but gone, with the exception of rural outlets.

The 2007 survey marked the first time that respondents were able to indicate connectivity speed categories of greater than 1.5mbps. By and large, however, the connectivity speeds identified by respondents remained essentially unchanged since the 2006 survey. It is important to note, however, that 12.9 percent of respondents reported that they did not know their connection speeds, as compared to 4.9 percent in 2006.

Figure 20: Public Library Outlets Type of Public Access Internet Service							
	Metropolitan Status			Poverty Level			
Type of connection	Urban	Suburban	Rural	Low	Medium	High	Overall
DSL	13.9% (n=379)	15.6% (n=798)	33.2% (n=2,666)	25.1% (n=3,350)	20.2% (n=473)	12.2% (n=20)	24.2% (n=3,843)
Cable	11.8% (n=323)	24.6% (n=1,262)	19.8% (n=1,589)	22.1% (n=2,953)	8.7% (n=205)	9.5% (n=16)	20.0% (n=3,174)
Leased Line	54.3% (n=1,482)	45.5% (n=2,334)	25.2% (n=2,024)	34.4% (n=4,590)	49.6% (n=1,163)	51.8% (n=85)	36.8% (n=5,839)
Municipal Networks (wireless or other)	4.6% (n=125)	2.8% (n=143)	4.3% (n=341)	3.8% (n=512)	3.6% (n=85)	7.1% (n=12)	3.8% (n=609)
Satellite	*	*	2.4% (n=196)	1.5% (n=200)	1.1% (n=26)	2.4% (n=4)	1.9% (n=231)
Fiber	17.9% (n=489)	14.6% (n=750)	8.0% (n=644)	11.5% (n=1,535)	13.3% (n=312)	21.3% (n=35)	11.9% (n=1,882)
Other	9.1% (n=248)	5.9% (n=301)	8.5% (n=679)	7.5% (n=998)	9.1% (n=214)	9.8% (n=16)	7.7% (n=1,228)
Don't Know	1.2% (n=33)	1.1% (n=55)	1.6% (n=126)	1.3% (n=176)	1.6% (n=38)	--	1.3% (n=214)

Will not total to 100%, as respondents could select more than one option.
Weighted missing values, n=8
Key: -- : No data to report
  * : Insufficient data to report

Figure 20 reports on the type of connections public library outlets are using to access the Internet. Leased lines were the most frequently reported type of connection (36.8 percent), followed by DSL (24.2 percent), and Cable (20 percent). Rural libraries were more likely than others to use DSL for Internet access (33.2 percent). Fiber was reported by 11.9 percent of libraries and was more likely to be available to urban and suburban libraries. Satellite was the least common type of Internet service, particularly for urban and suburban outlets.

Figure 21: Public Library Outlets Shared Wireless-Workstation Bandwidth							
	Metropolitan Status			Poverty Level			
	Urban	Suburban	Rural	Low	Medium	High	Overall
Yes, both the wireless connection and public access workstations share the same bandwidth/connection	56.2% (n=1,534)	50.1% (n=2,570)	47.2% (n=3,787)	50.2% (n=6,711)	47.1% (n=1,104)	45.3% (n=74)	49.7% (n=7,890)
No, the wireless connection is separate from the public access workstation bandwidth/connection	21.5% (n=587)	23.2% (n=1,189)	11.0% (n=881)	16.8% (n=2,248)	16.4% (n=385)	14.4% (n=24)	16.7% (n=2,657)
Don't know	5.6% (n=153)	7.1% (n=363)	13.6% (n=1,088)	10.2% (n=1,360)	9.2% (n=216)	16.9% (n=28)	10.1% (n=1,604)

Weighted missing values, n=8

Figure 21 shows the degree to which public Internet workstations share bandwidth or connections with wireless access. Nearly half of all public library outlets (49.7 percent) report sharing the same bandwidth/connection. A separate wireless connection from the one used by public access workstations was reported as being in use in 16.7 percent of outlets Suburban and urban outlets are 50 percent more likely to have separate connections than are rural libraries. Rural libraries were more likely to report not knowing if the bandwidth/connection was shared.

Figure 22: Public Library Outlets Public Access Internet Connection Adequacy							
	Metropolitan Status			**Poverty Level**			
Adequacy of Public Access Internet Connection	Urban	Suburban	Rural	Low	Medium	High	Overall
The connection speed is insufficient to meet patron needs	21.8% (n=595)	15.8% (n=808)	13.9% (n=1,114)	15.0% (n=2,003)	20.0% (n=470)	26.4% (n=43)	15.9% (n=2,517)
The connection speed is sufficient to meet patron needs at some times	37.8% (n=1,030)	40.4% (n=2,068)	33.4% (n=2,676)	36.2% (n=4,831)	38.1% (n=893)	30.3% (n=50)	36.4% (n=5,774)
The connection speed is sufficient to meet patron needs at all times	35.8% (n=975)	39.6% (n=2,030)	48.9% (n=3,922)	45.0% (n=6,009)	36.3% (n=852)	40.8% (n=67)	43.6% (n=6,928)
Don't know	1.2% (n=33)	1.4% (n=72)	*	1.1% (n=144)	1.2% (n=27)	--	1.1% (n=171)
Weighted missing values, n=8 Key: -- : No data to report * : Insufficient data to report							

Figure 22 shows the perceived adequacy of Internet connection speeds in public library outlets. Access speeds were inadequate for a majority (52.3 percent) of libraries reporting. Forty-three-point-six (43.6) percent of outlets report that connection speed is adequate to meet patron needs at all times, about 10 percent fewer outlets than in 2006 (53.5 percent). Rural libraries were more likely than urban and suburban libraries to report adequate access speeds. In 36.4 percent of public library outlets, the connection speed is sufficient to meet patron needs at some times and 15.9 percent reported the connection speed is insufficient at all times.

Figure 23: Possibility of Increasing Adequacy of Public Library Outlets Public Access Internet Connection							
	Metropolitan Status			**Poverty Level**			
Adequacy of Public Access Internet Connection	Urban	Suburban	Rural	Low	Medium	High	Overall
There is no interest in increasing the connection speed	8.5% (n=232)	17.1% (n=875)	20.9% (n=1,680)	18.4% (n=2,458)	13.5% (n=317)	7.1% (n=12)	17.6% (n=2,787)
The connection speed is already at the maximum level available	10.9% (n=299)	12.3% (n=632)	21.3% (n=1,708)	17.3% (n=2,316)	12.9% (n=302)	12.2% (n=20)	16.6% (n=2,638)
There is interest in increasing the branch's bandwidth, but the library cannot currently afford to	15.0% (n=410)	16.1% (n=824)	20.5% (n=1,642)	18.3% (n=2,445)	17.4% (n=408)	14.2% (n=23)	18.1% (n=2,876)
There are plans in place to increase the bandwidth within the next year	22.1% (n=602)	18.7% (n=956)	7.6% (n=609)	12.4% (n=1,655)	20.1% (n=473)	23.5% (n=39)	13.6% (n=2,167)
It is possible to increase the speed; however, there are no plans in place to increase the bandwidth within the next year	23.5% (n=642)	20.1% (n=1,028)	17.3% (n=1,387)	18.6% (n=2,483)	22.6% (n=531)	26.4% (n=43)	19.3% (n=3,057)
There is interest but the branch lacks the technical knowledge to increase the bandwidth in the library	1.1% (n=31)	1.3% (n=66)	1.8% (n=142)	1.6% (n=220)	*	2.4% (n=4)	1.5% (n=239)
Other	11.1% (n=301)	8.1% (n=413)	4.8% (n=382)	7.0% (n=935)	6.4% (n=150)	6.9% (n=11)	6.9% (n=1,096)
Weighted missing values, n=8 Key: * : Insufficient data to report							

Less than one-fifth of public library outlets (17.6 percent) reported no interest in increasing connection speed, while 16.6 percent reported they were at the maximum speed available. Rural library outlets were the least likely to want or be able to increase their connection speed, while high poverty outlets were the most likely to have plans in place to increase connection speed within the next year. Most interesting in Figure 23 are the reported barriers to increasing access speeds. Cost was reported by 18.1 percent of libraries, and 1.5 percent reported lack of technical expertise as barriers to increasing access speeds. Nineteen point three (19.3) percent reported no plans to increase access speeds even though it was possible to do so. Only 13.6 percent of public library outlets had plans in place to increase bandwidth in the next year.

Figure 24: Public Access Internet Services Critical to the Role of Public Library Outlets							
	Metropolitan Status			**Poverty Level**			
Public Internet Services	Urban	Suburban	Rural	Low	Medium	High	Overall
Provide education resources and databases for K-12 students	71.2% (n=1,938)	71.8% (n=3,680)	63.8% (n=5,118)	67.1% (n=8,972)	70.5% (n=1,650)	68.9% (n=113)	67.7% (n=10,735)
Provide education resources and databases for students in higher education	15.2% (n=414)	21.9% (n=1,124)	23.2% (n=1,858)	20.5% (n=2,741)	26.5% (n=620)	21.6% (n=36)	21.4% (n=3,396)
Provide education resources and databases for home schooling	8.5% (n=231)	12.4% (n=635)	17.9% (n=1,433)	15.2% (n=2,036)	11.1% (n=259)	2.4% (n=4)	14.5% (n=2,299)
Provide education resources and databases for adult/continuing education students	23.5% (n=639)	25.2% (n=1,289)	30.4% (n=2,436)	27.4% (n=3,657)	28.0% (n=656)	31.3% (n=51)	27.5% (n=4,364)
Provide information for local economic development	9.2% (n=249)	2.6% (n=132)	2.9% (n=236)	3.7% (n=490)	4.8% (n=113)	9.5% (n=16)	3.9% (n=618)
Provide information about state and local business opportunities	4.5% (n=122)	1.6% (n=82)	3.1% (n=250)	2.8% (n=369)	2.8% (n=66)	12.0% (n=20)	2.9% (n=455)
Provide information for college applicants	1.9% (n=51)	3.6% (n=184)	7.8% (n=627)	5.0% (n=664)	8.1% (n=190)	4.9% (n=8)	5.4% (n=862)
Provide information for local business marketing	*	1.6% (n=82)	*	1.1% (n=149)	*	2.4% (n=4)	1.0% (n=164)
Provide information about the library's community	17.9% (n=488)	18.0% (n=924)	10.3% (n=829)	14.4% (n=1,926)	12.8% (n=300)	9.0% (n=15)	14.1% (n=2,241)
Provide information or databases regarding investments	2.5% (n=67)	6.1% (n=314)	1.5% (n=122)	3.4% (n=450)	2.3% (n=54)	--	3.2% (n=503)
Provide access to local public and local government documents	9.6% (n=262)	5.2% (n=267)	7.0% (n=564)	6.9% (n=928)	6.4% (n=149)	9.5% (n=16)	6.9% (n=1,093)
Provide access to federal government documents	5.0% (n=137)	5.8% (n=295)	11.0% (n=885)	8.9% (n=1,196)	5.1% (n=118)	2.4% (n=4)	8.3% (n=1,318)
Provide computer and Internet skills training	43.7% (n=1,190)	31.4% (n=1,609)	24.0% (n=1,929)	28.5% (n=3,807)	36.6% (n=857)	37.9% (n=62)	29.8% (n=4,727)
Provide services for job seekers	44.0% (n=1,198)	44.1% (n=2,262)	44.0% (n=3,528)	44.1% (n=5,896)	42.9% (n=1,005)	52.8% (n=87)	44.0% (n=6,987)
Provide services to new citizens and residents	11.5% (n=314)	9.9% (n=506)	14.9% (n=1,193)	13.2% (n=1,766)	10.5% (n=247)	--	12.7% (n=2,013)
Other	10.9% (n=296)	14.8% (n=759)	11.5% (n=919)	13.0% (n=1,732)	9.4% (n=219)	13.7% (n=23)	12.4% (n=1,974)
Will not total to 100%, as respondents could select more than one option. Weighted missing values, n=14 Key: -- : No data to report * : Insufficient data to report							

Figure 24 shows the services provided to the community through public library outlets in their areas. The top three education support services reported by public library outlets were education resources for K-12 students (67.7 percent), and education resources and databases for adult/continuing education (27.5 percent) and students in higher education (21.4 percent). Providing services for job seekers was reported by 44 percent of public library outlets, and 29.8 percent reported that they provide computer and Internet skills training. Urban outlets were the most likely (43.7 percent) to provide computer and Internet skills training as part of the services they provide to the community.

Figure 25: Public Library Outlets Information Technology Training for Patrons							
	Metropolitan Status			**Poverty Level**			
Impacts of Training	Urban	Suburban	Rural	Low	Medium	High	Overall
No training offered	12.5% (n=342)	18.9% (n=967)	30.8% (n=2,474)	24.4% (n=3,263)	21.6% (n=508)	7.3% (n=12)	23.8% (n=3,783)
Facilitates local economic development	6.6% (n=178)	2.2% (n=113)	*	2.2% (n=296)	2.6% (n=60)	7.1% (n=12)	2.3% (n=367)
Offers technology training to those who would otherwise not have any	54.2% (n=1,474)	45.2% (n=2,314)	30.8% (n=2,470)	38.7% (n=5,176)	42.3% (n=989)	56.9% (n=93)	39.4% (n=6,259)
Helps students with their school assignments and school work	35.9% (n=976)	36.2% (n=1,857)	34.4% (n=2,759)	34.3% (n=4,587)	40.4% (n=946)	35.7% (n=59)	35.2% (n=5,592)
Helps business owners understand and use technology and/or information resources	1.7% (n=47)	1.6% (n=83)	1.6% (n=132)	1.6% (n=217)	1.9% (n=45)	--	1.7% (n=262)
Helps patrons complete job applications	24.8% (n=675)	18.9% (n=971)	21.9% (n=1,759)	20.8% (n=2,778)	24.6% (n=576)	31.4% (n=52)	21.5% (n=3,405)
Provides general technology skills	45.3% (n=1,232)	41.1% (n=2,104)	32.8% (n=2,628)	37.1% (n=4,962)	39.2% (n=917)	51.7% (n=85)	37.6% (n=5,964)
Provides information literacy skills	48.9% (n=1,329)	53.7% (n=2,752)	39.6% (n=3,173)	46.1% (n=6,158)	43.4% (n=1,015)	49.8% (n=82)	45.7% (n=7,255)
Helps users access and use electronic government services and resources	17.5% (n=477)	18.6% (n=953)	21.6% (n=1,734)	20.3% (n=2,717)	17.3% (n=404)	26.1% (n=43)	19.9% (n=3,164)
Other	3.8% (n=104)	2.2% (n=111)	2.9% (n=231)	2.7% (n=360)	3.5% (n=82)	2.4% (n=4)	2.8% (n=446)

Weighted missing values, n=14
Key: -- : No data to report
      * : Insufficient data to report

While Figure 24 focused on the Internet *services* that are critical to the role of libraries, Figure 25 identifies the impact of information technology *training* provided to patrons by public library outlet staff. Providing information literacy skills is the most commonly reported impact of the technology training provided, and is more often provided in suburban outlets (53.7 percent) than in urban (48.9 percent) and rural libraries (39.6 percent). Technology skills training was reported as the second and third most frequently provided information technology training by libraries. Helping students with school and homework assignments was reported by 35.2 percent of libraries, although there was a decrease of 13.5 percent from 2006 in high poverty outlets providing students with school work help. Only 1.7 percent of library outlets reported knowing if business owners participated in technology training or if they had specific training target to this user population. Unfortunately, rural outlets are the least likely to offer training of any kind (30.8

percent) and this is largely attributed to insufficient staff resources to provide formal technology training to the public.

Figure 26: Factors Affecting Public Library Outlets' Ability to Provide Public Access Internet Connection

Factors Affecting Connection	Metropolitan Status			Poverty Level			Overall
	Urban	Suburban	Rural	Low	Medium	High	
There is no space for workstations and/or necessary equipment	38.8% (n=7)	66.7% (n=23)	42.5% (n=37)	58.6% (n=63)	18.1% (n=4)	--	48.2% (n=67)
The library building cannot support the necessary infrastructure (e.g. power, cabling, other)	--	--	17.6% (n=15)	10.1% (n=11)	18.1% (n=4)	--	10.9% (n=15)
The library cannot afford the necessary equipment	--	22.2% (n=8)	30.7% (n=27)	24.2% (n=26)	18.1% (n=4)	51.6% (n=4)	24.7% (n=34)
The library does not have access to adequate telecommunications services	38.8% (n=7)	22.2% (n=8)	26.8% (n=23)	27.1% (n=29)	36.3% (n=9)	--	27.1% (n=38)
The library cannot afford the recurring telecommunications costs	--	11.1% (n=4)	18.5% (n=16)	10.4% (n=11)	36.3% (n=9)	--	14.3% (n=20)
The library does not have the staff necessary to install, maintain, and/or upgrade the necessary technology	--	11.1% (n=4)	25.6% (n=22)	20.5% (n=22)	--	51.6% (n=4)	18.7% (n=26)
The library does not control its access to Internet services	--	--	18.2% (n=16)	6.7% (n=7)	18.1% (n=4)	51.6% (n=4)	11.3% (n=16)
There is no interest among library staff or management in connecting the library to the Internet	--	--	--	--	--	--	--
There is no interest within the local community in connecting the library to the Internet	--	--	5.1% (n=4)	--	18.1% (n=4)	--	3.2% (n=4)
Other	61.2% (n=11)	22.2% (n=8)	25.9% (n=22)	24.2% (n=26)	45.6% (n=11)	48.4% (n=4)	29.3% (n=41)

Figure 26 shows the factors limiting public library outlets' ability to provide public Internet access to patrons. Almost half of these outlets that do not provide Internet access (48.2 percent) cited a lack of space for workstations and other necessary equipment as the primary factor affecting their ability to provide access. No outlets reported that access was limited due to lack of interest by library staff or management. More than half (51.6 percent) of high poverty outlets reported budget, staff, or lack of direct control limits their ability to provide public Internet access. Rural libraries reported more factors (9 of the 10 factors measured) limited the provision of Internet access than did libraries in urban and suburban communities. Space and cost were the two factors most frequently reported by rural and suburban libraries. A lack of access to adequate telecommunications services also was a highly reported factor by rural (26.8 percent) and suburban (22.2 percent) libraries.

NATIONAL SYSTEM LEVEL DATA

This section details the study findings for national system level data. A brief discussion of the findings follows each table.

Figure 27: Public Library Systems Public Access Internet Services

Internet services	Metropolitan Status			Poverty Level			Overall
	Urban	Suburban	Rural	Low	Medium	High	
Digital reference/Virtual reference	69.1% (n=426)	66.1% (n=1,811)	52.3% (n=2,940)	57.6% (n=4,621)	57.7% (n=515)	67.4% (n=42)	57.7% (n=5,178)
Licensed databases	96.2% (n=594)	92.7% (n=2,539)	81.0% (n=4,555)	84.8% (n=6,802)	92.8% (n=828)	91.8% (n=57)	85.6% (n=7,687)
e-books	67.2% (n=415)	48.6% (n=1,332)	30.0% (n=1,687)	38.2% (n=3,063)	37.3% (n=333)	62.1% (n=39)	38.3% (n=3,434)
Video conferencing	8.4% (n=52)	1.9% (n=52)	5.0% (n=280)	3.9% (n=316)	6.7% (n=60)	13.5% (n=8)	4.3% (n=384)
Online instructional courses/tutorials	44.0% (n=272)	30.7% (n=841)	35.1% (n=1,973)	33.7% (n=2,704)	39.0% (n=348)	54.0% (n=34)	34.4% (n=3,085)
Homework resources	77.0% (n=476)	73.4% (n=2,010)	64.6% (n=3,630)	68.0% (n=5,458)	67.9% (n=606)	81.1% (n=50)	68.1% (n=6,115)
Audio content (e.g. podcasts, audiobooks, other)	51.4% (n=317)	52.0% (n=1,425)	29.7% (n=1,670)	38.1% (n=3,053)	35.8% (n=320)	64.8% (n=40)	38.0% (n=3,413)
Video content	26.3% (n=162)	15.7% (n=431)	16.0% (n=898)	16.1% (n=1,289)	20.2% (n=181)	35.1% (n=22)	16.6% (n=1,491)
Digitized special collections (e.g., letters, postcards, documents, other)	37.4% (n=231)	27.4% (n=750)	16.2% (n=912)	20.5% (n=1,642)	24.9% (n=222)	45.9% (n=29)	21.1% (n=1,892)
Other	5.2% (n=32)	3.7% (n=100)	3.7% (n=208)	3.6% (n=289)	5.5% (n=49)	5.5% (n=3)	3.8% (n=341)

Will not total to 100%, as respondents could select more than one option.

As revealed by Figure 27, the most frequently offered public access Internet services by public library systems are licensed databases (85.6 percent), homework resources (68.1 percent), digital reference or virtual reference services (57.7 percent), e-books (38.3 percent) and audio content such as podcasts and audiobooks (38 percent). High-poverty outlets providing audio content services increased 22.7 percent over last year's study (42.1 percent). Rural libraries reported providing video conferencing, online instructional courses/tutorials and video content more frequently than did suburban libraries. Only in the case of audio content did more suburban library systems provide access than did urban library systems. Urban and high poverty library systems offer the greatest number of services overall.

Responding library systems were also able to list other services not included in the question options. Other services noted by library systems include: community information, interlibrary loans, genealogy databases, and obituary indexes.

Figure 28: Disaster/Emergency Roles and Services of Public Library Systems							
	Metropolitan Status			**Poverty Level**			
Disaster/emergency roles and services	Urban	Suburban	Rural	Low	Medium	High	Overall
The library building serves as an emergency shelter	24.1% (n=149)	19.9% (n=546)	17.2% (n=967)	18.5% (n=1,482)	19.0% (n=170)	16.1% (n=10)	18.5% (n=1,662)
The library staff provide emergency responder services	19.8% (n=122)	9.1% (n=248)	5.3% (n=300)	6.7% (n=537)	14.4% (n=128)	8.1% (n=5)	7.5% (n=671)
The library's equipment is used by first responders	9.2% (n=57)	5.2% (n=143)	6.0% (n=338)	5.4% (n=436)	10.9% (n=97)	5.4% (n=3)	6.0% (n=537)
The library's public computing and Internet access services are used by the public to access emergency relief services and benefits	46.7% (n=288)	30.9% (n=845)	30.8% (n=1,732)	29.5% (n=2,365)	51.4% (n=459)	67.5% (n=42)	31.9% (n=2,866)
Other	6.6% (n=41)	7.5% (n=205)	8.1% (n=454)	7.7% (n=622)	8.4% (n=75)	5.4% (n=3)	7.8% (n=700)
Will not total to 100%, as respondents could select more than one option.							

Figure 28 shows the roles public library systems play in the event of disaster or emergency situations. Thirty-one-point-nine (31.9 percent) of library systems indicated that their computing and Internet services would be used by the public to access relief services and benefits. Urban systems were the most likely to have their buildings serve as emergency shelters or have staff provide emergency responder services in the case of an emergency or disaster.

Among the other services reported by library systems include: libraries serving as command and control centers, temporary setups for local businesses, classrooms in the case of public school damage, and evacuation sites for local schools. It should be noted that many of the library systems that marked "other" also indicated having no disaster plan or have not had a situation in which emergency services were needed.

Figure 29: E-Government Roles and Services of Public Library Systems							
	Metropolitan Status			**Poverty Level**			
E-Government roles and services	Urban	Suburban	Rural	Low	Medium	High	Overall
Staff provide assistance to patrons applying for or accessing e-government services	55.7% (n=344)	50.6% (n=1,386)	57.2% (n=3,213)	54.5% (n=4,369)	59.3% (n=529)	70.3% (n=44)	55.0% (n=4,942)
Staff provide as-needed assistance to patrons for understanding how to access and use government websites, programs, and services	82.8% (n=511)	79.5% (n=2,177)	77.6% (n=4,360)	78.0% (n=6,260)	82.6% (n=738)	81.0% (n=50)	78.5% (n=7,048)
The library offers training classes regarding the use of government websites, programs, and electronic forms	18.6% (n=115)	7.2% (n=198)	7.8% (n=440)	7.8% (n=625)	12.6% (n=112)	24.3% (n=15)	8.4% (n=753)
The library is partnering with government agencies, non-profit organizations, and others to provide e-government services	25.4% (n=157)	10.8% (n=296)	12.4% (n=696)	11.9% (n=952)	19.4% (n=173)	37.8% (n=24)	12.8% (n=1,149)
Other	3.9% (n=24)	1.7% (n=45)	2.1% (n=116)	1.8% (n=148)	3.8% (n=34)	5.4% (n=3)	2.1% (n=185)
Will not total to 100%, as respondents could select more than one option.							

As Figure 29 indicates, access to and assistance with government websites, programs, and services are the most common services public library systems provide with regard to E-government (78.5 percent). Additionally, over half of public library systems (55 percent) provide assistance to patrons applying for or accessing E-government services. For most types of E-government services, library systems serving high poverty communities are most likely to offer them to the public. Rural libraries (12.4 percent) are more likely than suburban libraries (10.8 percent) to partner with government agencies, non-profit organizations and others to provide E-government services.

Figure 30: Public Library Systems Disaster/Emergency Plan							
	Metropolitan Status			Poverty Level			
Disaster/emergency plan	Urban	Suburban	Rural	Low	Medium	High	Overall
There is no current written plan, and one is not in the process of being developed	12.2% (n=75)	23.1% (n=632)	32.5% (n=1,827)	28.9% (n=2,316)	22.7% (n=202)	24.5% (n=15)	28.2% (n=2,534)
There is no current written plan, but one is in the process of being developed	13.3% (n=82)	24.1% (n=661)	21.7% (n=1,222)	21.7% (n=1,738)	24.0% (n=214)	19.0% (n=12)	21.9% (n=1,964)
There is a current written plan	31.2% (n=193)	16.7% (n=458)	13.3% (n=748)	15.4% (n=1,232)	16.7% (n=149)	29.7% (n=18)	15.6% (n=1,399)
There is a current written plan, but it is more than one year old	30.6% (n=189)	24.8% (n=680)	19.4% (n=1,093)	21.8% (n=1,747)	22.2% (n=198)	27.0% (n=17)	21.9% (n=1,964)
The library is involved in disaster and emergency planning activities at the local level (e.g. town, city, county)	30.7% (n=190)	16.5% (n=451)	13.1% (n=734)	14.8% (n=1,187)	18.4% (n=165)	37.8% (n=23)	15.3% (n=1,375)
The library's existing or plan that is under development, was developed in conjunction with local or other emergency service organizations (e.g. fire, police, disaster relief)	10.9% (n=67)	7.6% (n=208)	6.7% (n=379)	6.7% (n=536)	12.0% (n=108)	16.2% (n=10)	7.3% (n=654)
Do not know	2.9% (n=18)	2.4% (n=66)	3.6% (n=201)	3.2% (n=257)	3.2% (n=28)	--	3.2% (n=286)
Other	3.4% (n=21)	2.4% (n=66)	2.8% (n=157)	2.6% (n=209)	3.9% (n=35)	--	2.7% (n=244)
Will not total to 100%, as respondents could select more than one option. Key: -- : No data to report							

Figure 30 shows the degree to which public library systems have established emergency or disaster plans established. Twenty-eight point eight (28.8 percent) of the systems reported that they do not currently have any sort of plan in place, nor is one being developed. Of those, rural systems are the least likely to have a plan. Only 15.6 percent of library systems reported having a current, updated written plan in place. However, 15.3 percent of systems are in the process of

55

developing an emergency preparedness plan, while another 21.9 percent are updating existing plans that are more than a year old.

Figure 31: Public Library Systems as the Only Provider of Free Public Internet Access							
	Metropolitan Status			Poverty Level			
Free public access	Urban	Suburban	Rural	Low	Medium	High	Overall
Yes	49.5% (n=306)	71.4% (n=1,955)	76.5% (n=4,300)	74.6% (n=5,983)	61.4% (n=548)	48.6% (n=30)	73.1% (n=6,561)
No	33.1% (n=204)	16.4% (n=450)	16.2% (n=911)	16.3% (n=1,306)	26.3% (n=234)	40.6% (n=25)	17.4% (n=1,566)
Do not know	9.7% (n=60)	9.0% (n=247)	3.0% (n=167)	5.1% (n=410)	6.8% (n=61)	5.4% (n=3)	5.3% (n=475)
Other	4.7% (n=29)	1.6% (n=45)	3.1% (n=174)	2.7% (n=216)	3.4% (n=30)	2.7% (n=2)	2.8% (n=248)

Public library systems are commonly the only provider of free public Internet access in many communities. Figure 31 shows 73.1 percent of library systems reporting they are the only provider of free Internet access in their areas, while 76.5 percent of rural libraries are the only such provider. Seventeen point four (17.4) percent stated that there were other places in the library system service area providing free Internet access. Urban and suburban library systems were the least likely to know whether there were other sources of free public Internet access in their communities.

Figure 32: Percentage of Public Library Systems that Applied for an E-rate Discount							
	Metropolitan Status			Poverty Level			
	Urban	Suburban	Rural	Low	Medium	High	Overall
Applied	51.3% (n=317)	32.2% (n=883)	41.1% (n=2,310)	36.9% (n=2,960)	57.0% (n=509)	64.7% (n=40)	39.1% (n=3,509)
Another organization applied on the library's behalf	7.2% (n=44)	13.7% (n=376)	12.0% (n=676)	12.5% (n=1,007)	9.9% (n=88)	2.7% (n=2)	12.2% (n=1,096)
Did not apply	38.2% (n=236)	48.4% (n=1,325)	42.2% (n=2,374)	45.7% (n=3,664)	28.6% (n=256)	24.4% (n=15)	43.8% (n=3,935)
Do not know	1.8% (n=11)	4.8% (n=132)	3.8% (n=215)	4.1% (n=326)	3.2% (n=29)	5.5% (n=3)	4.0% (n=359)

Figure 32 shows the percentage of public library systems that applied for an E-rate discount in 2007. A total of 51.3 percent of systems applied for an E-rate discount, either directly (39.1 percent) or through some other organization (12.2 percent). Urban libraries (58.5 percent) and rural libraries (53.1 percent) were most likely to apply, while only 45.9 percent of suburban libraries reported applying in 2007. Suburban (48.4 percent) and low poverty (45.7 percent) systems were the least likely to apply for the discount.

Figure 33: Percentage Public Library System Receiving E-rate Discount							
	Metropolitan Status			Poverty Level			
E-rate Discount Categories	Urban	Suburban	Rural	Low	Medium	High	Overall
Internet connectivity	65.5% (n=236)	45.9% (n=578)	53.8% (n=1,607)	50.9% (n=2,019)	62.4% (n=372)	72.1% (n=30)	52.6% (n=2,422)
Telecommunications services	91.9% (n=332)	83.4% (n=1,049)	82.0% (n=2,450)	81.8% (n=3,246)	91.0% (n=543)	100.0% (n=42)	83.2% (n=3,831)
Internal connections cost	17.0% (n=61)	13.8% (n=174)	6.7% (n=201)	8.7% (n=344)	13.6% (n=81)	24.1% (n=10)	9.5% (n=436)
Will not total to 100%, as respondents could select more than one option.								

56

For those public library systems receiving E-rate discounts, Figure 33 illustrates which services those funds support. A large majority of systems (83.2 percent) indicate the funds are going towards telecommunications services, with 100 percent of high poverty systems reporting so. About half (52.6 percent) stated that E-rate funds went towards Internet connectivity, and only 9.5 percent reported the funds going toward Internal connection costs, which was the only category not showing a substantial increase in funding.

Figure 34: Public Library Systems' Reasons for Not Applying for E-rate Discounts							
	Metropolitan Status			**Poverty Level**			
Reasons	Urban	Suburban	Rural	Low	Medium	High	Overall
The E-rate application process is too complicated	36.1% (n=85)	36.6% (n=485)	38.7% (n=919)	37.3% (n=1,368)	44.7% (n=114)	44.5% (n=7)	37.8% (n=1,489)
The library staff did not feel the library would qualify fiscal year	7.0% (n=17)	13.3% (n=176)	8.1% (n=191)	10.1% (n=368)	6.2% (n=16)	--	9.8% (n=384)
Our total E-rate discount is fairly low and not worth the time needed to participate in the program	43.2% (n=102)	41.3% (n=547)	32.2% (n=765)	36.1% (n=1,324)	32.8% (n=84)	44.1% (n=7)	36.0% (n=1,415)
The library receives it as part of a consortium, so therefore does not apply individually	6.2% (n=15)	15.2% (n=201)	4.9% (n=116)	8.7% (n=317)	5.2% (n=13)	11.0% (n=2)	8.4% (n=332)
The library was denied funding in the past	1.1% (n=3)	3.4% (n=45)	3.0% (n=72)	3.1% (n=113)	2.3% (n=6)	--	3.0% (n=119)
The library did not apply because of the need to comply with CIPA's filtering requirements	36.1% (n=85)	33.8% (n=447)	33.8% (n=803)	34.1% (n=1,248)	31.0% (n=79)	55.5% (n=8)	33.9% (n=1,335)
The library has applied for E-rate in the past, but no longer finds it necessary	7.3% (n=17)	6.6% (n=87)	10.6% (n=253)	9.1% (n=333)	8.7% (n=22)	11.0% (n=2)	9.1% (n=357)
Other	12.3% (n=29)	11.8% (n=156)	18.4% (n=437)	15.5% (n=566)	21.8% (n=56)	--	15.8% (n=622)
Will not total to 100%, as respondents could select more than one option.							
Key: -- : No data to report							

Figure 34 shows the reasons why public library systems did not apply for E-rate discounts. The most popular reasons for not applying included the application process being too complicated (37.8 percent), the funding amount was not worth the time required to apply (36 percent), and because the filtering requirements of the Children's Internet Protection Act (CIPA), (33.9 percent). In fact, a substantial increase can be seen in all outlet types reporting over last year in the category of libraries not applying due to CIPA filtering requirements. Suburban and low poverty systems were the most likely to feel that they would not qualify fiscal year for E-rate discounts. Only 3 percent of library systems reported being denied E-rate discounts in the past as a reason for not applying in 2006.

The following figures present comparative responses by libraries on a range of technology-related expenditures and the sources of support for fiscal year 2006 and estimates for fiscal year 2007. In some cases libraries simply were asked to mark yes or no to the service support, and in other cases were asked to provide expenditure detail. Libraries also were asked to provide operating revenue figures for the current (2006) fiscal year and estimates for fiscal year 2007. These questions aided the detailed expenditure analysis by providing more up-to-date operating revenue than available in the most current NCES public library data (fiscal year 2004).

Figure 35: Fiscal Year 2006 State Funded Technology Expenditures for the Public Library Systems							
	Metropolitan Status			**Poverty Level**			
Fiscal Year (Fiscal Year) Expenditures	Urban	Suburban	Rural	Low	Medium	High	Overall
Staff only hardware	1.7% (n=10)	3.6% (n=98)	3.8% (n=215)	3.4% (n=271)	5.5% (n=50)	2.7% (n=2)	3.6% (n=323)
Do not know/none: Staff only hardware	58.2% (n=359)	65.2% (n=1,787)	60.6% (n=3,409)	62.8% (n=5,041)	53.3% (n=476)	62.2% (n=39)	61.9% (n=5,555)
Staff only software	1.7% (n=10)	3.4% (n=94)	4.2% (n=235)	3.6% (n=292)	5.1% (n=46)	2.7% (n=2)	3.8% (n=339)
Do not know/none: Staff only software	57.4% (n=354)	64.4% (n=1,763)	59.9% (n=3,364)	61.9% (n=4,969)	53.1% (n=474)	62.2% (n=39)	61.1% (n=5,482)
Public computing hardware	8.7% (n=54)	6.5% (n=177)	8.4% (n=470)	7.2% (n=581)	12.4% (n=110)	16.2% (n=10)	7.8% (n=701)
Do not know/none: Public computing hardware	54.3% (n=335)	63.0% (n=1,725)	57.5% (n=3,235)	59.9% (n=4,804)	51.1% (n=456)	56.8% (n=35)	59.0% (n=5,295)
Public computing software	7.2% (n=45)	5.6% (n=153)	7.6% (n=426)	6.3% (n=508)	12.5% (n=111)	5.4% (n=3)	6.9% (n=623)
Do not know/none: Public computing software	54.1% (n=334)	62.2% (n=1,704)	57.8% (n=3,248)	59.7% (n=4,793)	51.0% (n=455)	62.2% (n=39)	58.9% (n=5,287)
Telecommunications services (including internet connectivity)	15.5% (n=95)	16.6% (n=455)	20.7% (n=1,164)	18.4% (n=1,473)	25.5% (n=228)	21.6% (n=13)	19.1% (n=1,714)
Do not know/none: Telecommunications services (including internet connectivity)	50.9% (n=314)	58.4% (n=1,599)	52.1% (n=2,931)	55.1% (n=4,423)	43.3% (n=386)	56.8% (n=35)	54.0% (n=4,844)
Wireless access (hard/software)	3.6% (n=22)	5.7% (n=156)	4.3% (n=243)	4.9% (n=392)	2.5% (n=22)	10.9% (n=7)	4.7% (n=421)
Do not know/none: Wireless access (hard/software)	56.3% (n=347)	62.0% (n=1,697)	59.0% (n=3,316)	60.5% (n=4,852)	53.1% (n=474)	56.8% (n=35)	59.7% (n=5,361)
Instructional technology (video conferencing hard/software, projection equipment)	4.3% (n=27)	1.1% (n=31)	4.3% (n=239)	3.2% (n=261)	3.9% (n=34)	2.7% (n=2)	3.3% (n=297)
Do not know/none: Instructional technology (video conferencing hard/software, projection equipment)	54.8% (n=339)	63.9% (n=1,750)	59.4% (n=3,340)	61.1% (n=4,903)	54.7% (n=488)	59.5% (n=37)	60.5% (n=5,428)
Licensed resources	65.5% (n=405)	55.0% (n=1,508)	57.8% (n=3,250)	56.8% (n=4,556)	64.1% (n=572)	56.6% (n=35)	57.5% (n=5,163)
Do not know/none: Licensed resources	25.7% (n=159)	37.1% (n=1,016)	33.2% (n=1,865)	34.9% (n=2,797)	24.8% (n=221)	35.3% (n=22)	33.9% (n=3,040)

Figures 35 and 36 illustrate library system expenses paid directly by or from funds provided by state libraries, state legislatures, or other state agencies in fiscal year 2006 and estimated for fiscal year 2007. Anecdotally, library systems reported that operating expenditures by source are aggregated thereby making it very difficult to know what proportion of state funds go toward technology-related expenditures. Further, some states provide services directly and no funds are passed from the state to libraries. These factors appear to present themselves in the findings, especially regarding the significance of "do not know" responses.

In both fiscal years licensed resources were the most common expense paid for by the state library systems, followed by telecommunications services. Instructional technology, such as video conferencing and projection technology, was the least common in fiscal year 2006, and only paid for 3.3 percent of systems. High poverty library systems were much more likely than any other systems to have wireless access expenses paid, as and more likely to estimate that public computing hardware expenses could be covered in the future.

Figure 36: Fiscal Year 2007 State Funded Technology Expenditures for Public Library Systems								
Fiscal Year (Fiscal Year) Expenditures	Metropolitan Status			Poverty Level			Overall
	Urban	Suburban	Rural	Low	Medium	High	
Staff only hardware	1.7% (n=10)	1.8% (n=49)	2.1% (n=119)	1.9% (n=151)	2.9% (n=26)	2.7% (n=2)	2.0% (n=178)
Do not know/none: Staff only hardware	58.2% (n=359)	65.2% (n=1,787)	60.6% (n=3,409)	62.8% (n=5,041)	53.3% (n=476)	62.2% (n=39)	61.9% (n=5,555)
Staff only software	2.1% (n=13)	2.2% (n=59)	2.6% (n=147)	2.3% (n=185)	3.5% (n=31)	2.7% (n=2	2.4% (n=219)
Do not know/none: Staff only software	57.4% (n=354)	64.4% (n=1,763)	59.9% (n=3,364)	61.9% (n=4,969)	53.1% (n=474)	62.2% (n=39)	61.1% (n=5,482)
Public computing hardware	6.8% (n=42)	3.5% (n=97)	5.3% (n=297)	4.6% (n=367)	6.5% (n=58)	16.2% (n=10)	4.9% (n=436)
Do not know/none: Public computing hardware	54.3% (n=335)	63.0% (n=1,725)	57.5% (n=3,235)	59.9% (n=4,804)	51.1% (n=456)	56.8% (n=35)	59.0% (n=5,295)
Public computing software	7.0% (n=44)	3.9% (n=108)	5.2% (n=290)	4.6% (n=371)	7.5% (n=67)	5.4% (n=3)	4.9% (n=441)
Do not know/none: Public computing software	54.1% (n=334)	62.2% (n=1,704)	57.8% (n=3,248)	59.7% (n=4,793)	51.0% (n=455)	62.2% (n=39)	58.9% (n=5,287)
Telecommunications services (including internet connectivity)	13.5% (n=83)	15.2% (n=417)	16.8% (n=945)	15.5% (n=1,247)	20.8% (n=186)	21.6% (n=13)	16.1% (n=1,446)
Do not know/none: Telecommunications services (including internet connectivity)	50.9% (n=314)	58.4% (n=1,599)	52.1% (n=2,931)	55.1% (n=4,423)	43.3% (n=386)	56.8% (n=35)	54.0% (n=4,844)
Wireless access (hard/software)	3.2% (n=20)	2.9% (n=80)	3.3% (n=188)	3.2% (n=254)	3.0% (n=27)	10.9% (n=7)	3.2% (n=288)
Do not know/none: Wireless access (hard/software)	56.3% (n=347)	62.0% (n=1,697)	59.0% (n=3,316)	60.5% (n=4,852)	53.1% (n=474)	56.8% (n=35)	59.7% (n=5,361)
Instructional technology (video conferencing hard/software, projection equipment)	4.1% (n=25)	*	3.8% (n=212)	2.8% (n=226)	3.0% (n=26)	2.7% (n=2)	2.8% (n=254)
Do not know/none: Instructional technology (video conferencing hard/software, projection equipment)	54.8% (n=339)	63.9% (n=1,750)	59.4% (n=3,340)	61.1% (n=4,903)	54.7% (n=488)	59.5% (n=37)	60.5% (n=5,428)
Licensed resources	60.6% (n=374)	49.6% (n=1,358)	49.8% (n=2,800)	50.1% (n=4,017)	54.4% (n=485)	48.4% (n=30)	50.5% (n=4,532)
Do not know/none: Licensed resources	25.7% (n=159)	37.1% (n=1,016)	33.2% (n=1,865)	34.9% (n=2,797)	24.8% (n=221)	35.3% (n=22)	33.9% (n=3,040)
Key: * : Insufficient data to report								

As Figure 37 shows, the greatest technology-related expenditure is on staff ($55,126), followed by licensed resources ($39,788) and telecommunications services ($21,224). The proportions of expenditures for staff are consistent with overall spending by public libraries. Public libraries reported to NCES for fiscal year 2004 that 65.8 percent of total operating expenditures went to staffing, followed by other types of expenditures (building maintenance, computer hardware/software, etc.) (21 percent) and collections (13.2 percent). [16]

It should not be surprising to find that high poverty public libraries (often located in urban areas) report spending more on public computing software, instructional technology, and licensed resources than in other areas or non-high poverty systems. Urban and medium poverty library systems reported spending the most on wireless access ($5,497 and $8,606, respectively) as compared to the average ($1,377). This, too, aligns with other data reported regarding the slower adoption of wireless in rural communities.

The expenditures presented in Figures 37 and 38 clearly reflect that rural libraries spend less because they have proportionally smaller operating budgets that do suburban and urban libraries.

It was interesting to see an anticipated increase in technology related expenditures from fiscal year 2006 to fiscal year 2007. Overall, expenditures reported in Figure 38 indicate that high poverty public libraries anticipate spending more on instructional technology and licensed resources than other types of systems. As in fiscal year 2006, urban libraries anticipate spending the most in each of the remaining expenditure categories.

Figure 37: Fiscal Year 2006 Public Library System Technology-Related Expenditures							
	Metropolitan Status			Poverty Level			
Technology-Related Expenditures	Urban	Suburban	Rural	Low	Medium	High	Overall
Staff only hardware	$69,818 (n=236)	$10,342 (n=1,165)	$2,655 (n=2,155)	$7,322 (n=3,200)	$30,669 (n=340)	$25,114. (n=17)	$9,636 (n=3,556)
Staff only software	$28,102 (n=227)	$7,640 (n=1,141)	$1,393. (n=1,939)	$4,178 (n=2,963)	$15,826 (n=326)	$14,079 (n=18)	$5,381 (n=3,308)
Public computing hardware	$101,293 (n=255)	$24,320 (n=1,255)	$4,529 (n=2,363)	$13,056 (n=3,498)	$57,546 (n=350)	$49,361 (n=25)	$17,310 (n=3,873)
Public computing software	$27,839 (n=226)	$9,748 (n=1,114)	$1,412 (n=2,045)	$4,866 (n=3,038)	$14,201 (n=325)	$28,896 (n=22)	$5,917 (n=3,385)
Telecommunications services (including internet connectivity)	$154,043 (n=286)	$26,059 (n=1,385)	$4,117 (n=2,609)	$15,228 (n=3,856)	$76,269 (n=400)	$67,705. (n=23)	$21,224 (n=4,279)
Wireless access (hard/software)	$8,606 (n=211)	$1,390 (n=996)	$512 (n=1,779)	$927 (n=2,677)	$5,497 (n=295)	$635 (n=13)	$1,377. (n=2,986)
Instructional technology (video conferencing hard/software, projection equipment)	$15,672 (n=144)	$4,619 (n=735)	$776 (n=1,410)	$2,288 (n=2,065)	$1,681 (n=214)	$165,077 (n=10)	$2,948. (n=2,289)
Licensed resources	$193,122 (n=285)	$60,633 (n=1,197)	$3,593 (n=1,895)	$33,233 (n=3,012)	$83,130 (n=341)	$251,021 (n=23)	$39,788 (n=3,377)
Staff in technology support positions in the library or under contract to the library for such support	$366,427 (n=249)	$62,676 (n=1,076)	$9,446 (n=1,874)	$42,740 (n=2,822)	$149,026 (n=355)	$128,567 (n=22)	$55,126 (n=3,199)
Staff providing technology-related training to library staff or public	$48,508 (n=186)	$7,497 (n=773)	$2,394 (n=1,506)	$4,713 (n=2,193)	$30,624 (n=259)	$11,729 (n=13)	$7,470 (n=2,465)

---

[16] National Center for Education Statistics. Public Libraries in the United States: Fiscal Year 2004. (NCES 2006-349). Washington, DC: NCES, 2006. http://www.nces.ed.gov/pubs2006/2006349.pdf

Figure 38: Fiscal Year 2007 Public Library System Technology-Related Expenditures

Technology-Related Expenditures	Metropolitan Status			Poverty Level			Overall
	Urban	Suburban	Rural	Low	Medium	High	
Staff only hardware	$114,878 (n=214)	$8,395 (n=1,016)	$2,502 (n=1,813)	$5,331 (n=2,726)	$74,366 (n=304)	$35,878 (n=13)	$12,362 (n=3,043)
Staff only software	$28,666 (n=211)	$11,901 (n=1,048)	$1,168 (n=1,766)	$5,630 (n=2,733)	$17,786 (n=278)	$18,568 (n=13)	$6,802 (n=3,024)
Public computing hardware	$105,727 (n=241)	$10,568 (n=1,184)	$4,003 (n=2,025)	$8,655 (n=3,094)	$54,561 (n=343)	$47,533 (n=13)	$13,370 (n=3,450)
Public computing software	$26,629 (n=199)	$14,392 (n=1,055)	$1,703 (n=1,837)	$7,005 (n=2,774)	$12,811 (n=304)	$21,772 (n=13)	$7,639 (n=3,091)
Telecommunications services (including internet connectivity)	$174,876 (n=268)	$26,353 (n=1,235)	$4,291 (n=2,226)	$16,762 (n=3,344)	$85,223 (n=369)	$87,249 (n=17)	$23,845 (n=3,730)
Wireless access (hard/software)	$9,724 (n=196)	$1,419 (n=844)	$493. (n=1,557)	$991. (n=2,320)	$5,801 (n=270)	$1,000 (n=7)	$1,491 (n=2,597)
Instructional technology (video conferencing hard/software, projection equipment)	$12,205 (n=137)	$3,891 (n=721)	$288 (n=1,321)	$1,683 (n=1,973)	$2,927 (n=200)	$142,755 (n=7)	$2,230. (n=2,180)
Licensed resources	$217,850 (n=264)	$72,962 (n=1,138)	$4,068 (n=1,704)	$39,879 (n=2,769)	$97,820 (n=321)	$342,440. (n=17)	$47,497 (n=3,106)
Staff in technology support positions in the library or under contract to the library for such support	$389,104 (n=238)	$64,044. (n=1,023)	$10,398 (n=1,717)	$45,949 (n=2,633)	$158,025 (n=327)	$178,931 (n=18)	$59,076 (n=2,979)
Staff providing technology-related training to library staff or public	$52,695 (n=186)	$8,675 (n=818)	$2,347 (n=1,424)	$5,265 (n=2,176)	$35,585 (n=242)	$16,287 (n=10)	$8,331 (n=2,428)

Figure 39: Fiscal Year 2006 Public Library System Total Operating Expenditures

Sources of Funding	Fiscal Year 2006		
	Salaries (including benefits)	Collections	Other Expenditures
Local/county	$3,736,758. (n=6,230)	$217,095. (n=5,485)	$370,983 (n=5,637)
State (including state aid to public libraries, or state-supported tax programs)	$147,612 (n=3,288)	$41,750 (n=3,564)	$64,544 (n=3,645)
Federal	$1,704 (n=2,505)	$1,211 (n=2,423)	$11,585. (n=2,619)
Fees/fines	$11,139 (n=2,673)	$11,379 (n=2,870)	$28,192 (n=3,387)
Donations/local fund raising	$10,487 (n=2,855)	$10,885 (n=3,558)	$25,811 (n=3,748)
Grants (local, state or national grant programs)	$72,522 (n=2,846)	$17,760 (n=3,171)	$29,553 (n=3,673)
Reported average percent	82.7%	6.2%	11.0%

Figure 39 shows the average expenditure by source of funding for all public library systems reporting salaries, collections, and other expenditures. Local/county funding was the largest single source for all three categories of operating expenses. Federal funding was the smallest source for each. This finding is consistent with data reported annually by public libraries to the NCES (see footnote 6). Nationally, public libraries reported that 81.5 percent of operating revenue comes from local sources, 10 percent from state, and less than one (.5) percent from federal sources. About 8 percent comes from other revenue sources, such as fee/fines, donations and grants. As with fiscal year 2006 data in Figure 39, Figure 40 shows that local/county funding remains the largest single source for all three categories of operating expenses. The data presented in Figures 39-52 provide detail on "other expenditures" not available in the NCES annual studies.

Figure 40: Fiscal Year 2007 Public Library System Total Operating Expenditures			
	Fiscal Year 2007		
Sources of Funding	Salaries (including benefits)	Collections	Other Expenditures
Local/county	$1,279,118 (n=5,316)	$266,205 (n=4,707)	$430,805 (n=4,865)
State (including state aid to public libraries, or state-supported tax programs)	$156,214 (n=2,739)	$45,588 (n=3,020)	$49,040 (n=2,984)
Federal	$926 (n=2,090)	$843 (n=2,040)	$8,961 (n=2,209)
Fees/fines	$10,230 (n=2,282)	$12,813 (n=2,451)	$74,438 (n=2,996)
Donations/local fund raising	$8,538 (n=2,380)	$13,891 (n=2,841)	$24,836 (n=3,095)
Grants (local, state or national grant programs)	$31,656 (n=2,437)	$8,360 (n=2,544)	$13,215 (n=3,056)
Reported average percent	61.0%	14.3%	24.7%

The following figures (Figures 41-52) present operating expenditures reported for fiscal year 2006 and estimates for fiscal year 2007 by source, metropolitan status and poverty. It is important to consider that fiscal year 2006 figures may be mid-year reporting and only reflect expenditures to date. Fiscal year 2007 figures are estimates, and should be considered as figures for planning only.

When comparing Figures 41 and 42, certain trends emerge across several of the sources of funding. For example, rural public libraries expect to get more funding in fiscal year 2007 than they did in fiscal year 2006 from local and county sources for all expenditure categories, but less from grants and federal sources. Since grants and federal sources may be linked to specific incentive projects, it is not uncommon to see fluctuations in these particular revenue sources. There were only four specific instances when federal funding was not cited as the smallest source of funding, and those instances are listed below (see Figures 43, 51, and 52).

The potential impact of not receiving stable local funding is that libraries will rely more heavily on other sources of revenue, such as fines/fees, donations or grants to fill the revenue void. These inconsistent funding sources are an impractical solution to funding basic library services. This response to inadequate local funding also impacts libraries ability to plan and implement innovative services that may create efficiencies in overall library services.

Figure 41: Fiscal Year 2006 Rural Public Library System Total Operating Expenditures

	Fiscal Year 2006		
Sources of Funding	Salaries (including benefits)	Collections	Other Expenditures
Local/county	$187,998 (n=3,859)	$35,910 (n=3,268)	$66,021 (n=3,408)
State (including state aid to public libraries, or state-supported tax programs)	$53,001 (n=1,976)	$14,158 (n=2,161)	$16,557 (n=2,120)
Federal	$1,054 (n=1,519)	$794 (n=1,441)	$1,425 (n=1,560)
Fees/fines	$3,157 (n=1,622)	$2,427 (n=1,731)	$7,505 (n=2,045)
Donations/local fund raising	$3,934 (n=1,717)	$4,991 (n=2,128)	$8,436. (n=2,250)
Grants (local, state or national grant programs)	$6,063 (n=1,714)	$3,511 (n=1,891)	$6,793. (n=2,209)
Reported average percent	60.2%	14.6%	25.2%

Figure 42: Fiscal Year 2007 Rural Public Library System Total Operating Expenditures

	Fiscal Year 2007		
Sources of Funding	Salaries (including benefits)	Collections	Other Expenditures
Local/county	$210,652 (n=3,251)	$38,998 (n=2,783)	$72,691 (n=2,927)
State (including state aid to public libraries, or state-supported tax programs)	$49,468 (n=1,584)	$16,816 (n=1,789)	$16,413 (n=1,748)
Federal	$668 (n=1,236)	$627 (n=1,208)	$924. (n=1,283)
Fees/fines	$2,685 (n=1,352)	$2,200 (n=1,427)	$7,923 (n=1,707)
Donations/local fund raising	$3,736 (n=1,455)	$5,493. (n=1,704)	$7,609 (n=1,885)
Grants (local, state or national grant programs)	$5,456 (n=1,461)	$3,113 (n=1,489)	$5,242 (n=1,806)
Reported average percent	60.5%	14.9%	24.6%

Figure 43: Fiscal Year 2006 Suburban Public Library System Total Operating Expenditures

	Fiscal Year 2006		
Sources of Funding	Salaries (including benefits)	Collections	Other Expenditures
Local/county	$6,173,149 (n=1,927)	$313,825 (n=1,798)	$503,122 (n=1,802)
State (including state aid to public libraries, or state-supported tax programs)	$249,992 (n=1,096)	$41,230 (n=1,142)	$46,329. (n=1,256)
Federal	$866 (n=833)	$329 (n=823)	$16,616 (n=878)
Fees/fines	$21,191 (n=891)	$11,234 (n=965)	$32,406 (n=1,114)
Donations/local fund raising	$13,818 (n=971)	$11,439 (n=1,184)	$36,383 (n=1,256)
Grants (local, state or national grant programs)	$48,855 (n=951)	$10,631 (n=1,055)	$10,867 (n=1,207)
Reported average percent	86.3%	5.2%	8.6%

Figure 44: Fiscal Year 2007 Suburban Public Library System Total Operating Expenditures

Sources of Funding	Fiscal Year 2007		
	Salaries (including benefits)	Collections	Other Expenditures
Local/county	$1,870,915 (n=1,670)	$409,407 (n=1,552)	$460,374. (n=1,562)
State (including state aid to public libraries, or state-supported tax programs)	$270,299 (n=954)	$39,128 (n=996)	$46,365 (n=1,017)
Federal	$394 (n=718)	$94 (n=697)	$2,584. (n=771)
Fees/fines	$19,357 (n=784)	$11,548 (n=861)	$144,966 (n=1,083)
Donations/local fund raising	$8,746 (n=778)	$10,739 (n=928)	$21,796 (n=999)
Grants (local, state or national grant programs)	$63,543 (n=816)	$11,505 (n=881)	$7,459 (n=1,041)
Reported average percent	65.7%	14.2%	20.1%

Figure 45: Fiscal Year 2006 Urban Public Library System Total Operating Expenditures

Sources of Funding	Fiscal Year 2006		
	Salaries (including benefits)	Collections	Other Expenditures
Local/county	$24,000,181 (n=444)	$1,214,881 (n=419)	$2,251,246 (n=426)
State (including state aid to public libraries, or state-supported tax programs)	$494,639 (n=215)	$272,183 (n=261)	$528,147 (n=269)
Federal	$12,703 (n=153)	$9,530 (n=160)	$74,566 (n=182)
Fees/fines	$36,010 (n=160)	$101,351 (n=174)	$193,058 (n=228)
Donations/local fund raising	$58,564 (n=167)	$58,989 (n=247)	$132,190 (n=243)
Grants (local, state or national grant programs)	$827,660 (n=181)	$170,649 (n=225)	$312,856 (n=257)
Reported average percent	82.7%	5.9%	11.4%

Average percent by expenditure category (salaries, collections, other) are only calculated for metropolitan status, not poverty as there is little variation in distributions between them.

Figure 46: Fiscal Year 2007 Urban Public Library System Total Operating Expenditures

Sources of Funding	Fiscal Year 2007 Salaries (including benefits)	Collections	Other Expenditures
Local/county	$7,567,402 (n=395)	$1,368,853 (n=372)	$3,099,827 (n=375)
State (including state aid to public libraries, or state-supported tax programs)	$455,229 (n=201)	$291,474 (n=236)	$321,737 (n=219)
Federal	$6,065 (n=136)	$6,659 (n=135)	$107,290 (n=155)
Fees/fines	$31,087 (n=146)	$112,486 (n=163)	$254,304 (n=207)
Donations/local fund raising	$54,791 (n=148)	$96,041 (n=210)	$193,096 (n=211)
Grants (local, state or national grant programs)	$108,233 (n=160)	$37,203 (n=175)	$110,947 (n=209)
Reported average percent	57.8%	13.4%	28.7%

Figure 47: Fiscal Year 2006 Low Poverty Public Library System Total Operating Expenditures

Sources of Funding	Fiscal Year 2006 Salaries (including benefits)	Collections	Other Expenditures
Local/county	$2,506,352 (n=5,594)	$183,388 (n=4,908)	$305,426 (n=5,045)
State (including state aid to public libraries, or state-supported tax programs)	$128,075 (n=2,908)	$31,092 (n=3,145)	$54,779 (n=3,259)
Federal	$1,162 (n=2,255)	$735 (n=2,183)	$11,217 (n=2,320)
Fees/fines	$10,723 (n=2,409)	$9,668 (n=2,598)	$21,023 (n=3,004)
Donations/local fund raising	$9,124 (n=2,574)	$8,721 (n=3,200)	$22,570 (n=3,351)
Grants (local, state or national grant programs)	$77,867 (n=2,557)	$18,490 (n=2,833)	$29,193 (n=3,241)

Figure 48: Fiscal Year 2007 Low Poverty Public Library Systems Total Operating Expenditures

Sources of Funding	Fiscal Year 2007 Salaries (including benefits)	Collections	Other Expenditures
Local/county	$1,097,087 (n=4,753)	$231,231 (n=4,211)	$330,979 (n=4,361)
State (including state aid to public libraries, or state-supported tax programs)	$140,533 (n=2,417)	$34,443 (n=2,702)	$38,401 (n=2,664)
Federal	$712 (n=1,873)	$546 (n=1,829)	$8,692 (n=1,956)
Fees/fines	$10,140 (n=2,059)	$11,091 (n=2,207)	$70,980 (n=2,651)
Donations/local fund raising	$6,614 (n=2,144)	$10,149 (n=2,533)	$18,420 (n=2,770)
Grants (local, state or national grant programs)	$32,585 (n=2,179)	$7,927 (n=2,290)	$9,759 (n=2,722)

Comparing the 2006 fiscal year data (Figure 49) for medium poverty libraries with projected expenditures, one large difference is in the expected funding from local and county sources for salaries. The fiscal year 2006 data indicate that an average of $15,191,330 was allocated to salaries from local and county sources, and the fiscal year 2007 data indicate a sharp decrease ($2,632,932). However, when considered in a context of NCES 2004 expenditures as a percentage of overall operating expenditure the fiscal year 2007 estimates closely align with what actual operating expenditures are historically for public libraries.

Figure 49: Fiscal Year 2006 Medium Poverty Public Library System Total Operating Expenditures

Sources of Funding	Fiscal Year 2006		
	Salaries (including benefits)	Collections	Other Expenditures
Local/county	$15,191,332 (n=595)	$470,247 (n=537)	$858,791 (n=551)
State (including state aid to public libraries, or state-supported tax programs)	$302,773 (n=361)	$115,077 (n=397)	$148,965 (n=359)
Federal	$5,863 (n=236)	$5,719 (n=230)	$13,378 (n=282)
Fees/fines	$10,540 (n=252)	$25,191 (n=260)	$82,856 (n=366)
Donations/local fund raising	$23,651 (n=270)	$28,258 (n=343)	$53,753 (n=381)
Grants (local, state or national grant programs)	$23,609 (n=267)	$10,506 (n=315)	$30,618 (n=405)

Figure 50: Fiscal Year 2007 Medium Poverty Public Library System Total Operating Expenditures

Sources of Funding	Fiscal Year 2007		
	Salaries (including benefits)	Collections	Other Expenditures
Local/county	$2,632,932 (n=530)	$523,659 (n=465)	$1,248,789 (n=471)
State (including state aid to public libraries, or state-supported tax programs)	$277,593 (n=307)	$130,800 (n=302)	$138,041 (n=302)
Federal	$1,261 (n=205)	$3,537 (n=200)	$9,307 (n=240)
Fees/fines	$10,525 (n=213)	$26,323 (n=230)	$99,882 (n=329)
Donations/local fund raising	$24,824 (n=225)	$40,280 (n=293)	$80,806 (n=309)
Grants (local, state or national grant programs)	$24,465 (n=236)	$12,350 (n=236)	$43,104 (n=317)

Figure 51: Fiscal Year 2006 High Poverty Public Library System Total Operating Expenditures

Sources of Funding	Fiscal Year 2006		
	Salaries (including benefits)	Collections	Other Expenditures
Local/county	$5,307,782 (n=40)	$949,849 (n=40)	$1,906,767 (n=40)
State (including state aid to public libraries, or state-supported tax programs)	$190,244 (n=18)	$244,884 (n=22)	$121,257 (n=27)
Federal	$17,815 (n=15)	$1,495 (n=10)	$32,223 (n=17)
Fees/fines	$109,925 (n=12)	$84,105 (n=12)	$119,196 (n=17)
Donations/local fund raising	$7,185 (n=12)	$74,457 (n=15)	$38,849 (n=17)
Grants (local, state or national grant programs)	$43,713 (n=22)	$27,120 (n=24)	$56,866 (n=27)

Figure 52: Fiscal Year 2007 High Poverty Public Library System Total Operating Expenditures

Sources of Funding	Fiscal Year 2007		
	Salaries (including benefits)	Collections	Other Expenditures
Local/county	$5,671,002 (n=34)	$1,132,817 (n=32)	$1,997,230 (n=32)
State (including state aid to public libraries, or state-supported tax programs)	$199,286 (n=15)	$308,419 (n=17)	$129,399 (n=18)
Federal	$29,305 (n=12)	$1,285 (n=12)	$42,125 (n=13)
Fees/fines	$22,532 (n=10)	$64,065 (n=13)	$122,501 (n=17)
Donations/local fund raising	$54,467 (n=10)	$130,073 (n=15)	$54,645 (n=17)
Grants (local, state or national grant programs)	$16,881 (n=22)	$11,072 (n=18)	$10,173 (n=17)

Figures 53-67 present even more detail on types of technology-related expenditures by source of funding. This level of expenditure detail has not been captured before and, although response levels dropped off as more detail was requested, the data are still valuable in gaining a better understanding of patterns of spending in these broad technology categories. Categories of expenditures are summed and percentages also are provided for illustration purposes.

Mirroring earlier findings, the largest single source for technology-related expenditures comes from the local/county sources. Without exception, public libraries of every metropolitan status and poverty level indicated that technology-related expenditures for fiscal year 2006 and expected expenditures for fiscal year 2007 would in large part come from local and county sources.

With the exception of two instances (see Figures 57 and 63 below), federal funds were most likely to be applied to telecommunications expenses by all public libraries. Looking at Figure 53 specifically, it shows that a large proportion of funds from donations and grants were allocated to hardware expenditures. This tells us that libraries may not be in a position to rely on local tax support to fund technology, but are relying on external fundraising to provide what have become basic library services.

Figure 53: Fiscal Year 2006 Public Library System Total Technology-Related Operating Expenditures				
Fiscal Year 2006				
Sources of Funding	Salaries (including benefits)	Hardware	Software	Telecommunications
Local/county	$96,906 (n=3,205)	$32,677 (n=3,900)	$18,929 (n=3,726)	$23,786 (n=4,053)
State (including state aid to public libraries, or state-supported tax programs)	$6,865 (n=2,060)	$5,337 (n=2,248)	$3,130 (n=2,134)	$3,556 (n=2,148)
Federal	$173 (n=1,884)	$1,337 (n=1,887)	$343 (n=1,858)	$3,833 (n=2,088)
Fees/fines	$462 (n=1,917)	$769 (n=1,901)	$576 (n=1,892)	$304 (n=1,875)
Donations/local fund raising	$1,070 (n=1,919)	$7,342 (n=2,332)	$650 (n=2,139)	$487 (n=1,990)
Grants (local, state or national grant programs)	$3,854 (n=1,973)	$6,655 (n=2,577)	$1,030 (n=2,113)	$713 (n=2,042)
Reported average total	$109,330	$54,117	$24,658	$32,679
Average percent	49.5%	24.5%	11.2%	14.8%

Figures 55 and 56 provide a comparison of rural libraries' current fiscal year (2006) technology-related expenditures as well as next fiscal year's (2007) anticipated expenditures. According to the data, state funding is expected to be less across all technology-related expenditures when compared to the 2006 data.

Figure 54: Fiscal Year 2007 Public Library System Total Technology-Related Operating Expenditures				
Fiscal Year 2007				
Sources of Funding	Salaries (including benefits)	Hardware	Software	Telecommunications
Local/county	$90,972 (n=2,980)	$30,895 (n=3,612)	$23,198 (n=3,448)	$26,825 (n=3,766)
State (including state aid to public libraries, or state-supported tax programs)	$6,667 (n=1,964)	$3,882 (n=2,096)	$3,326 (n=2,043)	$2,982 (n=2,021)
Federal	$201 (n=1,820)	$417 (n=1,810)	$169 (n=1,803)	$6,396 (n=1,969)
Fees/fines	$360 (n=1,833)	$626 (n=1,825)	$882 (n=1,840)	$226 (n=1,828)
Donations/local fund raising	$1,117 (n=1,889)	$3743 (n=2,069)	$1,531 (n=2,035)	$418 (n=1,923)
Grants (local, state or national grant programs)	$1,454 (n=1,886)	$4,501 (n=2,231)	$933 (n=1,986)	$379 (n=1,957)
Reported average total	$100,771	$44,064	$30,039	$37,226
Average percent	47.5%	20.8%	14.2%	17.6%

Figure 55: Fiscal Year 2006 Rural Public Library Systems Total Technology-Related Operating Expenditures

Fiscal Year 2006

Sources of Funding	Salaries (including benefits)	Hardware	Software	Telecommunications
Local/county	$18,083 (n=1,751)	$6,140 (n=2,186)	$3,725 (n=2,100)	$3,586 (n=2,284)
State (including state aid to public libraries, or state-supported tax programs)	$2,843 (n=1,246)	$1,777 (n=1,348)	$1,044 (n=1,297)	$1,523 (n=1,304)
Federal	$75 (n=1,140)	$223 (n=1,134)	$41 (n=1,110)	$808 (n=1,277)
Fees/fines	$167 (n=1,157)	$87 (n=1,130)	$50 (n=1,123)	$124 (n=1,123)
Donations/local fund raising	$516 (n=1,161)	$1,396 (n=1,369)	$298 (n=1,236)	$345 (n=1,209)
Grants (local, state or national grant programs)	$1,104 (n=1,195)	$2,808 (n=1,529)	$67 (n=1,277)	$388 (n=1,243)
Reported average total	$22,788	$12,431	$5,225	$6,774
Average percent	48.3%	26.3%	11.1%	14.3%

Figure 56: Fiscal Year 2007 Rural Public Library System Total Technology-Related Operating Expenditures

Fiscal Year 2007

Sources of Funding	Salaries (including benefits)	Hardware	Software	Telecommunications
Local/county	$19,147 (n=1,635)	$5,940 (n=2,012)	$4,429 (n=1,929)	$3,823 (n=2,120)
State (including state aid to public libraries, or state-supported tax programs)	$2,720 (n=1,174)	$1,595 (n=1,232)	$965 (n=1,215)	$1,386 (n=1,202)
Federal	$93 (n=1,096)	$40 (n=1,075)	$37 (n=1,079)	$704 (n=1,191)
Fees/fines	$101 (n=1,096)	$129 (n=1,079)	$58 (n=1,096)	$48 (n=1,086)
Donations/local fund raising	$398 (n=1,137)	$1,092 (n=1,267)	$261 (n=1,188)	$344 (n=1,164)
Grants (local, state or national grant programs)	$728 (n=1,133)	$2,605 (n=1,359)	$325 (n=1,202)	$453 (n=1,192)
Reported average total	$23,187	$11,401	$6,075	$6,758
Average percent	48.9%	24.0%	12.8%	14.3%

Figure 57: Fiscal Year 2006 Suburban Public Library System Total Technology-Related Operating Expenditures

	Fiscal Year 2006			
Sources of Funding	Salaries (including benefits)	Hardware	Software	Telecommunications
Local/county	$140,710 (n=1,134)	$43,341 (n=1,381)	$30,843 (n=1,315)	$28,142 (n=1,440)
State (including state aid to public libraries, or state-supported tax programs)	$8,252 (n=683)	$3,830.38 (n=747)	$2,641 (n=701)	$2,598 (n=711)
Federal	$57 (n=628)	$1,036 (n=624)	$79 (n=628)	$731 (n=673)
Fees/fines	$952 (n=645)	$1,892 (n=652)	$1,559 (n=652)	$608 (n=635)
Donations/local fund raising	$772 (n=642)	$13,923 (n=819)	$1,007 (n=773)	$668 (n=659)
Grants (local, state or national grant programs)	$360 (n=655)	$4,740 (n=846)	$1,505 (n=690)	$589 (n=673)
Reported average total	$151,103	$68,762	$37,634	$33,336
Average percent	52.0%	23.6%	12.9%	11.5%

Figure 58: Fiscal Year 2007 Suburban Public Library System Total Technology-Related Operating Expenditures

	Fiscal Year 2007			
Sources of Funding	Salaries (including benefits)	Hardware	Software	Telecommunications
Local/county	$122,191 (n=1,061)	$34,432 (n=1,298)	$38,115 (n=1,231)	$28,301 (n=1,336)
State (including state aid to public libraries, or state-supported tax programs)	$7,343 (n=670)	$3,741 (n=722)	$3,192 (n=701)	$1,917 (n=705)
Federal	$60 (n=617)	$468 (n=617)	--	$903 (n=656)
Fees/fines	$718 (n=628)	$1,398 (n=638)	$2,430 (n=638)	$408 (n=631)
Donations/local fund raising	$557 (n=642)	$1,274 (n=684)	$3,357 (n=728)	$522 (n=645)
Grants (local, state or national grant programs)	$2,747 (n=638)	$4,313 (n=705)	$1,199 (n=659)	$249 (n=652)
Reported average total	$133,616	$45,626	$48,293	$32,300
Average percent	51.4%	17.6%	18.6%	12.4%
Key: -- : No data to report				

Figure 59: Fiscal Year 2006 Urban Public Library System Total Technology-Related Operating Expenditures

Fiscal Year 2006

Sources of Funding	Salaries (including benefits)	Hardware	Software	Telecommunications
Local/county	$373,508 (n=319)	$162,564 (n=333)	$71,206 (n=311)	$145,285 (n=328)
State (including state aid to public libraries, or state-supported tax programs)	$37,906 (n=131)	$44,190 (n=153)	$25,529 (n=136)	$28,780 (n=132)
Federal	$1,773 (n=116)	$12,526 (n=130)	$4,498 (n=121)	$46,991 (n=138)
Fees/fines	$682 (n=114)	$1,084 (n=119)	$151 (n=117)	$374 (n=117)
Donations/local fund raising	$8,226 (n=117)	$26,385 (n=145)	$1,887 (n=129)	$915 (n=122)
Grants (local, state or national grant programs)	$49,343 (n=123)	$43,973 (n=201)	$1,895 (n=146)	$4,591 (n=126)
Reported average total	$471,438	$290,722	$105,166	$226,936
Average percent	43.1%	26.6%	9.6%	20.7%

As revealed by Figure 59, urban public libraries were the only systems to report that funding from grants was mostly likely to be applied to salaries. Most other systems allocated a larger portion of grant funding to hardware expenditures. When compared with Figure 60, the total amount of grant money expected to be applied to salaries decreases significantly from $49,343 to $1,442. This reporting demonstrates the volatility of grant funding in general, and may also indicate the occurrence of a grant-funded technology project in an urban setting.

Figure 60: Fiscal Year 2007 Urban Public Library System Total Technology-Related Operating Expenditures

Fiscal Year 2007

Sources of Funding	Salaries (including benefits)	Hardware	Software	Telecommunications
Local/county	$388,276 (n=284)	$181,707 (n=302)	$85,293 (n=287)	$178,080 (n=309)
State (including state aid to public libraries, or state-supported tax programs)	$41,578 (n=120)	$24,543 (n=141)	$26,721 (n=127)	$26,374 (n=114)
Federal	$2,117 (n=107)	$3,601 (n=118)	$2,331 (n=113)	$91,691 (n=122)
Fees/fines	$902 (n=109)	$1,030 (n=108)	$79 (n=106)	$921 (n=112)
Donations/local fund raising	$11,843 (n=110)	$46,472 (n=118)	$3,034 (n=119)	$576 (n=114)
Grants (local, state or national grant programs)	$1,442 (n=114)	$20,661 (n=168)	$5,370 (n=125)	$350 (n=113)
Reported average total	$446,158	$278,014	$122,828	$297,992
Average percent	39.0%	24.3%	10.7%	26.0%

Figures 61-66 present reported technology-related operating expenditures by poverty. In Figures 63 and 64, a comparison of medium poverty libraries' expenditures by source, one of the major differences is in the amount of federal funding spent in fiscal year 2006 ($7,608) for hardware compared to the projected fiscal year 2007 expenditures ($2,314). This represents almost a two-thirds decrease in federal funding anticipated for these expenses. Further, Figure 63 illustrates one of the few instances where more federal funding was applied to hardware expenditures than telecommunications. Since telecommunications costs are more frequently paid from federal sources, this potential decline in funding could adversely affect how libraries fund other services.

Figure 61: Fiscal Year 2006 Low Poverty Public Library System Total Technology-Related Operating Expenditures

Sources of Funding	Salaries (including benefits)	Hardware	Software	Telecommunications
Local/county	$82,026 (n=2,817)	$23,013 (n=3,497)	$16,215 (n=3,318)	$15,948 (n=3,607)
State (including state aid to public libraries, or state-supported tax programs)	$4,566 (n=1,832)	$2,709 (n=1,994)	$2,584 (n=1,907)	$2,336 (n=1,938)
Federal	$72 (n=1,694)	$657 (n=1,702)	$43 (n=1,664)	$3,297 (n=1,863)
Fees/fines	$474 (n=1,722)	$755 (n=1,708)	$626 (n=1,708)	$313 (n=1,691)
Donations/local fund raising	$1,069 (n=1,719)	$6,126 (n=2,100)	$633 (n=1,936)	$429 (n=1,791)
Grants (local, state or national grant programs)	$4,081 (n=1,774)	$5,384 (n=2,289)	$996 (n=1,891)	$735 (n=1,842)
Reported average total	$92,288	$38,644	$21,097	$23,058
Average percent	52.7%	22.1%	12.0%	13.2%

Figure 62: Fiscal Year 2007 Low Poverty Public Library System Total Technology-Related Operating Expenditures

Sources of Funding	Salaries (including benefits)	Hardware	Software	Telecommunications
Local/county	$73,697 (n=2,634)	$19,956 (n=3,232)	$19,731 (n=3,081)	$17,027 (n=3,353)
State (including state aid to public libraries, or state-supported tax programs)	$4,392 (n=1,756)	$2,428 (n=1,867)	$2,491 (n=1,825)	$1,567 (n=1,822)
Federal	$85 (n=1,640)	$221 (n=1,633)	$18 (n=1,622)	$6,276 (n=1,763)
Fees/fines	$359 (n=1,653)	$653 (n=1,650)	$968 (n=1,664)	$184 (n=1,650)
Donations/local fund raising	$913 (n=1,701)	$1,185 (n=1,863)	$1,544 (n=1,850)	$373 (n=1,736)
Grants (local, state or national grant programs)	$1,503 (n=1,698)	$3,295 (n=1,976)	$691 (n=1,780)	$354 (n=1,770)
Reported average total	$80,949	$27,738	$25,443	$25,781
Average percent	50.6%	17.3%	15.9%	16.1%

Figure 63: Fiscal Year 2006 Medium Poverty Public Library System Total Technology-Related Operating Expenditures

Sources of Funding	Salaries (including benefits)	Hardware	Software	Telecommunications
Local/county	$209,286 (n=363)	$119,252 (n=376)	$41,192 (n=381)	$81,901 (n=419)
State (including state aid to public libraries, or state-supported tax programs)	$26,081 (n=220)	$26,247 (n=241)	$8,040 (n=217)	$15,557 (n=199)
Federal	$19 (n=181)	$7,608 (n=179)	$2,586 (n=186)	$6,799 (n=217)
Fees/fines	$328 (n=188)	$914 (n=186)	$122 (n=177)	$211 (n=177)
Donations/local fund raising	$1,105 (n=194)	$19,087 (n=222)	$849 (n=197)	$1,044 (n=192)
Grants (local, state or national grant programs)	$1,811 (n=189)	$14,595 (n=274)	$1,199 (n=212)	$522 (n=195)
Reported average total	$238,630	$187,703	$53,988	$106,034
Average percent	40.7%	32.0%	9.2%	18.1%

Figure 64: Fiscal Year 2007 Medium Poverty Public Library System Total Technology-Related Operating Expenditures

Sources of Funding	Salaries (including benefits)	Hardware	Software	Telecommunications
Local/county	$225,440 (n=326)	$121,182 (n=358)	$46,931 (n=345)	$95,134 (n=392)
State (including state aid to public libraries, or state-supported tax programs)	$26,785 (n=199)	$15,850 (n=221)	$10,630 (n=212)	$16,459 (n=192)
Federal	$22 (n=173)	$2,313 (n=171)	$1,142 (n=172)	$6,212 (n=197)
Fees/fines	$339 (n=173)	$384 (n=168)	$71 (n=169)	$620 (n=172)
Donations/local fund raising	$1,445 (n=179)	$27,758 (n=199)	$1,458 (n=179)	$857 (n=181)
Grants (local, state or national grant programs)	$887 (n=178)	$13,745 (n=245)	$3,118 (n=197)	$457 (n=178)
Reported average total	$254,918	$181,232	$63,350	$119,739
Average percent	41.2%	29.3%	10.2%	19.3%

Figure 65: Fiscal Year 2006 High Poverty Public Library System Total Technology-Related Operating Expenditures

Sources of Funding	Salaries (including benefits)	Hardware	Software	Telecommunications
Local/county	$140,651 (n=25)	$78,401 (n=27)	$38,689 (n=27)	$170,287 (n=27)
State (including state aid to public libraries, or state-supported tax programs)	$4,713 (n=8)	$20,958 (n=13)	$1,061 (n=10)	$675 (n=10)
Federal	$24,143 (n=8)	$6,210 (n=7)	$10,164 (n=8)	$46,300 (n=8)
Fees/fines	$1,128 (n=7)	$250 (n=7)	$30 (n=7)	$328 (n=7)
Donations/local fund raising	$282 (n=7)	$2,031 (n=10)	$8 (n=7)	$82 (n=7)
Grants (local, state or national grant programs)	$2,397 (n=10)	$61,627 (n=13)	$3,917 (n=10)	$262 (n=5)
Reported average total	$173,314	$169,477	$53,869	$217,934
Average percent	28.2%	27.6%	8.8%	35.5%

Figure 66: Fiscal Year 2007 High Poverty Public Library System Total Technology-Related Operating Expenditures

Sources of Funding	Salaries (including benefits)	Hardware	Software	Telecommunications
Local/county	$175,566 (n=20)	$170,116 (n=22)	$137,929 (n=22)	$307,207 (n=22)
State (including state aid to public libraries, or state-supported tax programs)	$5,601 (n=8)	$12,480 (n=8)	$83 (n=7)	$968 (n=7)
Federal	$26,720 (n=8)	--	$9,400 (n=8)	$36,222 (n=8)
Fees/fines	$1,118 (n=7)	$239 (n=7)	$29 (n=7)	$336 (n=7)
Donations/local fund raising	$35,694 (n=8)	$84 (n=7)	$10 (n=7)	$118 (n=7)
Grants (local, state or national grant programs)	$3,245 (n=10)	$16,543 (n=10)	$951 (n=8)	$3,918 (n=8)
Reported average total	$247,943	$199,461	$148,401	$348,770
Average percent	26.2%	21.1%	15.7%	36.9%

Key: -- : No data to report

Figures 65 and 66 compare fiscal year 2006 and anticipated fiscal year 2007 expenditures for high poverty public libraries. One of the largest differences these figures illustrate is between the total funding provided by donations applied to salary expenditures. Fiscal year 2006 data reveal an average of $282 from donations being applied to salaries, while Figure 66 indicates a jump to $35,694 in fiscal year 2007. This may be an anomaly, and will be an area of focus in future studies.

STATE SUMMARIES

Introduction

The survey sampled and received responses from all states and the District of Columbia. The survey did not, however, receive enough responses from all states for analysis purposes. The ensuing state tables provide selected summary survey data for the states for which there were adequate and representative responses (44 in all, plus the District of Columbia). States for which data could not be fully analyzed included Colorado, Hawaii, Nebraska, New Hampshire, Minnesota and Washington.

The survey data were weighted to enable state projections. The weighting used was based on three variables:

1) Metropolitan status of libraries in the state (urban, suburban, and rural);

2) Calculated poverty of the population served by the libraries in the state (less than 20 percent, 20-40 percent, and greater than 40 percent); and

3) Total number of libraries in the state. Thus, the data presented in the tables are statewide estimates.

The survey deployed a two-stage approach that included questions regarding sampled outlets (branches) and questions regarding an entire library system. Except for the categories relating to expenditures and Internet services available, all of the data included in the following state summaries was gathered at the outlet (branch) level.

Additional detailed state data tables are available at www.ala.org/plinternetfunding.

ALABAMA

Alabama has 208 public library systems with 284 physical library locations and 17 bookmobiles to serve almost 4.5 million residents. Alabama's public libraries are primarily organized as municipal government libraries (74.5 percent). The rest are organized as multi-jurisdictional libraries (17.8 percent) and as county libraries (7.2 percent).[17]

More state tables are available online at www.ala.org/plinternetfunding.

EXPENDITURES (library system data)		Alabama	U.S.
Total operating expenditures per capita[18]		$16.93	$30.49
Technology-related expenditures (FY2006)		$42,679	$166,181

CONNECTIVITY (library branch data)			
Average number of computers		12.7	10.7
Always sufficient computers available		19%	22%
Factors limiting library adding computers	Space	65%	76%
	Cost	83%	73%
Maximum Internet connection speed	769Kbps-1.5Mbps	23%	33%
	More than 1.5Mbps	29%	29%
Always adequate connection speed		48%	44%
Wireless availability		30%	54%

INTERNET SERVICES			
Internet services critical to role of library (library branch data)	Provide education resources & databases for K-12 students	87%	68%
	Provide services for job seekers	50%	44%
	Provide computer & Internet skills training	37%	30%
	Provide education resources & databases for adult/CE students	19%	28%
	Provide education resources & databases for students in higher ed	41%	21%
Internet services available (library system data)	Licensed databases	81%	86%
	Homework resources	93%	68%
	Digital/virtual reference	61%	58%
	E-books	26%	38%
	Audio content	28%	38%
Library offers IT training for patrons (branch)		71%	76%
Average hours open per week (branch)		45.7	45.2

---

[17] National Center for Education Statistics. Public Libraries in the United States: Fiscal Year 2004. (NCES 2006-349). Washington, DC: NCES, 2006. http://www.nces.ed.gov/pubs2006/2006349.pdf
[18] ibid

ALASKA

Alaska has 88 public library systems with 105 physical library locations and one bookmobile to serve almost 655,000 residents. Alaska's public libraries are primarily organized as municipal government libraries (46.6 percent). The rest are organized as association libraries within a municipality (25 percent), as county libraries (15.9 percent) and "other" – including libraries within the Native American Tribal Government and combined public/school libraries (8 percent).[19]

More state tables are available online at www.ala.org/plinternetfunding.

EXPENDITURES (library system data)		Alaska	U.S.
Total operating expenditures per capita[20]		$37.48	$30.49
Technology-related expenditures (FY 2006)		$12,189	$166,181
CONNECTIVITY (library branch data)			
Average number of computers		5.7	10.7
Always sufficient computers available		22%	22%
Factors limiting library adding computers	Space	77%	76%
	Cost	70%	73%
Maximum Internet connection speed	769Kbps-1.5Mbps	4%	33%
	More than 1.5Mbps	6%	29%
Always adequate connection speed		39%	44%
Wireless availability		57%	54%
INTERNET SERVICES			
Internet services critical to role of library (library branch data)	Provide education resources & databases for K-12 students	42%	68%
	Provide services for job seekers	47%	44%
	Provide computer & Internet skills training	19%	30%
	Provide education resources & databases for adult/CE students	14%	28%
	Provide education resources & databases for students in higher ed	26%	21%
Internet services available (library system data)	Licensed databases	74%	86%
	Homework resources	81%	68%
	Digital/virtual reference	40%	58%
	E-books	18%	38%
	Audio content	30%	38%
Library offers IT training for patrons (branch)		59%	76%
Average hours open per week (branch)		35.2	45.2

---

[19] National Center for Education Statistics. Public Libraries in the United States: Fiscal Year 2004. (NCES 2006-349). Washington, DC: NCES, 2006. http://www.nces.ed.gov/pubs2006/2006349.pdf
[20] ibid

ARIZONA

Arizona has 91 public library systems with 187 physical library locations and 11 bookmobiles to serve more than 5.4 million residents. Arizona's public libraries primarily are operated jointly by a county and city (40.7 percent). The rest are organized as municipal government libraries (25.3 percent) and as county libraries (25.3 percent).[21]

More state tables are available online at www.ala.org/plinternetfunding.

		Arizona	U.S.
EXPENDITURES (library system data)			
Total operating expenditures per capita[22]		$23.69	$30.49
Technology-related expenditures (FY 2006)		$626,343	$166,181
CONNECTIVITY (library branch data)			
Average number of computers		27.2	10.7
Always sufficient computers available		20%	22%
Factors limiting library adding computers	Space	81%	76%
	Cost	89%	73%
Maximum Internet connection speed	769Kbps-1.5Mbps	10%	33%
	More than 1.5Mbps	51%	29%
Always adequate connection speed		61%	44%
Wireless availability		60%	54%
INTERNET SERVICES			
Internet services critical to role of library (library branch data)	Provide education resources & databases for K-12 students	87%	68%
	Provide services for job seekers	30%	44%
	Provide computer & Internet skills training	27%	30%
	Provide education resources & databases for adult/CE students	32%	28%
	Provide education resources & databases for students in higher ed	38%	21%
Internet services available (library system data)	Licensed databases	92%	86%
	Homework resources	61%	68%
	Digital/virtual reference	32%	58%
	E-books	36%	38%
	Audio content	46%	38%
Library offers IT training for patrons (branch)		62%	76%
Average hours open per week (branch)		45.7	45.2

---

[21] National Center for Education Statistics. Public Libraries in the United States: Fiscal Year 2004. (NCES 2006-349). Washington, DC: NCES, 2006. http://www.nces.ed.gov/pubs2006/2006349.pdf
[22] ibid

ARKANSAS

Arkansas has 48 public library systems with 211 physical library locations and three bookmobiles to serve almost 2.7 million residents. Arkansas' public libraries are organized primarily as county libraries (43.8 percent). The rest are organized as multi-jurisdictional libraries (33.3 percent) and as municipal government libraries (18.8 percent).[23]

More state tables are available online at www.ala.org/plinternetfunding.

		Arkansas	U.S.
EXPENDITURES (library system data)			
Total operating expenditures per capita[24]		$15.49	$30.49
Technology-related expenditures (FY 2006)		$78,426	$166,181
CONNECTIVITY (library branch data)			
Average number of computers		8.0	10.7
Always sufficient computers available		33%	22%
Factors limiting library adding computers	Space	83%	76%
	Cost	70%	73%
Maximum Internet connection speed	769Kbps-1.5Mbps	20%	33%
	More than 1.5Mbps	32%	29%
Always adequate connection speed		36%	44%
Wireless availability		52%	54%
INTERNET SERVICES			
Internet services critical to role of library (library branch data)	Provide education resources & databases for K-12 students	75%	68%
	Provide services for job seekers	62%	44%
	Provide computer & Internet skills training	27%	30%
	Provide education resources & databases for adult/CE students	14%	28%
	Provide education resources & databases for students in higher ed	22%	21%
Internet services available (library system data)	Licensed databases	92%	86%
	Homework resources	54%	68%
	Digital/virtual reference	44%	58%
	E-books	21%	38%
	Audio content	29%	38%
Library offers IT training for patrons (branch)		53%	76%
Average hours open per week (branch)		38.8	45.2

---

[23] National Center for Education Statistics. Public Libraries in the United States: Fiscal Year 2004. (NCES 2006-349). Washington, DC: NCES, 2006. http://www.nces.ed.gov/pubs2006/2006349.pdf
[24] ibid

CALIFORNIA

California has 179 public library systems with 1,087 physical library locations and 63 bookmobiles to serve more than 36 million residents. California's public libraries are primarily organized as municipal government libraries (63.7 percent). Most of the rest are organized as county libraries (24.6 percent) and library districts (5 percent).[25]

More state tables are available online at www.ala.org/plinternetfunding.

EXPENDITURES (library system data)		California	U.S.
Total operating expenditures per capita[26]		$27.56	$30.49
Technology-related expenditures (FY 2006)		$518,835	$166,181
CONNECTIVITY (library branch data)			
Average number of computers		12.7	10.7
Always sufficient computers available		11%	22%
Factors limiting library adding computers	Space	84%	76%
	Cost	55%	73%
Maximum Internet connection speed	769Kbps-1.5Mbps	45%	33%
	More than 1.5Mbps	40%	29%
Always adequate connection speed		25%	44%
Wireless availability		49%	54%
INTERNET SERVICES			
Internet services critical to role of library (library branch data)	Provide education resources & databases for K-12 students	79%	68%
	Provide services for job seekers	27%	44%
	Provide computer & Internet skills training	38%	30%
	Provide education resources & databases for adult/CE students	31%	28%
	Provide education resources & databases for students in higher ed	17%	21%
Internet services available (library system data)	Licensed databases	91%	86%
	Homework resources	73%	68%
	Digital/virtual reference	76%	58%
	E-books	54%	38%
	Audio content	52%	38%
Library offers IT training for patrons (branch)		78%	76%
Average hours open per week (branch)		45.0	45.2

---

[25] National Center for Education Statistics. Public Libraries in the United States: Fiscal Year 2004. (NCES 2006-349). Washington, DC: NCES, 2006. http://www.nces.ed.gov/pubs2006/2006349.pdf
[26] ibid

COLORADO

Colorado has 115 public library systems with 241 physical library locations and 12 bookmobiles to serve about 4.4 million residents. Colorado's public libraries are primarily organized as library districts (41.7 percent) and municipal government libraries (38.3 percent). Most of the rest are organized as county libraries (12.2 percent) and multi-jurisdictional libraries (7 percent).[27]

More state tables are available online at www.ala.org/plinternetfunding.

EXPENDITURES (library system data)		Colorado	U.S.
Total operating expenditures per capita[28]		$39.29	$30.49
Technology-related expenditures (FY 2006)		$141,355	$166,181
CONNECTIVITY (library branch data)			
Average number of computers		--*	10.7
Always sufficient computers available		--	22%
Factors limiting library adding computers	Space	--	76%
	Cost	--	73%
Maximum Internet connection speed	769Kbps-1.5Mbps	--	33%
	More than 1.5Mbps	--	29%
Always adequate connection speed		--	44%
Wireless availability		--	54%
INTERNET SERVICES			
Internet services critical to role of library (library branch data)	Provide education resources & databases for K-12 students	--	68%
	Provide services for job seekers	--	44%
	Provide computer & Internet skills training	--	30%
	Provide education resources & databases for adult/CE students	--	28%
	Provide education resources & databases for students in higher ed	--	21%
Internet services available (library system data)	Licensed databases	59%	86%
	Homework resources	73%	68%
	Digital/virtual reference	58%	58%
	E-books	12%	38%
	Audio content	32%	38%
Library offers IT training for patrons (branch)		--	76%
Average hours open per week (branch)		--	45.2

---

[27] National Center for Education Statistics. Public Libraries in the United States: Fiscal Year 2004. (NCES 2006-349). Washington, DC: NCES, 2006. http://www.nces.ed.gov/pubs2006/2006349.pdf
[28] Ibid
* There was not enough outlet-level data reported to analyze at the state level.

CONNECTICUT

Connecticut has 194 public library systems with 244 physical library locations and seven bookmobiles to serve almost 3.5 million residents. Connecticut's public libraries are primarily organized as municipal government libraries (50.5 percent) or association libraries within a municipality (49.5 percent).[29]

More state tables are available online at www.ala.org/plinternetfunding.

		Conn.	U.S.
EXPENDITURES (library system data)			
Total operating expenditures per capita[30]		$41.97	$30.49
Technology-related expenditures (FY 2006)		$67,272	$166,181
CONNECTIVITY (library branch data)			
Average number of computers		10.0	10.7
Always sufficient computers available		33%	22%
Factors limiting library adding computers	Space	72%	76%
	Cost	68%	73%
Maximum Internet connection speed	769Kbps-1.5Mbps	53%	33%
	More than 1.5Mbps	40%	29%
Always adequate connection speed		44%	44%
Wireless availability		61%	54%
INTERNET SERVICES			
Internet services critical to role of library (library branch data)	Provide education resources & databases for K-12 students	66%	68%
	Provide services for job seekers	48%	44%
	Provide computer & Internet skills training	37%	30%
	Provide education resources & databases for adult/CE students	38%	28%
	Provide education resources & databases for students in higher ed	16%	21%
Internet services available (library system data)	Licensed databases	98%	86%
	Homework resources	75%	68%
	Digital/virtual reference	94%	58%
	E-books	23%	38%
	Audio content	39%	38%
Library offers IT training for patrons (branch)		77%	76%
Average hours open per week (branch)		50.7	45.2

---

[29] National Center for Education Statistics. Public Libraries in the United States: Fiscal Year 2004. (NCES 2006-349). Washington, DC: NCES, 2006. http://www.nces.ed.gov/pubs2006/2006349.pdf
[30] ibid

DELAWARE

Delaware has 21 public library systems with 33 physical library locations and two bookmobiles serving more than 4.2 million residents. Delaware's public libraries are organized primarily as library districts (52.4 percent) and county systems (28.6 percent). Another 19.1 percent are organized as municipal government or city/county libraries.[31]

More state tables are available online at www.ala.org/plinternetfunding.

		Delaware	U.S.
EXPENDITURES (library system data)			
Total operating expenditures per capita[32]		$24.83	$30.49
Technology-related expenditures (FY 2006)		$9,788	$166,181
CONNECTIVITY (library branch data)			
Average number of computers		11.0	10.7
Always sufficient computers available		18%	22%
Factors limiting library adding computers	Space	82%	76%
	Cost	64%	73%
Maximum Internet connection speed	769Kbps-1.5Mbps	36%	33%
	More than 1.5Mbps	24%	29%
Always adequate connection speed		39%	44%
Wireless availability		49%	54%
INTERNET SERVICES			
Internet services critical to role of library (library branch data)	Provide education resources & databases for K-12 students	49%	68%
	Provide services for job seekers	55%	44%
	Provide computer & Internet skills training	39%	30%
	Provide education resources & databases for adult/CE students	30%	28%
	Provide education resources & databases for students in higher ed	3%	21%
Internet services available (library system data)	Licensed databases	87%	86%
	Homework resources	56%	68%
	Digital/virtual reference	61%	58%
	E-books	56%	38%
	Audio content	44%	38%
Library offers IT training for patrons (branch)		88%	76%
Average hours open per week (branch)		52.6	45.2

---

[31] National Center for Education Statistics. Public Libraries in the United States: Fiscal Year 2004. (NCES 2006-349). Washington, DC: NCES, 2006. http://www.nces.ed.gov/pubs2006/2006349.pdf
[32] ibid

DISTRICT OF COLUMBIA

The District of Columbia has one public library system with 27 physical library locations and one bookmobile to serve about 554,000 residents.[33]

More state tables are available online at www.ala.org/plinternetfunding.

EXPENDITURES		D.C.	U.S.
Total operating expenditures per capita[34]		$50.44	$30.49
Technology-related expenditures (FY 2006)		--*	$166,181

CONNECTIVITY		D.C.	U.S.
Average number of computers		6.6	10.7
Always sufficient computers available		0%	22%
Factors limiting library adding computers	Space	47%	76%
	Cost	46%	73%
Maximum Internet connection speed	769Kbps-1.5Mbps	--*	33%
	More than 1.5Mbps	88%	29%
Always adequate connection speed		67%	44%
Wireless availability		100%	54%

INTERNET SERVICES		D.C.	U.S.
Internet services critical to role of library	Provide education resources & databases for K-12 students	91%	68%
	Provide services for job seekers	87%	44%
	Provide computer & Internet skills training	4%	30%
	Provide education resources & databases for adult/CE students	25%	28%
	Provide education resources & databases for students in higher ed	29%	21%
Internet services available	Licensed databases	100%	86%
	Homework resources	100%	68%
	Digital/virtual reference	100%	58%
	E-books	100%	38%
	Audio content	100%	38%
Library offers IT training for patrons		87%	76%
Average hours open per week		58.4	45.2

---

[33] National Center for Education Statistics. Public Libraries in the United States: Fiscal Year 2004. (NCES 2006-349). Washington, DC: NCES, 2006. http://www.nces.ed.gov/pubs2006/2006349.pdf
[34] Ibid
* -- signifies no data was reported.

FLORIDA

Florida has 70 public library systems with 498 physical library locations and 32 bookmobiles to serve almost 17.5 million residents. Florida's public libraries are primarily organized as county libraries (50 percent) and municipal government libraries (30 percent). Most of the rest are organized as multi-jurisdictional libraries (15.7 percent). [35]

More state tables are available online at www.ala.org/plinternetfunding.

		Florida	U.S.
EXPENDITURES (library system data)			
Total operating expenditures per capita[36]		$25.06	$30.49
Technology-related expenditures (FY 2006)		$1,476,629	$166,181
CONNECTIVITY (library branch data)			
Average number of computers		19.5	10.7
Always sufficient computers available		8%	22%
Factors limiting library adding computers	Space	72%	76%
	Cost	55%	73%
Maximum Internet connection speed	769Kbps-1.5Mbps	38%	33%
	More than 1.5Mbps	35%	29%
Always adequate connection speed		22%	44%
Wireless availability		55%	54%
INTERNET SERVICES			
Internet services critical to role of library (library branch data)	Provide education resources & databases for K-12 students	58%	68%
	Provide services for job seekers	26%	44%
	Provide computer & Internet skills training	50%	30%
	Provide education resources & databases for adult/CE students	19%	28%
	Provide education resources & databases for students in higher ed	19%	21%
Internet services available (library system data)	Licensed databases	93%	86%
	Homework resources	73%	68%
	Digital/virtual reference	88%	58%
	E-books	57%	38%
	Audio content	43%	38%
Library offers IT training for patrons (branch)		92%	76%
Average hours open per week (branch)		50.7	45.2

---

[35] National Center for Education Statistics. Public Libraries in the United States: Fiscal Year 2004. (NCES 2006-349). Washington, DC: NCES, 2006. http://www.nces.ed.gov/pubs2006/2006349.pdf
[36] ibid

GEORGIA

Georgia has 58 public library systems with 369 physical library locations and 26 bookmobiles to serve almost 8.5 million residents. Georgia's public libraries are organized as multi-jurisdictional libraries (56.9 percent) and as county libraries (43.1 percent). [37]

More state tables are available online at www.ala.org/plinternetfunding.

EXPENDITURES (library system data)		Georgia	U.S.
Total operating expenditures per capita[38]		$19.19	$30.49
Technology-related expenditures (FY 2006)		$384,931	$166,181

CONNECTIVITY (library branch data)		Georgia	U.S.
Average number of computers		14.7	10.7
Always sufficient computers available		26%	22%
Factors limiting library adding computers	Space	79%	76%
	Cost	86%	73%
Maximum Internet connection speed	769Kbps-1.5Mbps	47%	33%
	More than 1.5Mbps	33%	29%
Always adequate connection speed		53%	44%
Wireless availability		45%	54%

INTERNET SERVICES			
Internet services critical to role of library (library branch data)	Provide education resources & databases for K-12 students	71%	68%
	Provide services for job seekers	37%	44%
	Provide computer & Internet skills training	27%	30%
	Provide education resources & databases for adult/CE students	34%	28%
	Provide education resources & databases for students in higher ed	36%	21%
Internet services available (library system data)	Licensed databases	95%	86%
	Homework resources	48%	68%
	Digital/virtual reference	51%	58%
	E-books	40%	38%
	Audio content	23%	38%
Library offers IT training for patrons (branch)		74%	76%
Average hours open per week (branch)		49.3	45.2

---

[37] National Center for Education Statistics. Public Libraries in the United States: Fiscal Year 2004. (NCES 2006-349). Washington, DC: NCES, 2006. http://www.nces.ed.gov/pubs2006/2006349.pdf
[38] ibid

HAWAII

Hawaii has only one public library system with 51 physical library locations and one bookmobile to serve about 1.2 million residents.[39]

More state tables are available online at www.ala.org/plinternetfunding.

EXPENDITURES		Hawaii	U.S.
Total operating expenditures per capita[40]		$21.70	$30.49
Technology-related expenditures (FY 2006)		No data	$166,181
CONNECTIVITY			
Average number of computers		--*	10.7
Always sufficient computers available		--	22%
Factors limiting library adding computers	Space	--	76%
	Cost	--	73%
Maximum Internet connection speed	769Kbps-1.5Mbps	--	33%
	More than 1.5Mbps	--	29%
Always adequate connection speed		--	44%
Wireless availability		--	54%
INTERNET SERVICES			
Internet services critical to role of library	Provide education resources & databases for K-12 students	--	68%
	Provide services for job seekers	--	44%
	Provide computer & Internet skills training	--	30%
	Provide education resources & databases for adult/CE students	--	28%
	Provide education resources & databases for students in higher ed	--	21%
Internet services available	Licensed databases	100%	86%
	Homework resources	No data	68%
	Digital/virtual reference	No data	58%
	E-books	100%	38%
	Audio content	100%	38%
Library offers IT training for patrons		--	76%
Average hours open per week		--	45.2

---

[39] National Center for Education Statistics. Public Libraries in the United States: Fiscal Year 2004. (NCES 2006-349). Washington, DC: NCES, 2006. http://www.nces.ed.gov/pubs2006/2006349.pdf

[40] Ibid

* Hawaii did not respond to outlet-level questions.

IDAHO

Idaho has 104 public library systems with 143 physical library locations and seven bookmobiles to serve about 1.2 million residents. Idaho's public libraries are organized as library districts (51 percent) or municipal government libraries (49 percent). [41]

More state tables are available online at www.ala.org/plinternetfunding.

EXPENDITURES (library system data)		Idaho	U.S.
Total operating expenditures per capita[42]		$24.00	$30.49
Technology-related expenditures (FY 2006)		$48,433	$166,181

CONNECTIVITY (library branch data)			
Average number of computers		7.2	10.7
Always sufficient computers available		20%	22%
Factors limiting library adding computers	Space	82%	76%
	Cost	78%	73%
Maximum Internet connection speed	769Kbps-1.5Mbps	23%	33%
	More than 1.5Mbps	36%	29%
Always adequate connection speed		38%	44%
Wireless availability		50%	54%

INTERNET SERVICES			
Internet services critical to role of library (library branch data)	Provide education resources & databases for K-12 students	61%	68%
	Provide services for job seekers	40%	44%
	Provide computer & Internet skills training	14%	30%
	Provide education resources & databases for adult/CE students	39%	28%
	Provide education resources & databases for students in higher ed	14%	21%
Internet services available (library system data)	Licensed databases	87%	86%
	Homework resources	71%	68%
	Digital/virtual reference	48%	58%
	E-books	10%	38%
	Audio content	26%	38%
Library offers IT training for patrons (branch)		58%	76%
Average hours open per week (branch)		38.7	45.2

---

[41] National Center for Education Statistics. Public Libraries in the United States: Fiscal Year 2004. (NCES 2006-349). Washington, DC: NCES, 2006. http://www.nces.ed.gov/pubs2006/2006349.pdf
[42] ibid

ILLINOIS

Illinois has 626 public library systems with 789 physical library locations and 27 bookmobiles to serve almost 11.4 million residents. Illinois' public libraries are organized as municipal government libraries (51 percent) or library districts (49 percent). [43]

More state tables are available online at www.ala.org/plinternetfunding.

EXPENDITURES (library system data)		Illinois	U.S.
Total operating expenditures per capita[44]		$46.43	$30.49
Technology-related expenditures (FY 2006)		$91,214	$166,181
CONNECTIVITY (library branch data)			
Average number of computers		12.6	10.7
Always sufficient computers available		23%	22%
Factors limiting library adding computers	Space	72%	76%
	Cost	71%	73%
Maximum Internet connection speed	769Kbps-1.5Mbps	34%	33%
	More than 1.5Mbps	27%	29%
Always adequate connection speed		48%	44%
Wireless availability		57%	54%
INTERNET SERVICES			
Internet services critical to role of library	Provide education resources & databases for K-12 students	65%	68%
	Provide services for job seekers	49%	44%
	Provide computer & Internet skills training	26%	30%
	Provide education resources & databases for adult/CE students	28%	28%
	Provide education resources & databases for students in higher ed	22%	21%
Internet services available (library system data)	Licensed databases	76%	86%
	Homework resources	62%	68%
	Digital/virtual reference	59%	58%
	E-books	31%	38%
	Audio content	38%	38%
Library offers IT training for patrons (branch)		77%	76%
Average hours open per week (branch)		49.3	45.2

---

[43] National Center for Education Statistics. Public Libraries in the United States: Fiscal Year 2004. (NCES 2006-349). Washington, DC: NCES, 2006. http://www.nces.ed.gov/pubs2006/2006349.pdf
[44] ibid

INDIANA

Indiana has 239 public library systems with 438 physical library locations and 38 bookmobiles to serve about 5.8 million residents. All of Indiana's public libraries are organized as library districts (100 percent).[45]

More state tables are available online at www.ala.org/plinternetfunding.

		Indiana	U.S.
EXPENDITURES (library system data)			
Total operating expenditures per capita[46]		$45.16	$30.49
Technology-related expenditures (FY 2006)		--*	$166,181
CONNECTIVITY (library branch data)			
Average number of computers		15.6	10.7
Always sufficient computers available		20%	22%
Factors limiting library adding computers	*Space*	78%	76%
	Cost	76%	73%
Maximum Internet connection speed	*769Kbps-1.5Mbps*	36%	33%
	More than 1.5Mbps	34%	29%
Always adequate connection speed		37%	44%
Wireless availability		64%	54%
INTERNET SERVICES			
Internet services critical to role of library (library branch data)	*Provide education resources & databases for K-12 students*	70%	68%
	Provide services for job seekers	50%	44%
	Provide computer & Internet skills training	29%	30%
	Provide education resources & databases for adult/CE students	19%	28%
	Provide education resources & databases for students in higher ed	16%	21%
Internet services available (library system data)	*Licensed databases*	--	86%
	Homework resources	--	68%
	Digital/virtual reference	--	58%
	E-books	--	38%
	Audio content	--	38%
Library offers IT training for patrons (branch)		91%	76%
Average hours open per week (branch)		49.9	45.2

---

[45] National Center for Education Statistics. Public Libraries in the United States: Fiscal Year 2004. (NCES 2006-349). Washington, DC: NCES, 2006. http://www.nces.ed.gov/pubs2006/2006349.pdf
[46] Ibid
* There was not enough system-level data reported to analyze at the state level.

IOWA

Iowa has 540 public library systems with 564 physical library locations and five bookmobiles to serve more than 2.9 million residents. Iowa's public libraries are primarily organized as municipal government libraries (98.7 percent). [47]

More state tables are available online at www.ala.org/plinternetfunding.

		Iowa	U.S.
EXPENDITURES (library system data)			
Total operating expenditures per capita[48]		$26.85	$30.49
Technology-related expenditures (FY 2006)		$23,587	$166,181
CONNECTIVITY (library branch data)			
Average number of computers		6.0	10.7
Always sufficient computers available		33%	22%
Factors limiting library adding computers	Space	64%	76%
	Cost	80%	73%
Maximum Internet connection speed	769Kbps-1.5Mbps	15%	33%
	More than 1.5Mbps	14%	29%
Always adequate connection speed		56%	44%
Wireless availability		46%	54%
INTERNET SERVICES			
Internet services critical to role of library (library branch data)	Provide education resources & databases for K-12 students	78%	68%
	Provide services for job seekers	46%	44%
	Provide computer & Internet skills training	29%	30%
	Provide education resources & databases for adult/CE students	26%	28%
	Provide education resources & databases for students in higher ed	22%	21%
Internet services available (library system data)	Licensed databases	72%	86%
	Homework resources	66%	68%
	Digital/virtual reference	38%	58%
	E-books	5%	38%
	Audio content	15%	38%
Library offers IT training for patrons (branch)		74%	76%
Average hours open per week (branch)		35.8	45.2

---

[47] National Center for Education Statistics. Public Libraries in the United States: Fiscal Year 2004. (NCES 2006-349). Washington, DC: NCES, 2006. http://www.nces.ed.gov/pubs2006/2006349.pdf
[48] ibid

KANSAS

Kansas has 325 public library systems with 374 buildings and 5 bookmobiles serving nearly 2.3 million residents. The majority of Kansas public libraries serve communities with fewer than 10,000 residents (90.5 percent).[49]

More state tables are available online at www.ala.org/plinternetfunding.

		Kansas	U.S.
EXPENDITURES (library system data)			
Total operating expenditures per capita[50]		$37.34	$30.49
Technology-related expenditures (FY 2006)		--*	$166,181
CONNECTIVITY (library branch data)			
Average number of computers		6.7	10.7
Always sufficient computers available		26%	22%
Factors limiting library adding computers	Space	70%	76%
	Cost	78%	73%
Maximum Internet connection speed	769Kbps-1.5Mbps	25%	33%
	More than 1.5Mbps	17%	29%
Always adequate connection speed		46%	44%
Wireless availability		50%	54%
INTERNET SERVICES			
Internet services critical to role of library (library branch data)	Provide education resources & databases for K-12 students	54%	68%
	Provide services for job seekers	49%	44%
	Provide computer & Internet skills training	24%	30%
	Provide education resources & databases for adult/CE students	36%	28%
	Provide education resources & databases for students in higher ed	23%	21%
Internet services available (library system data)	Licensed databases	--	86%
	Homework resources	--	68%
	Digital/virtual reference	--	58%
	E-books	--	38%
	Audio content	--	38%
Library offers IT training for patrons (branch)		71%	76%
Average hours open per week (branch)		37.6	45.2

---

[49] National Center for Education Statistics. Public Libraries in the United States: Fiscal Year 2004. (NCES 2006-349). Washington, DC: NCES, 2006. http://www.nces.ed.gov/pubs2006/2006349.pdf

[50] Ibid

* There was not enough system-level data reported to analyze at the state level.

KENTUCKY

Kentucky has 116 public library systems with 190 physical library locations and 86 bookmobiles (more than any other state) to serve about 4 million residents. Kentucky's public libraries are primarily organized as library districts (89.7 percent) and as county libraries (9.5 percent).[51]

More state tables are available online at www.ala.org/plinternetfunding.

		Kentucky	U.S.
EXPENDITURES (library system data)			
Total operating expenditures per capita[52]		$21.17	$30.49
Technology-related expenditures (FY 2006)		--*	$166,181
CONNECTIVITY (library branch data)			
Average number of computers		14.3	10.7
Always sufficient computers available		24%	22%
Factors limiting library adding computers	Space	79%	76%
	Cost	69%	73%
Maximum Internet connection speed	769Kbps-1.5Mbps	40%	33%
	More than 1.5Mbps	34%	29%
Always adequate connection speed		37%	44%
Wireless availability		60%	54%
INTERNET SERVICES			
Internet services critical to role of library (library branch data)	Provide education resources & databases for K-12 students	69%	68%
	Provide services for job seekers	31%	44%
	Provide computer & Internet skills training	26%	30%
	Provide education resources & databases for adult/CE students	32%	28%
	Provide education resources & databases for students in higher ed	60%	21%
Internet services available (library system data)	Licensed databases	--	86%
	Homework resources	--	68%
	Digital/virtual reference	--	58%
	E-books	--	38%
	Audio content	--	38%
Library offers IT training for patrons (branch)		83%	76%
Average hours open per week (branch)		52.6	45.2

---

[51] National Center for Education Statistics. Public Libraries in the United States: Fiscal Year 2004. (NCES 2006-349). Washington, DC: NCES, 2006. http://www.nces.ed.gov/pubs2006/2006349.pdf
[52] Ibid
* There was not enough system-level data reported to analyze at the state level.

LOUISIANA

Louisiana has 66 public library systems with 335 physical library locations and 27 bookmobiles to serve almost 4.5 million residents. Louisiana's public libraries are primarily organized as county/parish libraries (90.9 percent). [53]

More state tables are available online at www.ala.org/plinternetfunding.

EXPENDITURES (library system data)		Louisiana	U.S.
Total operating expenditures per capita[54]		$25.99	$30.49
Technology-related expenditures (FY 2006)		$247,180	$166,181

CONNECTIVITY (library branch data)		Louisiana	U.S.
Average number of computers		7.0	10.7
Always sufficient computers available		24%	22%
Factors limiting library adding computers	*Space*	87%	76%
	Cost	58%	73%
Maximum Internet connection speed	*769Kbps-1.5Mbps*	47%	33%
	More than 1.5Mbps	5%	29%
Always adequate connection speed		22%	44%
Wireless availability		17%	54%

INTERNET SERVICES			
Internet services critical to role of library (library branch data)	*Provide education resources & databases for K-12 students*	84%	68%
	Provide services for job seekers	55%	44%
	Provide computer & Internet skills training	31%	30%
	Provide education resources & databases for adult/CE students	24%	28%
	Provide education resources & databases for students in higher ed	25%	21%
Internet services available (library system data)	*Licensed databases*	94%	86%
	Homework resources	53%	68%
	Digital/virtual reference	54%	58%
	E-books	13%	38%
	Audio content	13%	38%
Library offers IT training for patrons (branch)		76%	76%
Average hours open per week (branch)		49.3	45.2

---

[53] National Center for Education Statistics. Public Libraries in the United States: Fiscal Year 2004. (NCES 2006-349). Washington, DC: NCES, 2006. http://www.nces.ed.gov/pubs2006/2006349.pdf
[54] ibid

MAINE

Maine has 269 public library systems with 276 physical library locations to serve almost 1.2 million residents. Maine's public libraries are primarily organized as association libraries within a municipality (61.7 percent) and as municipal government libraries (38.3 percent). [55]

More state tables are available online at www.ala.org/plinternetfunding.

EXPENDITURES (library system data)		Maine	U.S.
Total operating expenditures per capita[56]		$26.58	$30.49
Technology-related expenditures (FY 2006)		$17,459	$166,181
CONNECTIVITY (library branch data)			
Average number of computers		5.8	10.7
Always sufficient computers available		42%	22%
Factors limiting library adding computers	Space	74%	76%
	Cost	82%	73%
Maximum Internet connection speed	769Kbps-1.5Mbps	26%	33%
	More than 1.5Mbps	20%	29%
Always adequate connection speed		59%	44%
Wireless availability		78%	54%
INTERNET SERVICES			
Internet services critical to role of library (library branch data)	Provide education resources & databases for K-12 students	57%	68%
	Provide services for job seekers	33%	44%
	Provide computer & Internet skills training	17%	30%
	Provide education resources & databases for adult/CE students	37%	28%
	Provide education resources & databases for students in higher ed	15%	21%
Internet services available (library system data)	Licensed databases	78%	86%
	Homework resources	55%	68%
	Digital/virtual reference	47%	58%
	E-books	17%	38%
	Audio content	16%	38%
Library offers IT training for patrons (branch)		69%	76%
Average hours open per week (branch)		34.6	45.2

---

[55] National Center for Education Statistics. Public Libraries in the United States: Fiscal Year 2004. (NCES 2006-349). Washington, DC: NCES, 2006. http://www.nces.ed.gov/pubs2006/2006349.pdf
[56] ibid

MARYLAND

Maryland has 24 library systems with 179 physical library buildings and 11 bookmobiles serving more than 5.4 million residents. All of the libraries are organized as county/parish libraries (100 percent).[57]

More state tables are available online at www.ala.org/plinternetfunding.

EXPENDITURES (library system data)		Maryland	U.S.
Total operating expenditures per capita[58]		$36.30	$30.49
Technology-related expenditures (FY 2006)		$1,408,173	$166,181

CONNECTIVITY (library branch data)			
Average number of computers		14.5	10.7
Always sufficient computers available		13%	22%
Factors limiting library adding computers	Space	86%	76%
	Cost	81%	73%
Maximum Internet connection speed	769Kbps-1.5Mbps	41%	33%
	More than 1.5Mbps	52%	29%
Always adequate connection speed		34%	44%
Wireless availability		55%	54%

INTERNET SERVICES			
Internet services critical to role of library (library branch data)	Provide education resources & databases for K-12 students	89%	68%
	Provide services for job seekers	36%	44%
	Provide computer & Internet skills training	20%	30%
	Provide education resources & databases for adult/CE students	43%	28%
	Provide education resources & databases for students in higher ed	23%	21%
Internet services available (library system data)	Licensed databases	100%	86%
	Homework resources	100%	68%
	Digital/virtual reference	100%	58%
	E-books	76%	38%
	Audio content	70%	38%
Library offers IT training for patrons (branch)		98%	76%
Average hours open per week (branch)		49.7	45.2

---

[57] National Center for Education Statistics. Public Libraries in the United States: Fiscal Year 2004. (NCES 2006-349). Washington, DC: NCES, 2006. http://www.nces.ed.gov/pubs2006/2006349.pdf
[58] ibid

MASSACHUSETTS

Massachusetts has 370 public library systems with 485 physical library locations and five bookmobiles to serve more than 6.4 million residents. Massachusetts' public libraries are primarily organized as municipal government libraries (93.2 percent). Most of the rest are organized as association libraries within a municipality (6.5 percent).[59]

More state tables are available online at www.ala.org/plinternetfunding.

EXPENDITURES (library system data)		Mass.	U.S.
Total operating expenditures per capita[60]		$32.97	$30.49
Technology-related expenditures (FY 2006)		$44,003	$166,181

CONNECTIVITY (library branch data)			
Average number of computers		9.7	10.7
Always sufficient computers available		22%	22%
Factors limiting library adding computers	Space	71%	76%
	Cost	73%	73%
Maximum Internet connection speed	769Kbps-1.5Mbps	27%	33%
	More than 1.5Mbps	21%	29%
Always adequate connection speed		35%	44%
Wireless availability		63%	54%

INTERNET SERVICES			
Internet services critical to role of library (library branch data)	Provide education resources & databases for K-12 students	70%	68%
	Provide services for job seekers	24%	44%
	Provide computer & Internet skills training	26%	30%
	Provide education resources & databases for adult/CE students	35%	28%
	Provide education resources & databases for students in higher ed	17%	21%
Internet services available (library system data)	Licensed databases	98%	86%
	Homework resources	66%	68%
	Digital/virtual reference	77%	58%
	E-books	77%	38%
	Audio content	68%	38%
Library offers IT training for patrons (branch)		77%	76%
Average hours open per week (branch)		41.8	45.2

---

[59] National Center for Education Statistics. Public Libraries in the United States: Fiscal Year 2004. (NCES 2006-349). Washington, DC: NCES, 2006. http://www.nces.ed.gov/pubs2006/2006349.pdf
[60] ibid

MICHIGAN

Michigan has 384 public library systems with 658 physical library locations and 17 bookmobiles to serve almost 9.9 million residents. Michigan's public libraries are primarily organized as municipal government libraries (52.6 percent) and library districts (36.7 percent).[61]

More state tables are available online at www.ala.org/plinternetfunding.

EXPENDITURES (library system data)		Michigan	U.S.
Total operating expenditures per capita[62]		$33.42	$30.49
Technology-related expenditures (FY 2006)		$152,729	$166,181
CONNECTIVITY (library branch data)			
Average number of computers		10.9	10.7
Always sufficient computers available		18%	22%
Factors limiting library adding computers	Space	76%	76%
	Cost	64%	73%
Maximum Internet connection speed	769Kbps-1.5Mbps	40%	33%
	More than 1.5Mbps	26%	29%
Always adequate connection speed		46%	44%
Wireless availability		48%	54%
INTERNET SERVICES			
Internet services critical to role of library (library branch data)	Provide education resources & databases for K-12 students	68%	68%
	Provide services for job seekers	60%	44%
	Provide computer & Internet skills training	26%	30%
	Provide education resources & databases for adult/CE students	25%	28%
	Provide education resources & databases for students in higher ed	28%	21%
Internet services available (library system data)	Licensed databases	85%	86%
	Homework resources	71%	68%
	Digital/virtual reference	55%	58%
	E-books	50%	38%
	Audio content	25%	38%
Library offers IT training for patrons (branch)		74%	76%
Average hours open per week (branch)		45.6	45.2

---

[61] National Center for Education Statistics. Public Libraries in the United States: Fiscal Year 2004. (NCES 2006-349). Washington, DC: NCES, 2006. http://www.nces.ed.gov/pubs2006/2006349.pdf
[62] ibid

MISSISSIPPI

Mississippi has 49 public library systems with 241 physical library locations and two bookmobiles to serve almost 2.9 million residents. Mississippi's public libraries are organized as county/parish libraries (34.7 percent), multi-jurisdictional libraries (34.7 percent), and as jointly operated city/county libraries (26.5 percent).[63]

More state tables are available online at www.ala.org/plinternetfunding.

EXPENDITURES (library system data)		Miss.	U.S.
Total operating expenditures per capita[64]		$13.24	$30.49
Technology-related expenditures (FY 2006)		$86,679	$166,181
CONNECTIVITY (library branch data)			
Average number of computers		5.9	10.7
Always sufficient computers available		25%	22%
Factors limiting library adding computers	Space	70%	76%
	Cost	82%	73%
Maximum Internet connection speed	769Kbps-1.5Mbps	24%	33%
	More than 1.5Mbps	22%	29%
Always adequate connection speed		30%	44%
Wireless availability		23%	54%
INTERNET SERVICES			
Internet services critical to role of library (library branch data)	Provide education resources & databases for K-12 students	86%	68%
	Provide services for job seekers	54%	44%
	Provide computer & Internet skills training	23%	30%
	Provide education resources & databases for adult/CE students	24%	28%
	Provide education resources & databases for students in higher ed	26%	21%
Internet services available (library system data)	Licensed databases	95%	86%
	Homework resources	53%	68%
	Digital/virtual reference	40%	58%
	E-books	12%	38%
	Audio content	20%	38%
Library offers IT training for patrons (branch)		71%	76%
Average hours open per week (branch)		36.0	45.2

---

[63] National Center for Education Statistics. Public Libraries in the United States: Fiscal Year 2004. (NCES 2006-349). Washington, DC: NCES, 2006. http://www.nces.ed.gov/pubs2006/2006349.pdf
[64] ibid

MISSOURI

Missouri has 151 public library systems with 360 physical library locations and 32 bookmobiles to serve about 5 million residents. Missouri's public libraries are primarily organized as library districts (88.1 percent). Most of the rest are organized as municipal government libraries (9.3 percent) and association libraries within a municipality (2 percent).[65]

More state tables are available online at www.ala.org/plinternetfunding.

EXPENDITURES (library system data)		Missouri	U.S.
Total operating expenditures per capita[66]		$31.36	$30.49
Technology-related expenditures (FY 2006)		$90,439	$166,181

CONNECTIVITY (library branch data)		Missouri	U.S.
Average number of computers		10.8	10.7
Always sufficient computers available		33%	22%
Factors limiting library adding computers	Space	65%	76%
	Cost	83%	73%
Maximum Internet connection speed	769Kbps-1.5Mbps	46%	33%
	More than 1.5Mbps	34%	29%
Always adequate connection speed		58%	44%
Wireless availability		42%	54%

INTERNET SERVICES		Missouri	U.S.
Internet services critical to role of library (library branch data)	Provide education resources & databases for K-12 students	65%	68%
	Provide services for job seekers	44%	44%
	Provide computer & Internet skills training	35%	30%
	Provide education resources & databases for adult/CE students	27%	28%
	Provide education resources & databases for students in higher ed	37%	21%
Internet services available (library system data)	Licensed databases	90%	86%
	Homework resources	63%	68%
	Digital/virtual reference	48%	58%
	E-books	38%	38%
	Audio content	20%	38%
Library offers IT training for patrons (branch)		84%	76%
Average hours open per week (branch)		47.7	45.2

---

[65] National Center for Education Statistics. Public Libraries in the United States: Fiscal Year 2004. (NCES 2006-349). Washington, DC: NCES, 2006. http://www.nces.ed.gov/pubs2006/2006349.pdf
[66] ibid

MONTANA

Montana has 79 public library systems with 108 physical library locations and three bookmobiles to serve almost 900,000 residents. Montana's public libraries are primarily organized as municipal government libraries (35.4 percent) and county/parish libraries (34.2 percent). The rest are organized as jointly operated city/county libraries (16.5 percent) and multi-jurisdictional libraries (13.9 percent).[67]

More state tables are available online at www.ala.org/plinternetfunding.

		Montana	U.S.
EXPENDITURES (library system data)			
Total operating expenditures per capita[68]		$18.01	$30.49
Technology-related expenditures (FY 2006)		$20,668	$166,181
CONNECTIVITY (library branch data)			
Average number of computers		5.7	10.7
Always sufficient computers available		28%	22%
Factors limiting library adding computers	Space	64%	76%
	Cost	93%	73%
Maximum Internet connection speed	769Kbps-1.5Mbps	28%	33%
	More than 1.5Mbps	10%	29%
Always adequate connection speed		44%	44%
Wireless availability		56%	54%
INTERNET SERVICES			
Internet services critical to role of library (library branch data)	Provide education resources & databases for K-12 students	30%	68%
	Provide services for job seekers	55%	44%
	Provide computer & Internet skills training	39%	30%
	Provide education resources & databases for adult/CE students	23%	28%
	Provide education resources & databases for students in higher ed	14%	21%
Internet services available (library system data)	Licensed databases	91%	86%
	Homework resources	57%	68%
	Digital/virtual reference	58%	58%
	E-books	40%	38%
	Audio content	30%	38%
Library offers IT training for patrons (branch)		74%	76%
Average hours open per week (branch)		34.4	45.2

---

[67] National Center for Education Statistics. Public Libraries in the United States: Fiscal Year 2004. (NCES 2006-349). Washington, DC: NCES, 2006. http://www.nces.ed.gov/pubs2006/2006349.pdf
[68] ibid

NEVADA

Nevada has 22 public library systems with 85 physical library locations and four bookmobiles to serve its more than 2.5 million residents. Nevada's public libraries are organized primarily as county library systems (50 percent), and library districts (40 percent). The rest are organized as municipal and multi-jurisdictional libraries (9.1 percent).[69]

More state tables are available online at www.ala.org/plinternetfunding.

EXPENDITURES (library system data)		Nevada	U.S.
Total operating expenditures per capita[70]		$27.13	$30.49
Technology-related expenditures (FY 2006)		$46,322	$166,181

CONNECTIVITY (library branch data)			
Average number of computers		6.8	10.7
Always sufficient computers available		23%	22%
Factors limiting library adding computers	Space	64%	76%
	Cost	61%	73%
Maximum Internet connection speed	769Kbps-1.5Mbps	36%	33%
	More than 1.5Mbps	18%	29%
Always adequate connection speed		44%	44%
Wireless availability		29%	54%

INTERNET SERVICES			
Internet services critical to role of library (library branch data)	Provide education resources & databases for K-12 students	69%	68%
	Provide services for job seekers	33%	44%
	Provide computer & Internet skills training	15%	30%
	Provide education resources & databases for adult/CE students	24%	28%
	Provide education resources & databases for students in higher ed	23%	21%
Internet services available (library system data)	Licensed databases	75%	86%
	Homework resources	58%	68%
	Digital/virtual reference	50%	58%
	E-books	19%	38%
	Audio content	31%	38%
Library offers IT training for patrons (branch)		71%	76%
Average hours open per week (branch)		35.4	45.2

---

[69] National Center for Education Statistics. Public Libraries in the United States: Fiscal Year 2004. (NCES 2006-349). Washington, DC: NCES, 2006. http://www.nces.ed.gov/pubs2006/2006349.pdf
[70] ibid

NEW JERSEY

New Jersey has 306 public library systems with 454 physical library locations and 15 bookmobiles to serve more than 8.3 million residents. New Jersey's public libraries are primarily organized as municipal government libraries (75.8 percent). The rest are organized as county libraries (4.6 percent), association libraries within a municipality (17.3 percent), and multi-jurisdictional libraries (2 percent).[71]

More state tables are available online at www.ala.org/plinternetfunding.

EXPENDITURES (library system data)		N.J.	U.S.
Total operating expenditures per capita[72]		$43.52	$30.49
Technology-related expenditures (FY 2006)		$115,723	$166,181

CONNECTIVITY (library branch data)		N.J.	U.S.
Average number of computers		12.0	10.7
Always sufficient computers available		31%	22%
Factors limiting library adding computers	Space	81%	76%
	Cost	59%	73%
Maximum Internet connection speed	769Kbps-1.5Mbps	35%	33%
	More than 1.5Mbps	31%	29%
Always adequate connection speed		39%	44%
Wireless availability		84%	54%

INTERNET SERVICES		N.J.	U.S.
Internet services critical to role of library (library branch data)	Provide education resources & databases for K-12 students	69%	68%
	Provide services for job seekers	48%	44%
	Provide computer & Internet skills training	42%	30%
	Provide education resources & databases for adult/CE students	19%	28%
	Provide education resources & databases for students in higher ed	18%	21%
Internet services available (library system data)	Licensed databases	92%	86%
	Homework resources	76%	68%
	Digital/virtual reference	60%	58%
	E-books	27%	38%
	Audio content	61%	38%
Library offers IT training for patrons (branch)		83%	76%
Average hours open per week (branch)		56.3	45.2

---

[71] National Center for Education Statistics. Public Libraries in the United States: Fiscal Year 2004. (NCES 2006-349). Washington, DC: NCES, 2006. http://www.nces.ed.gov/pubs2006/2006349.pdf
[72] ibid

NEW MEXICO

New Mexico has 92 public library systems with 120 physical library locations and four bookmobiles to serve its more than 1.6 million residents. New Mexico's public libraries are organized primarily as municipal government libraries (59.8 percent). Another 19.6 percent are organized as Native American Tribal Government libraries or in school districts.[73]

More state tables are available online at www.ala.org/plinternetfunding.

		N.M.	U.S.
EXPENDITURES (library system data)			
Total operating expenditures per capita[74]		$22.33	$30.49
Technology-related expenditures (FY 2006)		$66,787	$166,181
CONNECTIVITY (library branch data)			
Average number of computers		12.0	10.7
Always sufficient computers available		34%	22%
Factors limiting library adding computers	*Space*	86%	76%
	Cost	59%	73%
Maximum Internet connection speed	*769Kbps-1.5Mbps*	31%	33%
	More than 1.5Mbps	12%	29%
Always adequate connection speed		44%	44%
Wireless availability		34%	54%
INTERNET SERVICES			
Internet services critical to role of library (library branch data)	*Provide education resources & databases for K-12 students*	55%	68%
	Provide services for job seekers	30%	44%
	Provide computer & Internet skills training	27%	30%
	Provide education resources & databases for adult/CE students	50%	28%
	Provide education resources & databases for students in higher ed	44%	21%
Internet services available (library system data)	*Licensed databases*	90%	86%
	Homework resources	67%	68%
	Digital/virtual reference	58%	58%
	E-books	9%	38%
	Audio content	26%	38%
Library offers IT training for patrons (branch)		81%	76%
Average hours open per week (branch)		48.8	45.2

---

[73] National Center for Education Statistics. Public Libraries in the United States: Fiscal Year 2004. (NCES 2006-349). Washington, DC: NCES, 2006. http://www.nces.ed.gov/pubs2006/2006349.pdf
[74] ibid

NEW YORK

New York has 753 public library systems with 1,081 physical library locations and 9 bookmobiles to serve its more than 18.9 million residents. New York's public libraries are predominantly (92.2 percent) single library outlets (one building library) and organized primarily as non-profit associations (47.9 percent), municipal government libraries (27 percent) and library districts (23.8 percent).[75]

More state tables are available online at www.ala.org/plinternetfunding.

EXPENDITURES (library system data)		N.Y.	U.S.
Total operating expenditures per capita[76]		$47.74	$30.49
Technology-related expenditures (FY 2006)		$448,662	$166,181

CONNECTIVITY (library branch data)		N.Y.	U.S.
Average number of computers		11.0	10.7
Always sufficient computers available		19%	22%
Factors limiting library adding computers	Space	73%	76%
	Cost	83%	73%
Maximum Internet connection speed	769Kbps-1.5Mbps	32%	33%
	More than 1.5Mbps	32%	29%
Always adequate connection speed		52%	44%
Wireless availability		70%	54%

INTERNET SERVICES		N.Y.	U.S.
Internet services critical to role of library (library branch data)	Provide education resources & databases for K-12 students	72%	68%
	Provide services for job seekers	44%	44%
	Provide computer & Internet skills training	35%	30%
	Provide education resources & databases for adult/CE students	28%	28%
	Provide education resources & databases for students in higher ed	22%	21%
Internet services available (library system data)	Licensed databases	91%	86%
	Homework resources	74%	68%
	Digital/virtual reference	66%	58%
	E-books	33%	38%
	Audio content	42%	38%
Library offers IT training for patrons (branch)		85%	76%
Average hours open per week (branch)		43.5	45.2

---

[75] National Center for Education Statistics. Public Libraries in the United States: Fiscal Year 2004. (NCES 2006-349). Washington, DC: NCES, 2006. http://www.nces.ed.gov/pubs2006/2006349.pdf
[76] ibid

NORTH CAROLINA

North Carolina has 75 public library systems with 381 physical library locations and 39 bookmobiles to serve its more than 8.4 million residents. North Carolina's public libraries are organized primarily as county (53.3 percent) libraries. Another 20 percent are organized as multi-jurisdictional libraries, and 16 percent are municipal or city government libraries.[77]

More state tables are available online at www.ala.org/plinternetfunding.

EXPENDITURES (library system data)		N.C.	U.S.
Total operating expenditures per capita[78]		$18.66	$30.49
Technology-related expenditures (FY 2006)		$241,749	$166,181

CONNECTIVITY (library branch data)			
Average number of computers		15.0	10.7
Always sufficient computers available		14%	22%
Factors limiting library adding computers	Space	83%	76%
	Cost	70%	73%
Maximum Internet connection speed	769Kbps-1.5Mbps	15%	33%
	More than 1.5Mbps	45%	29%
Always adequate connection speed		32%	44%
Wireless availability		37%	54%

INTERNET SERVICES			
Internet services critical to role of library (library branch data)	Provide education resources & databases for K-12 students	78%	68%
	Provide services for job seekers	44%	44%
	Provide computer & Internet skills training	23%	30%
	Provide education resources & databases for adult/CE students	35%	28%
	Provide education resources & databases for students in higher ed	31%	21%
Internet services available (library system data)	Licensed databases	98%	86%
	Homework resources	75%	68%
	Digital/virtual reference	74%	58%
	E-books	95%	38%
	Audio content	93%	38%
Library offers IT training for patrons (branch)		77%	76%
Average hours open per week (branch)		47.5	45.2

---

[77] National Center for Education Statistics. Public Libraries in the United States: Fiscal Year 2004. (NCES 2006-349). Washington, DC: NCES, 2006. http://www.nces.ed.gov/pubs2006/2006349.pdf
[78] ibid

NORTH DAKOTA

North Dakota has 83 public library systems with 91 physical library locations and 14 bookmobiles to serve its 551,000 residents. North Dakota's public libraries are organized primarily as municipal government libraries (66.3 percent). Another 14.5 percent are organized as multi-jurisdictional libraries, as county libraries (10.8 percent), and as city/county libraries (8.4 percent).[79]

More state tables are available online at www.ala.org/plinternetfunding.

EXPENDITURES (library system data)		N.D.	U.S.
Total operating expenditures per capita[80]		$18.66	$30.49
Technology-related expenditures (FY 2006)		$37,063	$166,181

CONNECTIVITY (library branch data)			
Average number of computers		6.2	10.7
Always sufficient computers available		58%	22%
Factors limiting library adding computers	Space	72%	76%
	Cost	72%	73%
Maximum Internet connection speed	769Kbps-1.5Mbps	21%	33%
	More than 1.5Mbps	19%	29%
Always adequate connection speed		55%	44%
Wireless availability		19%	54%

INTERNET SERVICES			
Internet services critical to role of library (library branch data)	Provide education resources & databases for K-12 students	73%	68%
	Provide services for job seekers	49%	44%
	Provide computer & Internet skills training	26%	30%
	Provide education resources & databases for adult/CE students	34%	28%
	Provide education resources & databases for students in higher ed	15%	21%
Internet services available (library system data)	Licensed databases	79%	86%
	Homework resources	51%	68%
	Digital/virtual reference	37%	58%
	E-books	60%	38%
	Audio content	30%	38%
Library offers IT training for patrons (branch)		55%	76%
Average hours open per week (branch)		36.1	45.2

---

[79] National Center for Education Statistics. Public Libraries in the United States: Fiscal Year 2004. (NCES 2006-349). Washington, DC: NCES, 2006. http://www.nces.ed.gov/pubs2006/2006349.pdf
[80] ibid

OHIO

Ohio has 250 public library systems with 717 physical library locations and 75 bookmobiles to serve its more than 11.4 million residents. Ohio's public libraries are organized primarily by school district (60.4 percent) and county (22.8 percent).[81]

More state tables are available online at www.ala.org/plinternetfunding.

		Ohio	U.S.
EXPENDITURES (library system data)			
Total operating expenditures per capita[82]		$53.12	$30.49
Technology-related expenditures (FY 2006)		$286,976	$166,181
CONNECTIVITY (library branch data)			
Average number of computers		10.6	10.7
Always sufficient computers available		10%	22%
Factors limiting library adding computers	*Space*	86%	76%
	Cost	54%	73%
Maximum Internet connection speed	*769Kbps-1.5Mbps*	50%	33%
	More than 1.5Mbps	35%	29%
Always adequate connection speed		57%	44%
Wireless availability		67%	54%
INTERNET SERVICES			
Internet services critical to role of library (library branch data)	*Provide education resources & databases for K-12 students*	68%	68%
	Provide services for job seekers	42%	44%
	Provide computer & Internet skills training	34%	30%
	Provide education resources & databases for adult/CE students	20%	28%
	Provide education resources & databases for students in higher ed	15%	21%
Internet services available (library system data)	*Licensed databases*	95%	86%
	Homework resources	87%	68%
	Digital/virtual reference	81%	58%
	E-books	57%	38%
	Audio content	63%	38%
Library offers IT training for patrons (branch)		86%	76%
Average hours open per week (branch)		57.1	45.2

---

[81] National Center for Education Statistics. Public Libraries in the United States: Fiscal Year 2004. (NCES 2006-349). Washington, DC: NCES, 2006. http://www.nces.ed.gov/pubs2006/2006349.pdf
[82] ibid

OKLAHOMA

Oklahoma has 112 public library systems with 206 physical library locations and four bookmobiles to serve almost 2.9 million residents. Oklahoma's public libraries are primarily organized as municipal government libraries (88.4 percent). Most of the rest are organized as multi-jurisdictional libraries (6.3 percent) and as county libraries (4.5 percent).[83]

More state tables are available online at www.ala.org/plinternetfunding.

EXPENDITURES (library system data)		Oklahoma	U.S.
Total operating expenditures per capita[84]		$23.51	$30.49
Technology-related expenditures (FY 2006)		$21,848	$166,181

CONNECTIVITY (library branch data)			
Average number of computers		8.8	10.7
Always sufficient computers available		21%	22%
Factors limiting library adding computers	Space	79%	76%
	Cost	80%	73%
Maximum Internet connection speed	769Kbps-1.5Mbps	44%	33%
	More than 1.5Mbps	37%	29%
Always adequate connection speed		58%	44%
Wireless availability		52%	54%

INTERNET SERVICES			
Internet services critical to role of library (library branch data)	Provide education resources & databases for K-12 students	47%	68%
	Provide services for job seekers	56%	44%
	Provide computer & Internet skills training	27%	30%
	Provide education resources & databases for adult/CE students	24%	28%
	Provide education resources & databases for students in higher ed	23%	21%
Internet services available (library system data)	Licensed databases	90%	86%
	Homework resources	70%	68%
	Digital/virtual reference	48%	58%
	E-books	20%	38%
	Audio content	30%	38%
Library offers IT training for patrons (branch)		87%	76%
Average hours open per week (branch)		42.5	45.2

---

[83] National Center for Education Statistics. Public Libraries in the United States: Fiscal Year 2004. (NCES 2006-349). Washington, DC: NCES, 2006. http://www.nces.ed.gov/pubs2006/2006349.pdf
[84] ibid

OREGON

Oregon has 125 public library systems with 210 physical library locations and 11 bookmobiles to serve its more than 3.2 million residents. Oregon's public libraries are organized primarily by municipal government (68.8 percent). Another 13 percent are organized as library districts, 12 percent as county libraries, 3.2 percent as association libraries, and the remaining 2.4 percent by school districts.[85]

More state tables are available online at www.ala.org/plinternetfunding.

EXPENDITURES (library system data)		Oregon	U.S.
Total operating expenditures per capita[86]		$40.22	$30.49
Technology-related expenditures (FY 2006)		$44,357	$166,181

CONNECTIVITY (library branch data)			
Average number of computers		11.2	10.7
Always sufficient computers available		9%	22%
Factors limiting library adding computers	*Space*	66%	76%
	Cost	82%	73%
Maximum Internet connection speed	*769Kbps-1.5Mbps*	41%	33%
	More than 1.5Mbps	30%	29%
Always adequate connection speed		49%	44%
Wireless availability		38%	54%

INTERNET SERVICES			
Internet services critical to role of library (library branch data)	*Provide education resources & databases for K-12 students*	58%	68%
	Provide services for job seekers	67%	44%
	Provide computer & Internet skills training	21%	30%
	Provide education resources & databases for adult/CE students	25%	28%
	Provide education resources & databases for students in higher ed	4%	21%
Internet services available (library system data)	*Licensed databases*	98%	86%
	Homework resources	46%	68%
	Digital/virtual reference	77%	58%
	E-books	24%	38%
	Audio content	29%	38%
Library offers IT training for patrons (branch)		59%	76%
Average hours open per week (branch)		39.6	45.2

---

[85] National Center for Education Statistics. Public Libraries in the United States: Fiscal Year 2004. (NCES 2006-349). Washington, DC: NCES, 2006. http://www.nces.ed.gov/pubs2006/2006349.pdf
[86] ibid

PENNSYLVANIA

Pennsylvania has 455 public library systems with 632 physical library locations and 11 bookmobiles to serve its more than 11.9 million residents. Pennsylvania's public libraries are organized primarily as association libraries (85.5 percent). The rest (14.5 percent) are organized in other ways, including combined public/school libraries.[87]

More state tables are available online at www.ala.org/plinternetfunding.

EXPENDITURES (library system data)		Penn.	U.S.
Total operating expenditures per capita[88]		$23.51	$30.49
Technology-related expenditures (FY 2006)		$30,345	$166,181

CONNECTIVITY (library branch data)		Penn.	U.S.
Average number of computers		10.0	10.7
Always sufficient computers available		15%	22%
Factors limiting library adding computers	Space	79%	76%
	Cost	80%	73%
Maximum Internet connection speed	769Kbps-1.5Mbps	24%	33%
	More than 1.5Mbps	38%	29%
Always adequate connection speed		43%	44%
Wireless availability		58%	54%

INTERNET SERVICES		Penn.	U.S.
Internet services critical to role of library (library branch data)	Provide education resources & databases for K-12 students	74%	68%
	Provide services for job seekers	60%	44%
	Provide computer & Internet skills training	27%	30%
	Provide education resources & databases for adult/CE students	26%	28%
	Provide education resources & databases for students in higher ed	12%	21%
Internet services available (library system data)	Licensed databases	98%	86%
	Homework resources	65%	68%
	Digital/virtual reference	78%	58%
	E-books	62%	38%
	Audio content	46%	38%
Library offers IT training for patrons (branch)		75%	76%
Average hours open per week (branch)		51.4	45.2

---

[87] National Center for Education Statistics. Public Libraries in the United States: Fiscal Year 2004. (NCES 2006-349). Washington, DC: NCES, 2006. http://www.nces.ed.gov/pubs2006/2006349.pdf
[88] ibid

RHODE ISLAND

Rhode Island has 48 public library systems with 72 physical library locations and two bookmobiles to serve its more than 1.07 million residents. Rhode Island's public libraries are organized in two ways – municipal government (45.8 percent) and nonprofit associations (54.2 percent).[89]

More state tables are available online at www.ala.org/plinternetfunding.

		R.I.	U.S.
EXPENDITURES (library system data)			
Total operating expenditures per capita[90]		$38.51	$30.49
Technology-related expenditures (FY 2006)		$160,787	$166,181
CONNECTIVITY (library branch data)			
Average number of computers		7.4	10.7
Always sufficient computers available		18%	22%
Factors limiting library adding computers	*Space*	76%	76%
	Cost	30%	73%
Maximum Internet connection speed	*769Kbps-1.5Mbps*	29%	33%
	More than 1.5Mbps	34%	29%
Always adequate connection speed		51%	44%
Wireless availability		65%	54%
INTERNET SERVICES			
Internet services critical to role of library (library branch data)	*Provide education resources & databases for K-12 students*	87%	68%
	Provide services for job seekers	41%	44%
	Provide computer & Internet skills training	37%	30%
	Provide education resources & databases for adult/CE students	15%	28%
	Provide education resources & databases for students in higher ed	9%	21%
Internet services available (library system data)	*Licensed databases*	100%	86%
	Homework resources	70%	68%
	Digital/virtual reference	55%	58%
	E-books	27%	38%
	Audio content	9%	38%
Library offers IT training for patrons (branch)		87%	76%
Average hours open per week (branch)		47.2	45.2

---

[89] National Center for Education Statistics. Public Libraries in the United States: Fiscal Year 2004. (NCES 2006-349). Washington, DC: NCES, 2006. http://www.nces.ed.gov/pubs2006/2006349.pdf
[90] ibid

SOUTH CAROLINA

South Carolina has 42 public library systems with 183 physical library locations and 35 bookmobiles to serve its more than 4.1 million residents. South Carolina's public libraries are predominantly library systems with central and branch libraries, and are organized primarily as county libraries (92.9 percent).[91]

More state tables are available online at www.ala.org/plinternetfunding.

		S.C.	U.S.
EXPENDITURES (library system data)			
Total operating expenditures per capita[92]		$21.06	$30.49
Technology-related expenditures (FY 2006)		$70,555	$166,181
CONNECTIVITY (library branch data)			
Average number of computers		10.8	10.7
Always sufficient computers available		14%	22%
Factors limiting library adding computers	Space	90%	76%
	Cost	54%	73%
Maximum Internet connection speed	769Kbps-1.5Mbps	71%	33%
	More than 1.5Mbps	10%	29%
Always adequate connection speed		38%	44%
Wireless availability		39%	54%
INTERNET SERVICES			
Internet services critical to role of library (library branch data)	Provide education resources & databases for K-12 students	68%	68%
	Provide services for job seekers	32%	44%
	Provide computer & Internet skills training	7%	30%
	Provide education resources & databases for adult/CE students	52%	28%
	Provide education resources & databases for students in higher ed	25%	21%
Internet services available (library system data)	Licensed databases	96%	86%
	Homework resources	74%	68%
	Digital/virtual reference	53%	58%
	E-books	26%	38%
	Audio content	29%	38%
Library offers IT training for patrons (branch)		51%	76%
Average hours open per week (branch)		45.5	45.2

---

[91] National Center for Education Statistics. Public Libraries in the United States: Fiscal Year 2004. (NCES 2006-349). Washington, DC: NCES, 2006. http://www.nces.ed.gov/pubs2006/2006349.pdf
[92] ibid

SOUTH DAKOTA

South Dakota has 125 public library systems with 144 physical library locations and 8 bookmobiles to serve its more than 671,000 residents. South Dakota's public libraries are organized primarily as municipal government (63.2 percent) libraries. Most of the rest are organized as multi-jurisdictional libraries (16 percent), as county libraries (8 percent), and as city/county libraries (7.2 percent).[93]

More state tables are available online at www.ala.org/plinternetfunding.

		S.D.	U.S.
EXPENDITURES (library system data)			
Total operating expenditures per capita[94]		$27.89	$30.49
Technology-related expenditures (FY 2006)		$39,015	$166,181
CONNECTIVITY (library branch data)			
Average number of computers		7.2	10.7
Always sufficient computers available		38%	22%
Factors limiting library adding computers	*Space*	71%	76%
	Cost	86%	73%
Maximum Internet connection speed	*769Kbps-1.5Mbps*	14%	33%
	More than 1.5Mbps	27%	29%
Always adequate connection speed		40%	44%
Wireless availability		40%	54%
INTERNET SERVICES			
Internet services critical to role of library (library branch data)	*Provide education resources & databases for K-12 students*	70%	68%
	Provide services for job seekers	30%	44%
	Provide computer & Internet skills training	16%	30%
	Provide education resources & databases for adult/CE students	41%	28%
	Provide education resources & databases for students in higher ed	36%	21%
Internet services available (library system data)	*Licensed databases*	85%	86%
	Homework resources	74%	68%
	Digital/virtual reference	71%	58%
	E-books	54%	38%
	Audio content	32%	38%
Library offers IT training for patrons (branch)		55%	76%
Average hours open per week (branch)		36.5	45.2

---

[93] National Center for Education Statistics. Public Libraries in the United States: Fiscal Year 2004. (NCES 2006-349). Washington, DC: NCES, 2006. http://www.nces.ed.gov/pubs2006/2006349.pdf
[94] ibid

TENNESSEE

Tennessee has 184 public library systems with 286 physical library locations and two bookmobiles to serve its more than 5.7 million residents. Tennessee's public libraries are organized primarily as municipal government (55.4 percent) and county (40.8 percent).[95]

More state tables are available online at www.ala.org/plinternetfunding.

EXPENSES		Tennessee	U.S.
EXPENDITURES (library system data)			
Total operating expenditures per capita[96]		$16.02	$30.49
Technology-related expenditures (FY 2006)		$70,672	$166,181
CONNECTIVITY (library branch data)			
Average number of computers		8.5	10.7
Always sufficient computers available		24%	22%
Factors limiting library adding computers	Space	81%	76%
	Cost	75%	73%
Maximum Internet connection speed	769Kbps-1.5Mbps	17%	33%
	More than 1.5Mbps	27%	29%
Always adequate connection speed		58%	44%
Wireless availability		38%	54%
INTERNET SERVICES			
Internet services critical to role of library (library branch data)	Provide education resources & databases for K-12 students	72%	68%
	Provide services for job seekers	56%	44%
	Provide computer & Internet skills training	21%	30%
	Provide education resources & databases for adult/CE students	32%	28%
	Provide education resources & databases for students in higher ed	28%	21%
Internet services available (library system data)	Licensed databases	81%	86%
	Homework resources	53%	68%
	Digital/virtual reference	54%	58%
	E-books	72%	38%
	Audio content	57%	38%
Library offers IT training for patrons (branch)		75%	76%
Average hours open per week (branch)		42.9	45.2

---

[95] National Center for Education Statistics. Public Libraries in the United States: Fiscal Year 2004. (NCES 2006-349). Washington, DC: NCES, 2006. http://www.nces.ed.gov/pubs2006/2006349.pdf
[96] ibid

TEXAS

Texas has 555 public library systems with 847 physical library locations and 12 bookmobiles to serve its more than 20.2 million residents. Texas's public libraries are organized primarily by municipal government (55.5 percent), county (20.9 percent), and as association libraries (17.3 percent).[97]

More state tables are available online at www.ala.org/plinternetfunding.

EXPENDITURES (library system data)		Texas	U.S.
Total operating expenditures per capita[98]		$16.93	$30.49
Technology-related expenditures (FY 2006)		$108,708	$166,181

CONNECTIVITY (library branch data)			
Average number of computers		13.9	10.7
Always sufficient computers available		26%	22%
Factors limiting library adding computers	*Space*	77%	76%
	Cost	82%	73%
Maximum Internet connection speed	*769Kbps-1.5Mbps*	29%	33%
	More than 1.5Mbps	32%	29%
Always adequate connection speed		48%	44%
Wireless availability		63%	54%

INTERNET SERVICES			
Internet services critical to role of library (library branch data)	*Provide education resources & databases for K-12 students*	66%	68%
	Provide services for job seekers	44%	44%
	Provide computer & Internet skills training	33%	30%
	Provide education resources & databases for adult/CE students	28%	28%
	Provide education resources & databases for students in higher ed	23%	21%
Internet services available (library system data)	*Licensed databases*	86%	86%
	Homework resources	70%	68%
	Digital/virtual reference	44%	58%
	E-books	49%	38%
	Audio content	25%	38%
Library offers IT training for patrons (branch)		74%	76%
Average hours open per week (branch)		46.2	45.2

---

[97] National Center for Education Statistics. Public Libraries in the United States: Fiscal Year 2004. (NCES 2006-349). Washington, DC: NCES, 2006. http://www.nces.ed.gov/pubs2006/2006349.pdf
[98] ibid

UTAH

Utah has 72 public library systems with 113 physical library locations and 23 bookmobiles serving about 2.4 million residents. Utah's public libraries are organized primarily as municipal government libraries (61 percent) and county library systems (39 percent).[99]

More state tables are available online at www.ala.org/plinternetfunding.

EXPENDITURES (library system data)		Utah	U.S.
Total operating expenditures per capita[100]		$27.90	$30.49
Technology-related expenditures (FY 2006)		$87,210	$166,181
CONNECTIVITY (library branch data)			
Average number of computers		10.2	10.7
Always sufficient computers available		24%	22%
Factors limiting library adding computers	Space	83%	76%
	Cost	74%	73%
Maximum Internet connection speed	769Kbps-1.5Mbps	27%	33%
	More than 1.5Mbps	31%	29%
Always adequate connection speed		42%	44%
Wireless availability		46%	54%
INTERNET SERVICES			
Internet services critical to role of library (library branch data)	Provide education resources & databases for K-12 students	60%	68%
	Provide services for job seekers	35%	44%
	Provide computer & Internet skills training	21%	30%
	Provide education resources & databases for adult/CE students	20%	28%
	Provide education resources & databases for students in higher ed	51%	21%
Internet services available (library system data)	Licensed databases	100%	86%
	Homework resources	77%	68%
	Digital/virtual reference	37%	58%
	E-books	72%	38%
	Audio content	66%	38%
Library offers IT training for patrons (branch)		73%	76%
Average hours open per week (branch)		47.2	45.2

---

[99] National Center for Education Statistics. Public Libraries in the United States: Fiscal Year 2004. (NCES 2006-349). Washington, DC: NCES, 2006. http://www.nces.ed.gov/pubs2006/2006349.pdf
[100] ibid

VERMONT

Vermont has 189 public library systems with 191 physical library locations and 10 bookmobiles to serve about 577,000 residents. Vermont's public libraries are primarily organized as municipal government libraries (53.4 percent) and association libraries within a municipality (40.2 percent).[101]

More state tables are available online at www.ala.org/plinternetfunding.

		Vermont	U.S.
EXPENDITURES (library system data)			
Total operating expenditures per capita[102]		$27.50	$30.49
Technology-related expenditures (FY 2006)		$5,181	$166,181
CONNECTIVITY (library branch data)			
Average number of computers		4.7	10.7
Always sufficient computers available		27%	22%
Factors limiting library adding computers	Space	74%	76%
	Cost	80%	73%
Maximum Internet connection speed	769Kbps-1.5Mbps	12%	33%
	More than 1.5Mbps	22%	29%
Always adequate connection speed		56%	44%
Wireless availability		67%	54%
INTERNET SERVICES			
Internet services critical to role of library (library branch data)	Provide education resources & databases for K-12 students	44%	68%
	Provide services for job seekers	33%	44%
	Provide computer & Internet skills training	28%	30%
	Provide education resources & databases for adult/CE students	32%	28%
	Provide education resources & databases for students in higher ed	11%	21%
Internet services available (library system data)	Licensed databases	82%	86%
	Homework resources	62%	68%
	Digital/virtual reference	43%	58%
	E-books	1%	38%
	Audio content	13%	38%
Library offers IT training for patrons (branch)		67%	76%
Average hours open per week (branch)		33.0	45.2

---

[101] National Center for Education Statistics. Public Libraries in the United States: Fiscal Year 2004. (NCES 2006-349). Washington, DC: NCES, 2006. http://www.nces.ed.gov/pubs2006/2006349.pdf
[102] ibid

VIRGINIA

Virginia has 90 public library systems with 341 physical library locations and 33 bookmobiles to serve 7.3 million residents. Virginia's public libraries are primarily organized as county/parish libraries (40 percent), municipal government libraries (25.6 percent) and as multi-jurisdictional libraries (25.6 percent).[103]

More state tables are available online at www.ala.org/plinternetfunding.

EXPENDITURES (library system data)		Virginia	U.S.
Total operating expenditures per capita[104]		$28.84	$30.49
Technology-related expenditures (FY 2006)		$120,515	$166,181

CONNECTIVITY (library branch data)		Virginia	U.S.
Average number of computers		20.7	10.7
Always sufficient computers available		19%	22%
Factors limiting library adding computers	Space	90%	76%
	Cost	73%	73%
Maximum Internet connection speed	769Kbps-1.5Mbps	46%	33%
	More than 1.5Mbps	41%	29%
Always adequate connection speed		43%	44%
Wireless availability		58%	54%

INTERNET SERVICES			
Internet services critical to role of library (library branch data)	Provide education resources & databases for K-12 students	83%	68%
	Provide services for job seekers	44%	44%
	Provide computer & Internet skills training	54%	30%
	Provide education resources & databases for adult/CE students	11%	28%
	Provide education resources & databases for students in higher ed	12%	21%
Internet services available (library system data)	Licensed databases	100%	86%
	Homework resources	81%	68%
	Digital/virtual reference	52%	58%
	E-books	56%	38%
	Audio content	21%	38%
Library offers IT training for patrons (branch)		84%	76%
Average hours open per week (branch)		52.7	45.2

---

[103] National Center for Education Statistics. Public Libraries in the United States: Fiscal Year 2004. (NCES 2006-349). Washington, DC: NCES, 2006. http://www.nces.ed.gov/pubs2006/2006349.pdf
[104] ibid

WASHINGTON

Washington has 66 public library systems with 330 physical library locations and 19 bookmobiles to serve about 6 million residents. Washington's public libraries are organized as municipal government libraries (65.2 percent) and library districts (34.8 percent).[105]

More state tables are available online at www.ala.org/plinternetfunding.

EXPENDITURES (library system data)		Wash.	U.S.
Total operating expenditures per capita[106]		$42.58	$30.49
Technology-related expenditures (FY 2006)		$195,958	$166,181
CONNECTIVITY (library branch data)			
Average number of computers		--*	10.7
Always sufficient computers available		--	22%
Factors limiting library adding computers	Space	--	76%
	Cost	--	73%
Maximum Internet connection speed	769Kbps-1.5Mbps	--	33%
	More than 1.5Mbps	--	29%
Always adequate connection speed		--	44%
Wireless availability		--	54%
INTERNET SERVICES			
Internet services critical to role of library (library branch data)	Provide education resources & databases for K-12 students	--	68%
	Provide services for job seekers	--	44%
	Provide computer & Internet skills training	--	30%
	Provide education resources & databases for adult/CE students	--	28%
	Provide education resources & databases for students in higher ed	--	21%
Internet services available (library system data)	Licensed databases	86%	86%
	Homework resources	52%	68%
	Digital/virtual reference	31%	58%
	E-books	6%	38%
	Audio content	No data	38%
Library offers IT training for patrons (branch)		--	76%
Average hours open per week (branch)		--	45.2

---

[105] National Center for Education Statistics. Public Libraries in the United States: Fiscal Year 2004. (NCES 2006-349). Washington, DC: NCES, 2006. http://www.nces.ed.gov/pubs2006/2006349.pdf
[106] Ibid
* There was not enough outlet-level data reported to analyze at the state level.

WEST VIRGINIA

West Virginia has 97 public library systems with 174 physical library locations and seven bookmobiles to serve just over 1.8 million residents. West Virginia's public libraries are primarily organized as municipal government libraries (49.5 percent) and county/parish libraries (33 percent).[107]

More state tables are available online at www.ala.org/plinternetfunding.

EXPENDITURES (library system data)		W.V.	U.S.
Total operating expenditures per capita[108]		$14.57	$30.49
Technology-related expenditures (FY 2006)		$35,555	$166,181
CONNECTIVITY (library branch data)			
Average number of computers		7.2	10.7
Always sufficient computers available		27%	22%
Factors limiting library adding computers	Space	80%	76%
	Cost	80%	73%
Maximum Internet connection speed	769Kbps-1.5Mbps	35%	33%
	More than 1.5Mbps	25%	29%
Always adequate connection speed		46%	44%
Wireless availability		28%	54%
INTERNET SERVICES			
Internet services critical to role of library (library branch data)	Provide education resources & databases for K-12 students	86%	68%
	Provide services for job seekers	28%	44%
	Provide computer & Internet skills training	34%	30%
	Provide education resources & databases for adult/CE students	26%	28%
	Provide education resources & databases for students in higher ed	48%	21%
Internet services available (library system data)	Licensed databases	86%	86%
	Homework resources	52%	68%
	Digital/virtual reference	31%	58%
	E-books	6%	38%
	Audio content	No data	38%
Library offers IT training for patrons (branch)		73%	76%
Average hours open per week (branch)		42.3	45.2

---

[107] National Center for Education Statistics. Public Libraries in the United States: Fiscal Year 2004. (NCES 2006-349). Washington, DC: NCES, 2006. http://www.nces.ed.gov/pubs2006/2006349.pdf
[108] ibid

WISCONSIN

Wisconsin has 380 public library systems with 456 physical library locations and 10 bookmobiles to serve about 5.5 million residents. Wisconsin's public libraries are primarily organized as municipal government libraries (89.2 percent).[109]

More state tables are available online at www.ala.org/plinternetfunding.

		Wisconsin	U.S.
EXPENDITURES (library system data)			
Total operating expenditures per capita[110]		$32.81	$30.49
Technology-related expenditures (FY 2006)		$42,799	$166,181
CONNECTIVITY (library branch data)			
Average number of computers		7.7	10.7
Always sufficient computers available		17%	22%
Factors limiting library adding computers	Space	74%	76%
	Cost	75%	73%
Maximum Internet connection speed	769Kbps-1.5Mbps	35%	33%
	More than 1.5Mbps	27%	29%
Always adequate connection speed		45%	44%
Wireless availability		44%	54%
INTERNET SERVICES			
Internet services critical to role of library (library branch data)	Provide education resources & databases for K-12 students	54%	68%
	Provide services for job seekers	55%	44%
	Provide computer & Internet skills training	31%	30%
	Provide education resources & databases for adult/CE students	28%	28%
	Provide education resources & databases for students in higher ed	12%	21%
Internet services available (library system data)	Licensed databases	80%	86%
	Homework resources	58%	68%
	Digital/virtual reference	70%	58%
	E-books	83%	38%
	Audio content	67%	38%
Library offers IT training for patrons (branch)		77%	76%
Average hours open per week (branch)		43.2	45.2

---

[109] National Center for Education Statistics. Public Libraries in the United States: Fiscal Year 2004. (NCES 2006-349). Washington, DC: NCES, 2006. http://www.nces.ed.gov/pubs2006/2006349.pdf
[110] ibid

WYOMING

Wyoming has 23 public library systems with 74 physical library locations and two bookmobiles to serve just over 500,000 residents. All of Wyoming's public libraries are organized as county libraries.[111]

More state tables are available online at www.ala.org/plinternetfunding.

EXPENDITURES (library system data)		Wyoming	U.S.
Total operating expenditures per capita[112]		$38.32	$30.49
Technology-related expenditures (FY 2006)		$110,547	$166,181

CONNECTIVITY (library branch data)			
Average number of computers		7.1	10.7
Always sufficient computers available		27%	22%
Factors limiting library adding computers	Space	84%	76%
	Cost	63%	73%
Maximum Internet connection speed	769Kbps-1.5Mbps	38%	33%
	More than 1.5Mbps	10%	29%
Always adequate connection speed		41%	44%
Wireless availability		58%	54%

INTERNET SERVICES			
Internet services critical to role of library (library branch data)	Provide education resources & databases for K-12 students	77%	68%
	Provide services for job seekers	20%	44%
	Provide computer & Internet skills training	27%	30%
	Provide education resources & databases for adult/CE students	20%	28%
	Provide education resources & databases for students in higher ed	17%	21%
Internet services available (library system data)	Licensed databases	100%	86%
	Homework resources	57%	68%
	Digital/virtual reference	44%	58%
	E-books	70%	38%
	Audio content	83%	38%
Library offers IT training for patrons (branch)		61%	76%
Average hours open per week (branch)		37.8	45.2

---

[111] National Center for Education Statistics. Public Libraries in the United States: Fiscal Year 2004. (NCES 2006-349). Washington, DC: NCES, 2006. http://www.nces.ed.gov/pubs2006/2006349.pdf

[112] ibid

Section II:
Findings from the State Library Agency Chief Officers' Qualitative Questionnaire

EXECUTIVE SUMMARY

Every day, public libraries provide technology access and public computing services to millions of residents and visitors in their communities. For residents of rural areas, public libraries are often the only point of public access to computers and the Internet. Public libraries frequently are able to offer higher access speeds than those available to most residential users, making libraries an attractive site of public access for e-government services, downloadable media, distance education, and e-commerce activities (e.g., online banking, airline transactions).

Providing this public technology access presents both challenges and opportunities for public libraries, urban and rural. The 43 states that participated in this questionnaire represent 86 percent of all states in the U.S. When asked to comment on the status of technology access and funding for the public libraries in their state, especially with regard to broadband connections, areas of network vulnerability, challenges, unexpected successes, and ways in which external agents might be able to improve current conditions, the Chief Officers of State Library Agencies (COSLA) responded as follows:

Broadband Connectivity
Twenty-eight states (65 percent) reported that over 90 percent of their public libraries currently have broadband connectivity (defined as a connection that is direct, "always on," and not a dial-up connection). All but one reported that more than 50 percent of their public libraries currently have broadband connectivity.

How Broadband Connectivity is Achieved
Public libraries are using a variety of means to obtain the connections to the broadband capacity they need, and often use <u>more than one</u> approach. The most common ways that public libraries achieve broadband connectivity are through:
- Local telecommunications companies (79 percent);
- Local city/county government (65 percent); and
- Local school districts (63 percent).

Major Broadband Barriers
Twenty-four states (56 percent) identified high cost as the principal major barrier to broadband connectivity. Twenty-one (49 percent) reported that the capacity for connectivity did not exist in all parts of their state. Eighteen respondents (42 percent) reported few or no barriers to their state's public library broadband connectivity. Sixteen (37 percent) reported the lack of local library staff expertise as a major barrier to implementing or sustaining broadband connectivity. Other major barriers reported are slow and unreliable connections.

Vulnerably Networked Public Libraries

The concept of "vulnerably networked" was derived from work completed by Charles R. McClure and Joe Ryan as part of the *2006 Public Libraries and the Internet* study.[113] The researchers determined a range of characteristics that identified successfully networked libraries, including infrastructure requirements (e.g., telecommunications, computers, and trained staff). From that list, this study attempted to understand which public libraries did not meet these characteristics, or were at risk of not meeting them. For the purposes of this study "at risk" was defined as a public library being unable to offer, in whole or in part, access to electronic services via an infrastructure capable of supporting internal or external networked services. Measurable criteria with which to more accurately identify vulnerably networked public library in each state were collected to create a new *Checklist for the Identification of Vulnerably Networked Public Libraries* (Table 71).

Thirty-four respondents (79 percent) provided an actual estimate of the number of vulnerably networked libraries. Twenty-five reported that approximately 27 percent of their public libraries were vulnerable, while seven indicated that they did not have any vulnerable libraries.

Challenges Faced by Vulnerably Networked Public Libraries

When asked to identify the connectivity, IT, economic, political, staff and other challenges that may be faced during the next three years by vulnerably networked public libraries in their state, respondents most often mentioned:

Connectivity/Telecommunications Challenges: No connection; no availability; lack of local public library system/consortia affiliation or partnership; increased broadband demand; cost/affordability; expanding connection options; lack of state or local telecommunications expertise; lack of dependability and reliability; and wireless.

Information Technology (IT) Challenges: Planning for IT upgrade, replacement and maintenance; building renovation (wiring & space); IT filtering, security & management; the need for library-dedicated, locally available IT support; the importance of public training; and the need for library supported IT solutions.

Economic Challenges: Vulnerable local economies; the need to consolidate previously unplanned geographic distribution of libraries; increased demand coupled with unpredictable, flat or declining revenue streams; nonexistent or flawed public library funding strategies; flawed public library funding structures; lack of external affiliation and partnerships; overdependence on external financing of core resources and services; and the impact of E-rate.

Political Challenges: Internet safety concerns; the low priority placed on libraries and telecommunications; need for partnerships; libraries as a state or local funding responsibility; the need for a statewide telecommunications policy and state universal fund approach; E-rate: and the need for advocacy.

---

[113] Bertot, John, Charles R. McClure, Paul T. Jaeger and Joe Ryan. "Public Libraries and the Internet 2006: Study Results and Findings," September 2006. http://www.ii.fsu.edu/projectFiles/plinternet/2006/2006_plinternet.pdf

Staff Challenges: Staff IT training; insufficient staff, not just a lack of IT staff; unprepared staff, not just staff unprepared for IT; lack of leadership; difficulty hiring and retaining IT staff; the use of volunteers; and the lack of education among library boards regarding the importance of technology access.

Other Challenges: Inability to plan and budget for future technology needs; and uncertainty regarding how to measure and show the value of current IT-based services.

"Unexpectedly" Successfully Networked Public Libraries

Respondents were asked to identify "unexpectedly" successfully networked public libraries in their states. For the purposes of this study, an unexpectedly successfully networked public library or library system is one with a limited local economic or population base that has maintained broadband connectivity, IT, and has developed networked services even though its population served, or economic, or political or community circumstances suggested it would be unlikely to do so. Chief Officers reported nearly 100 public libraries in rural and/or economically depressed areas with "unexpectedly" successful technology access, most notable for their broadband connections; IT use and maintenance; and number of services based on IT (wireless being the "hot" new service). Important factors contributing to this "unexpected" success included: good fundraising skills; strong partnerships with local governments, consortia, and schools; and "visionary" leadership.

External Partner Assistance Needed

When asked to identify the types of assistance that external partners (including the state library, ALA, external funders and others) might provide to their state's vulnerably networked public libraries to demonstrably improve (within a 3-5 year timeframe) and sustain their networked resources and services, the Chief Officers responded with their three priority recommendations for assistance that would have a demonstrable impact:

- Obtain enough broadband to meet public library demand at an affordable price;
- Provide adequate IT to make efficient/effective use of broadband connection and meet users' needs for other IT-based services; and
- Provide library networked services of interest to their communities.

Future action to assist with these priorities is critical. The Chief Officers cited the impending substantially increased broadband demand, due to factors that include:

1. Transition from text- to graphic-based integrated library systems (ILS);
2. Increased demand due to "large" throughputs (e.g., downloads of e-books, music, video, games, etc.); and
3. Rising overall public usage.

METHODOLOGY

State Library Agencies have played a critical role in sustaining public libraries, particularly by providing development funds for the deployment of new library information technologies and services. In recognition of this leadership role, the ALA Office for Research and Statistics inaugurated an annual questionnaire of these agencies in 2006-07. Specific areas surveyed were:

- The current status of public libraries' broadband connectivity;

- Defining the 2007 vulnerably networked public libraries and challenges they will face during the next three years: A vulnerably networked public library may not: have a broadband connection; be able to raise funds to maintain/replace IT; support access to high-graphic databases or downloadable audio; have a library controlled Web site; or may offer only limited IT services (e.g., public Internet workstations; online catalog);

- Defining and learning from the 2007 "unexpectedly" successfully networked public libraries: This is a public library or system that has maintained broadband connectivity, IT, and has developed networked services, despite various factors that suggested it would be unlikely to do so; and

- Identifying ways potential external partner assistance can effectively meet the challenges faced by vulnerably networked public libraries to demonstrably improve technology access and funding.

The questionnaire was administered via an MS Word attachment to an e-mail announcement to the Chief Officers of State Library Agencies (COSLA) listserv in December 2006.[114] Several reminders were posted to the same listserv. Eighty-six percent of states (43) responded as of May 15, 2007. See Appendix B for the questionnaire.

---

[114] The study team supplemented the COSLA listserv announcement with in-person and e-mail follow-up.

FINDINGS

Broadband Connectivity

Figure 67 summarizes the percentage of public libraries that have broadband connectivity.[115]

Figure 67: What percentage of public libraries in your state have broadband connectivity?		
Percentage	States Responding	% total responding
Under 25%	NR	0% N=0
Between 26% and 50%	KS[116]	2% N=1
Between 51% and 75%	AK, ID, TX,	7% N=3
Between 76% and 90%	AR, AZ, IL, KY, MA, MI, ND, NE, NM, VA	23% N=10
Over 90%	AL, CA, CT, DE, FL, GA, IA, IN, LA, MD, MN, MS, MO, NJ, NC, NV, OH, OK, OR, PA, RI, SC, TN, UT, WA, WI, WV, WY	65% N=28
No response to question	NY	2% N=1

Sixty-five percent (28) responded that over 90 percent of their public libraries currently have broadband connections. All but one responded that more than 50 percent of their public libraries currently have broadband connections.

Achieving Broadband Connectivity

Figure 68 summarizes the methods by which public libraries achieve broadband connectivity. Respondents were encouraged to check <u>as many</u> of the provided options as applied.

Public libraries use a variety of means to obtain broadband connections, and may use <u>more than one</u> means to obtain the needed broadband capacity. The most common methods used by public libraries to obtain broadband connectivity are through:
- Local telecommunications companies (77 percent);
- Local city/county government (65 percent); and
- Local school districts (63 percent).

"Other" means identified included local cable and satellite and "entrepreneurial" public and regional library systems becoming Internet providers for themselves.

Figure 68: How do public libraries in your state achieve broadband connectivity?		
How achieved:	States Responding	% total responses
Directly through a local telecommunications company	AK, AL, AR, AZ, CA, FL, ID, IL, IA, IN, KS, KY, LA, MA, MI, MN, MS, MO, ND, NE, NM, NC, NV, OK, OR, PA, TN, TX, UT, VA, WA, WI, WV, WY	79% (34/43) N=34
Through the local school district	AK, AL, AR, AZ, FL. ID, IL, IA, IN, KS, MI, MN, MO, NM, NB, NC, NV, OK, OR, PA, TX, UT, VA, WA, WI, WV, WY	63% N=27
Through the local city/county government	AK, AL, AZ, CA, DE, FL, ID, IL, IA, IN, KS, MA, MI, MN, MO, NB, NM, NC, NV, OK, OR, PA, TX, UT, VA, WA, WI, WY	65% N=28

---

[115] The questionnaire defined broadband connectivity as a connection that is direct, "always on," not a dial-up connection.
[116] Kansas defined broadband as T-1.

Through a regional telecom. network	AL, AZ, CA, FL, ID, IL, IA, KS, MI, OR, PA, TN, VA, WA, WI	35% N=15
Through a regional **library** telecom. network	AL, AZ, CA, FL, IL, MA, MI, MN, NV, OH, OR, PA, WI	30% N=13
Through a state telecom. network (education, research, etc.)	AL, AR, CT, FL, IL, IN, KS, KY, LA, MN, MO, ND, NE, NC, OK, OR, RI, SC, TX, UT, VA, WA, WI, WV, WY	58% N=25
Though a state telecom. **library** network	DE, GA, MD, MS, NJ, RI, WY	16% N=7
Other (Describe):	LA, MA, SC	7% N=3
No response to question	NY	2% N=2

Major Barriers to Broadband Connectivity

Figure 69 summarizes the major barriers to the achievement of broadband connectivity by public libraries. Respondents were encouraged to check <u>as many</u> of the provided options as applied.

Figure 69: What are major barriers to state's public library broadband connectivity?

Barrier	States Responding	% total responses
Few or no barriers	AL, AR, CT, FL, GA, IA, MD, MS, MO, NJ, OH, OK, OR, SC, TN, WI, WV, WY	42% N=18
Capacity for connectivity does not exist in all parts of the state	AK, AZ, CA, DE, ID, IL, KS, KY, LA, MA, MI, MN, NE, NM, NV, NY, OR, PA, TX, VA, WA	49% N=21
Too many telecommunications companies for any statewide coordination	ID, IL, NC, NV, NY, TX, VA	16% N=7
Broadband connectivity cost is too high	AK, AZ, CA, ID, IL, IN, KS, KY, LA, MA, MI, NE, NJ, NM, NC, NV, OR, PA, TX, TN, UT, VA, WA, WI	56% N=24
State telecommunication policy	AK, CA, ID, KS, MA, NC, NY	16% N=7
No local expertise by library staff at local level	AK, CA, IL, KS, KY, LA, MI, ND, NE, NM, OK, OR, PA, RI, TX, VA, WA	40% N=17
Other	AZ, OK, WI	7% N=3

Twenty-four states(56 percent) identified the high cost of broadband connectivity as the principal major barrier.

Twenty-one (49 percent) noted that it is not possible to obtain a broadband connection in all parts of the state. For example, some telecommunications providers have refused to provide broadband service to some locales, claiming that the cost of upgrading the existing infrastructure and/or maintaining the upgraded infrastructure is too high to be profitable. *"The return on investment for telco's in rural areas is insufficient to support broadband infrastructure build-out without a technology breakthrough or subsidy support."* Another respondent reported that, *"Due to their geographic location, there are a number of libraries with satellite access. While technically, those libraries have "broadband" access; their connections are unreliable and ineffective."*

Eighteen responded (42 percent) that there are few or no barriers to public library broadband connectivity in their states. In one state, the Division of the Chief Information Officer has developed a consortium of K-12 educational entities and the public libraries, and files for E-Rate discounts. All of the state's public libraries and their branches are connected to a high-speed network with either MetroEthernet fiber connections or DIA fiber between the headquarters and the Internet. Either MetroEthernet or T-1 connects branches to the headquarters.

Seventeen (40 percent) noted that the lack of local library expertise is a major barrier. This includes the public library's ability to:

- Assess the library's telecommunications needs;
- Identify commercial providers and negotiate favorable rates;
- Identify public and subsidized opportunities for reduced rate broadband connections and complete the application processes (e.g., E-rate or participation in state or regional networks);
- Develop technology plans and apply for available funding such as E-rate; and
- Develop, maintain and upgrade internal library infrastructure to make maximum use of the broadband connection.

Several respondents commented that the issue of lack of expertise was even more basic, particularly in public libraries with little or no broadband connections. In these cases, local expertise was perceived as the ability to see the need for a broadband connection, and then act to motivate stakeholders in the communities to obtain or expand a public library's broadband connections. Expertise also includes the ability to explain the local utility and importance of the Internet services that can become possible with a broadband connection, including the provision of statewide databases, virtual reference and e-government services.

Several states noted the uneven costs required to obtain the same level of connectivity, due in part to lack of competition and "one vendor" communities. For example, *"Costs of T-1 access for libraries in our state range from a low of $425 per month to a high of $1,125 per month."*

When invited to identify "other" issues impeding access, respondents mentioned the reliability/dependability of existing broadband connections, as well as the likelihood of substantially increased near-term demand. For these respondents, the issue of reliability/dependability included the actual/real consistent speed of a library's contracted connection; often the actual speed delivered was much less than that purchased. Dependability referred to the lack of redundant connections. As one state commented, *"Each population center should have [at least] two paths in & out for reliable telecom. Lack of redundant paths can devastate whole regions when outages occur."* A number of respondents pointed out the high likelihood of substantially increased broadband demand due to increased graphics, bandwidth-heavy downloads (e-books, audio, video, games, etc), and rising overall usage.

Vulnerably Networked Public Libraries

The definition for a "vulnerably networked public library" is a work-in-progress and was initially outlined in the research completed by Charles R. McClure and Joe Ryan as part of the *2006 Public Libraries and the Internet* study. Through analysis of trends in prior Internet study data, a list of characteristics was developed. These were tested and expanded through a series of focus groups. From this, a range of characteristics that identified "successfully networked libraries" was developed and, inversely, the concept of potentially "vulnerably networked" libraries was derived.

The questionnaire developed for this study offered an initial definition from the 2006 research, asked for an estimate of the number of vulnerably networked public libraries within their states, asked for assistance refining the definition, and invited respondents to describe and discuss the specific challenges vulnerably networked public libraries may face during the next three years.

The following definition was provided to the Chief Officers: "A vulnerably networked public library is at risk of being unable to offer, in whole or in part:

- Access to electronic services within the library (e.g., offers public access Internet capable workstations, an OPAC or ILS); or,
- Network services external to the library (e.g., offers a library Web site with content easily updated and controlled by the local library); or,
- Infrastructure to support internal or external networked services (e.g., library has sufficient broadband connectivity; ability to maintain or replace IT; or, has access to or employs locally available, library dedicated, IT staff)."

Although characteristics should be considered on a library-by-library basis, it is important to understand that vulnerability may be relative within a range of comparable libraries. Realistically, comparability should be considered within a context of library operating revenue and expenditures and/or population of community served in relation to similar libraries in the state. Further comparison is possible by poverty rates, metropolitan status (somewhat similar to population served), or other criteria, but respondents were not asked to consider these during this study.

Figure 70 summarizes these estimates of "vulnerable libraries" by state. Thirty-four respondents provided estimates of their vulnerably networked libraries, while seven states indicated that they did not have <u>any</u> vulnerable libraries. Of the 25 responses for which an estimated percentage was provided, an average 27 percent of a state's public libraries are considered vulnerable.[117]

Figure 70: Estimate the number of "vulnerably networked public libraries" in your state									
State	Number	State	Number	State	Number	State	Number	State	Number
AL	0%	IL	125/651 (19%)	MN	NR	ND	15/87 (17%)	UT	20/70 (29%)
AK	33%	IN	140/238 (59%)	MS	0%	OH	25/251 (10%)	VA	NR
AR	75-80	IA	50-60	MO	70/165 (42%)	OK	50%	WA	20-30/66 (30-45%)
AZ	10%	KS	NR	NE	75/275 (27%)	OR	35 (27%)	WI	22%
CA	NR[118]	KY	NR	NV	6/85 (7%)	PA	204/629 (32%)	WV	0%
CT	20/195 (10%)	LA	80%	NJ	50/460 (11%)	RI	20-25/49 (41-51%)	WY	0%
DE	NR	MD	0%	NM	15/79 (19%)	SC	0%		
FL	47/515 (9%)	MA	370/370 (100%)[119]	NY	NR	TN	60/301 (20%)	NR	9 (21%)
GA	0%	MI	70-90/383 (18-23%)	NC	NR	TX	350/551 (64%)		
ID	NR								

---

[117] Calculated using the 25 respondents where a percentage of vulnerable libraries in the state could be tallied.
[118] NR indicates no response to the question.
[119] A 2006 Massachusetts Board of Library Commissioners study, along with previous work, identifies 63 public libraries that are not part of any automated network that may have only a low bandwidth connection.

Revised Vulnerably Networked Public Library Definition

When invited to provide measurable criteria that would better specify and help to more accurately identify "vulnerably networked public libraries" in their state, the Chief Officers suggested additional measurable criteria that could be used to refine the definition. Figure 71 summarizes this revised definition, and the additional characteristics in the form of a checklist. In the 2006 study, states were asked to provide characteristics of "successfully networked public libraries." In this study, states were asked to provide characteristics of "vulnerable" libraries, and those characteristics are purposefully presented as "negative" statements. The revised definition and characteristics were not tested in this study. However, if used in the future, it is important to keep with the original methodology and retain response meaning – an affirmative (yes) response would mean the deficiency in the characteristic was present in the public library being studied.

Figure 71: Checklist for the Identification of Vulnerably Networked Public Libraries

A vulnerably networked public library does not offer or is at risk of being unable to support certain basic infrastructure, internal network services and external network services. The checklist is divided into infrastructure, internal and external service categories. A library is vulnerable if the answer is "yes" to the first item in any of the three categories. A library may be vulnerable if the answer is "yes" to other items.

Infrastructure	Characteristics	Yes/No
Broadband	Does not have a reliable broadband connection, adequate library IT to support the connection, or does not provide adequate broadband access based on demand.	
Funding	The community economic health is threatened[120] or library funding, in general, is in jeopardy.	
Local IT budget line item	IT funding is not included as a local budget line item.	
External IT funding	Does not or cannot secure external IT funding (e.g., state, E-rate).	
High broadband cost	Costs to the public library or community to obtain broadband are substantially higher than other communities in the state.	
IT replacement	Unable to maintain or replace library's IT based on its IT replacement plan (or it does not have IT replacement plan).[121]	
Hours of operation	Hours of operation are below state averages for communities of similar size.	
System member	Does not belong to a library system that offers (among other benefits) interlibrary loan.	
Library staff	The number of library staff or staff qualifications (where they exist) is below state averages for communities of similar size	
Library dedicated IT support	Does not employ or have access to locally available, library dedicated, IT staff.[122]	
Staff training	All library staff does not attend at least one externally offered IT training session annually.	
Building	The library wiring has not been updated in 10 years. Or, the library has no IT space that is climate controlled, secure with backup power.	
Internal network services	**Characteristics**	**Yes/No**
Workstations	None or not enough networked public access Internet workstations (with basic software and printing capacity).	
ILS	Does not offer access to an integrated library system.	
External library services	No local library access to free, external (e.g., state/system) library network services (e.g., databases, virtual reference).	
Public training	Does not offer regular public training sessions in computer, Internet, software or database use.	

---

[120] E.g., a mining or timber industry town whose mineral or wood has run out.
[121] This would include evidence of lack of IT, inordinate downtime where IT based services were unavailable or evidence of old or malfunctioning IT where available. Replacement plan may be part of library IT plan.
[122] Library dedicated means there is specific IT staff knowledgeable about library specific IT applications and issues and that staff is available on demand to respond to requests for IT support.

External network services	Characteristics	Yes/No
Library Web site	Does not offer a local library Web site with dynamic, easily updated and locally controlled content.	
Web access to library services	Does not offer local library Web site access to (free/low cost) available internal or external (e.g., state/system) library services (e.g., databases; virtual reference; OPAC).	

Challenges Faced by Vulnerably Networked Public Libraries

When asked to identify the connectivity, IT, economic, political, staff and other challenges that may be faced during the next three years by the vulnerably networked public libraries in their state, the summarized responses were as follows:

Connectivity/Telecommunications Challenges

1. No connection; no availability: There are still public libraries in most states without broadband connections. Most state libraries can readily identify these vulnerably networked public libraries. Identified connection challenges included:
   - Geography and weather, making even satellite reception unreliable;
   - Cost: high costs, uneven costs, and local libraries that are unwilling to pay ongoing costs, due to the difficulty in obtaining funds for service they are not sure are needed;
   - No available service: ISPs claim it is not economical to provide service in certain areas;
   - No dependable connections: Connections may be slow or uneven; not available at certain times of the day or not on certain days; and repairs are slow; and
   - No field level IT support and expertise is available to assist local public libraries that are not presently connected to investigate broadband providers and assess alternatives, handle negotiations, establish connections, and provide ongoing maintenance.

2. Lack of local public library system/consortia affiliation or partnership: There are still independent local public libraries without any affiliation to larger organizations with common interest. Specifically, a number of respondents commented that those public libraries who aggregate their broadband demand into district, system and consortia purchases, or obtain bandwidth as part of local government or school partnerships receive better rates and service. Isolated, unaffiliated libraries need to be encouraged to band together for this and other purposes.

3. Increased broadband demand: Public libraries in most states have already experienced or anticipate rapid growth in broadband demand, driven by new applications with more intensive broadband use. Challenging issues include:
   - Whether capacity will be available: Some states have begun a systematic effort to ensure future capacity;
   - Whether capacity will be available everywhere: It is likely that the same geographic connectivity gaps will persist;
   - Whether capacity will be available at an affordable cost: Respondents report that public libraries are currently unable to purchase sufficient bandwidth to meet identified demand; and
   - Whether some public libraries are willing to address this issue at all: Of special concern are reports regarding public libraries and local funders who are unaware of their existing and future broadband needs; unwilling to address existing broadband needs; unwilling to plan for future needs; or lack the capacity to do so.

4. Cost /Affordability: Respondents report a wide variation in prices for the same level of broadband connection within their states or even within regions of their state. (e.g., costs of T-1 access for libraries in one state ranges from a low of $425 per month to a high of $1,125 per month.) Challenges include:
   - Libraries are currently unable to afford existing broadband demand;
   - Flat or declining budgets: One state reported that even when libraries were offered funds for a network upgrade, they declined the offer because they could not afford the ongoing costs of a higher capacity connection;
   - Variation in special rates: Some libraries receive free connections, but not others;
   - The public and key stakeholders seem unaware of the high value/rate of return that can be derived from the public good benefits of library (and school) broadband connectivity; and
   - Broadband costs, already an issue, will move to the top of the list as public demand increases, especially because state and local funding remain flat.

5. Expanding connection options: Public libraries in most states presently use a number of ways to connect to the Internet. The most common is a connection via a local ISP, school or local government. Sometimes the connection is via a state network. Occasionally, the connection is free or subsidized, but sometimes the cost for the same level service varies dramatically. Increased sharing of strategies, tactics and evidence at state, system, and local public library levels may prove useful in expanding connection options.

6. Lack of state or local telecommunications expertise: As with IT expertise, there is a wide divide between libraries that have dedicated access to telecommunications expertise and those that do not.

    At the state level: State libraries that have the telecommunications capacity to lobby executive, legislative and regulatory leaders, as well as commercial ISPs, obtain better service for libraries. Exploring the natural affinities and common needs of related potential partners at the state level to jointly access broadband takes time and expertise. However, many potential partnerships with economic development, small business, health, local government agencies cannot be pursued without state library level telecommunications expertise. Planning for state or regional library services would benefit from a telecommunications assessment. Local libraries cannot participate in or take advantage of state library-funded services, such as downloadable media, if local libraries do not have the bandwidth to participate or do not know how to connect the state service to their local library IT. In turn, State libraries cannot demonstrate the value/use of these services if the local libraries are not connected.

    At the local public library level: Those with access to telecommunications expertise tend to plan better; educate key community decision makers; pay less for telecommunications; and are more efficient. Where local library expertise is available, it can be shared with local schools, government, library systems and even the state library.

7. Dependability and Reliability: In many cases, there is a substantial difference between a contract's stated connectivity speed and the actual connectivity level experienced. Challenges include:
   - Connectivity speeds that vary throughout the day, and by day of the week;
   - Common outages and lack of redundant circuits; and
   - Lack of an identified champion to monitor or advocate for improved services on behalf of all public libraries.

8. Wireless: Library and community (municipal or county) wireless access is widely accepted as a current indicator of an exceptionally well-networked public library. Although it makes sense for many libraries to participate in wireless efforts led by local governments, schools and communities, the diffusion of wireless service availability appears haphazard, rather than systematic.

Information Technology (IT) Challenges

1. Planning for IT upgrade, replacement and maintenance: The presence of an IT replacement plan, evidence the plan is realistic and an IT line item in local government budget(s) are indicators of a successfully networked public library. One state reported that many libraries *"lack technology plans that progress into the future and focus instead on maintaining current levels of service with current technology."*

2. Building renovation (wiring & space): IT infrastructure often requires building alterations that are cost-prohibitive and/or impossible for outdated structures to accommodate.

3. IT filtering, security & management: Libraries spend a lot of time trying to figure out how to make their IT secure; a lot of money also is spent on filtering software. As LANs and WANs become the norm, more time and money managing IT (e.g., computer scheduling, print management, etc.) will be required. A useful development is software licensing (and management) at the system/consortia rather than the local library level.

4. Library-dedicated, locally available IT support: The difference between library-paid IT staff and all other approaches is readily apparent, especially when successfully networked libraries consistently note the presence of dedicated locally available IT support. Alternative approaches have been used with varying success, including: local government and schools providing library IT support; system or consortia support; state library support through regional systems; state library-supported statewide IT helpdesks; and state library support with outsourced/contracted labor. One state estimates that about 80 percent of its libraries do not have technical staff and rely on the state library for assistance.

5. Public training: The lack of public training to motivate the use of available technology and to explain how to use such networks services as databases and virtual reference remains a barrier to the widespread adoption and use of these technology services. Successfully networked libraries consistently offer public training in the use of network services; vulnerable public libraries do not.

6. Need for library-supported IT solutions: Some state libraries, using open source software, are developing library-tailored solutions to address persistent library IT problems. Current examples include state library-initiated programs to develop public library Web sites hosted remotely with content managed by local library (e.g., Plinkit Collaborative http://www.plinkit.org/; Georgia Public Library Service's open source-based ILS Evergreen http://www.open-ils.org/)

Economic Challenges

1. Vulnerable local economies: A number of respondents' comments focused on places with undiversified economies: one industry, one commodity (oil, mineral), one agricultural product towns. During boom times, libraries in these types of communities may have few problems, but they also have no economic savings plan with which to mitigate hardship during those times when the local economy goes bust.

2. Consolidating previously unplanned geographic distribution of libraries: Communities with more than one library, or adjacent communities with public libraries, may be unable to support all of them adequately, resulting in two or more vulnerable libraries, rather than one successful library.

3. Increased demand coupled with unpredictable, flat or declining revenue streams: There is a severe lack of stable and predictable funding, caused by economic downturns, poor management or politics. IT financing requires predictable revenue over several years in order to pay off debt; unfortunately, many states reported flat or declining revenues at state library and local library levels. Unpredictable funding presents a challenge as IT costs rise and the demand for IT services increase.

4. Nonexistent or flawed public library funding strategies: Not every public library board and management team has the capacity to develop a public library funding strategy that can effectively plan for and manage available funding. This challenge impacts every area of library operations, including IT infrastructure and service.

5. Flawed public library funding structures: Many public libraries support general operations on revenue derived from flawed or outdated funding mechanisms that may take a long time to modify, if even that is possible (e.g., In one state, some libraries operate on 10-year millage funding structure that requires anticipating funding needs far into the future; another state reports tax caps that have frozen library income).

6. Lack of external affiliation and partnerships: In general, successfully networked libraries are members of systems or consortia in active partnerships with local governments and schools. Vulnerable public libraries lack these arrangements, and tend to pay more for less, presuming they can even obtain access to network resources and services at all.

7. Overdependence on external financing of core resources and services: Vulnerable libraries largely depend upon external funding (e.g., E-rate, state technology funding) to support their broadband connection and IT infrastructure (e.g., routers, servers, workstations) and some IT-based services (e.g., state/consortia databases, virtual reference). Funding for these services may be vulnerable.

8. E-rate impact: With the 10th anniversary of the E-rate, it is clear that this source of funding has become an essential way in which a public library finances its IT. While successfully networked libraries apply for E-rate, vulnerable libraries often do not. Respondents agree the E-rate application process is overly cumbersome and requires a fairly accurate prediction of future IT, which many libraries find difficult to forecast. Smart public libraries apply as part of a group (system, consortia, state) or make use of an application aggregator, thus eliminating the need for staff in smaller libraries to track a cumbersome process and

paperwork. An obvious place for state library and Department of Education collaboration is in facilitating a universal and easy E-rate application process. Help also is needed because state IT and network agencies may not themselves understand E-rate requirements and its potential impact when state contracts are bid or other "statewide actions" are taken.

Political Challenges

1. Internet safety concerns: Internet safety, pornography, filtering, and copyright infringement are all challenging issues, or at least distractions that sap or misdirect library advocates' energy and the votes of political decision makers.

2. Libraries are a low priority: A number of respondents commented that library and telecommunication infrastructure issues are a low priority at the state and local levels.

3. Library telecommunications are a low priority: It is difficult to get the attention of key stakeholders on various basic telecommunications issues (e.g., the public good of supporting a library broadband connectivity right of way for broadband connection access.)

4. Need for partnerships: There is mixed success reported at the state and local levels regarding efforts to establish alliances with natural allies (e.g., culture; education; economic development; employment; health; tourism), as related to the deployment of IT services.

5. Confusion about funding responsibility: Some respondents are unclear about who is responsible for funding public libraries (state, county, municipal). There is much confusion and a loss of revenue when one of these units balks at funding.

6. Statewide telecommunications policy & state universal fund approach: Although several states reported having "library inclusive" state telecommunications policies and universal service funds, in other states these policies and approaches remain either untried or have failed. Commercial telecommunications providers remain a strong lobbying force with which to contend.

7. E-rate: Efforts to garner state-level support for continued E-rate funding have had mixed success. Efforts to coordinate E-rate regulation with state bidding and other state activities also have been problematic in some states.

8. Need for advocacy: The need for library advocacy to overcome political challenges remains essential.

Staff Challenges

1. Staff IT training: Library managers may require training in order to communicate library needs to IT staff. All staff, even IT personnel, finds it difficult to keep up with new IT and their potential impacts on libraries. Further challenges include uncoordinated and poorly advertised IT training opportunities within (and across) states. Although distance learning approaches have been attempted in order to reach remote library staff, the effectiveness of these learning opportunities has not been consistently evaluated.

2. Insufficient staff, not just a lack of IT staff: Vulnerable public libraries, particularly the smaller ones, lack not only IT staff, but enough library staff to meet their various public demands. This lack of staff also affects the ability to release staff to attend trainings, as well as staff's ability to provide trainings to the public.

3. Unprepared staff, not just staff unprepared for IT: The need for staff training in many areas of librarianship is not limited to IT. Systematic training lasting more than one session is particularly difficult to find. Coordinated, well-advertised training remains a challenge, as do the difficulties in freeing staff time and paying the costs of transportation and accommodation, as needed.

4. Poorly trained staff remains a barrier to the successful introduction of networked services: Even where IT is adequate and a networked service is available, this service is under-utilized. Untrained staff is a contributing cause; those who do not understand a service's use cannot motivate use, and often do not know themselves how to use the service effectively.

5. Leadership: The qualifications of those who serve as staff, especially in rural libraries, reflect the level of available local funding for personnel. Many local people who become rural library directors do not have the educational or professional background needed to run a public library.

6. Can't hire, can't keep: Rural public libraries find it especially difficult to find, hire or retain IT staff. High staff turnover remains a negative contributing factor.

7. Volunteers: Although volunteers make significant contributions to successful public libraries, fully utilizing these volunteer contributions remains an ongoing challenge.

8. Library Boards: Effective IT innovation cannot occur without Board champions. However, effective Board training, like staff training in this area, remains an ongoing challenge.

Other Challenges

1. Inability to plan and budget for future technology needs: Libraries in all states lack the capacity to plan for and budget for future technology needs. In addition, libraries often lack the motivation to do so, due to unpredictable fluctuation in local revenues.

2. Uncertainty regarding how to measure and show value of current IT-based services: Challenges include: understanding how a library measures use of IT-based services; how to value usage; how to systematically communicate usage evidence; and how to advocate for support. For example, one state reported many of its libraries do not understand how to capture usage of their IT resources (both the PAC and electronic resources) to show the value of increased funding for such budget items. Libraries are uncomfortable talking about the increased utilization of electronic resources and the demands it places upon the organization, because they are unable to show the benefit of such services and fear the discussion as the use of more traditional library services simultaneously declines.

"Unexpectedly" Successfully Networked Public Libraries

An "unexpectedly" successfully networked public library or library system is one with a limited local economic or population base that has maintained broadband connectivity, IT and has developed networked services, even though its population served, or economic, or political or community circumstances suggest it would be unlikely to do so.

The characteristics that respondents mostly frequently mentioned when asked to described these "unexpected" successes are found in Figure 72.

Figure 72: "Unexpectedly" Successfully Networked Public Library Characteristics	
Why unexpectedly successful?	Instances mentioned by Chief Officers
Good IT use & maintenance	26
Wireless (incl. county Wifi)	17
Fund raising	16
Good development of IT-based services (e.g., networked bookmobile; Web site; networked ILS)	14
Partnerships	Local government (8); Consortia (3); School (2); Volunteer (1)
Leadership	13
Unusually large broadband connection	9
IT networking	5
Good local IT expertise	5
Offers public training	3
Staff training	2

External Partner Assistance Needed by Vulnerably Networked Public Libraries

Respondents were asked to identify the types of assistance that external partners (including the state library, ALA, external funders and others) might provide to vulnerably networked public libraries to demonstrably improve (within a 3-5 year timeframe) and sustain their networked resources and services. From these, the researcher offers three priorities:

- Obtain enough broadband to meet public library demand at an affordable price;
- Provide adequate IT to make efficient/effective use of broadband connection and meet users' needs for other IT-based services; and
- Provide library networked services of interest to their communities.

Comments are summarized below, grouped by priority need, in order to facilitate future discussion of the challenges and the ways in which specific leveraged assistance by external agents could address these challenges.

PRIORITY: Obtain enough broadband to meet public library demand at an affordable price

Challenges & Recommended Means of Leveraged Assistance

Public libraries and systems use multiple means to obtain broadband connections. Individual public libraries and systems may not know about the potential means used to obtain connections or how to effectively obtain and manage it.

Assistance Needed: Conduct needed research, collating the results in a manual that identifies all of the various ways to obtain a broadband connection, discusses pros and cons, and provides step-by-step plans for obtaining and managing each type of connection. Distribute this manual to each state library, consortia, system and individual public library.

State libraries may influence or exert control over connection means. Individual State Libraries may not know enough about all of the potential means for connectivity or how to exercise effective influence or control.

Assistance Needed: Conduct needed research, collating the results in a manual that identifies all of the various ways to obtain a broadband connection, discusses pros and cons, with strategies and tactics that state libraries might pursue with each connection option.

Potential may exist at the state or federal level for libraries to obtain free or subsidized broadband connections (separate from E-rate) through Universal Service Funds or directly from commercial ISPs. State libraries may not be aware of these options and how to pursue them; a coordinated advocacy campaign may be necessary.

Assistance Needed: Conduct needed research to identify ways in which public libraries have obtained free or subsidized connections. Disseminate these successful strategies and tactics, along with supporting evidence, to state libraries and/or consortia, systems and individual public libraries. A coordinated advocacy campaign, if launched, must identify and collect evidence demonstrating "the public good value" of library (and other related organizations) broadband connectivity. Evidence must be widely disseminated to encourage acceptance by key stakeholders as an underlying assumption for support.

Aggregating demand and spreading costs among participants appears to be a more efficient and effective strategy.

Assistance Needed: Identify ways to encourage public library membership in aggregations (such as consortia and systems) for the purpose of obtaining better or more affordable broadband connections.

Telecommunications expertise may be missing to help negotiate and obtain connections; take advantage of opportunities; and resolve connection issues.

Assistance Needed: State libraries, consortia, systems and public libraries with direct access to dedicated telecommunications expertise are demonstrably better off than those without. However, like broadband connections, perhaps libraries must experience the benefit of such expertise before being willing to pay for it. If so, explore ways in which such expertise can be shared.

PRIORITY: Provide adequate IT to make efficient/ effective use of broadband connection and meet users' needs for other IT-based services.

Challenges & Recommended Means of Leveraged Assistance

Public libraries need adequate IT to take advantage of new applications and software, meet user demands, and to continue to play a role in education for 21st century citizenry.

Assistance Needed: Inventory existing public library IT needs. Develop and adopt minimum standards for use as leverage to obtain funding. Actively seek IT funding from external sources.

There are definite IT innovations that all libraries and communities should have (e.g., workstations; Internet connection; broadband; library Web site with local content control and updates; wireless.)

Assistance Needed: Create a common mantra: "Not every library has this IT, and it should." Help public libraries understand the need for IT and motivate its use; it is not enough merely to have the technology.

Public libraries need to develop realistic funding plans for replacing existing IT and obtaining new IT (e.g., wireless) as needed. These plans should include local participation.

Assistance Needed: Encourage external funders of public library IT to include "match" requirements for: (a) specific local buy-in; (b) a local IT budget line item; (c) IT plan including IT replacement; (d) proof of IT replacement plan; and (e) E-rate participation. In addition, encourage external funders to consider requiring: 1) system/consortia membership (if available and if membership benefits include: reduced broadband costs; library dedicated IT and telecommunications expertise; and shared ILS including interlibrary loan); and 2) the establishment by local libraries (via Friends or other legal entity) of a local endowment fund to sustain future IT purchases.

Clarify whether states, like local governments, bear responsibility for sustained local public library IT funding. Clarify whether states bear responsibility to sustain public library IT when local economies fail.

Assistance Needed: If so, find ways that external and private funding can be used as leverage to prod state government through their state libraries to: (a) fund library IT where they do not currently do so; (b) fund vulnerably networked public libraries; and (c) encourage local planning and local savings (endowments) to enable public libraries to continue to meet IT (and other demands) throughout cyclical downturns in local economies. Conduct additional research to identify other ways to protect public library IT investment during cyclical local economic downturns.

State libraries and public libraries benefit from dedicated library IT expertise to identify and capitalize on opportunities, plan, select and maintain IT, and in other related areas.

Assistance Needed: Encourage external agents to consider requiring libraries and library systems serving populations of a certain size to have IT personnel. Encourage external agents to consider requirements for IT expertise or stimulate IT service availability. Since little research has been done on the effectiveness (strengths, weaknesses) of the external provision of IT expertise (e.g., system level support; outsourcing; state help desks; school or local government IT support), explore whether standards could be devised, if helpful, (X contact hours per Y), and identify the roles, responsibilities, and tactics that would improve service delivery.

Public libraries may benefit from aggregating IT purchases.

Assistance Needed: Seek targeted external funding to stimulate the creation or improvement of group library IT (e.g., hardware, software, services, etc) purchase organizations (e.g., state, consortia, system, etc.). Conduct additional research to identify effective ways to stimulate improvements in this area.

PRIORITY: Provide library networked services of interest to their communities.

Challenges & Recommended Means of Leveraged Assistance:

A basic networked library service package in 2007 might include: networked library workstations with broadband Internet access; ILS (with interlibrary loan); access to a basic digital collection (e-books, videos, games, databases, newspapers, reference); and a library Web site (locally controlled content and updates), with organized, access to safe, local and remote network collections, services and e-government.

Assistance Needed: The development and external support of a basic networked library service package standard (perhaps adjusted biennially) might increase the likelihood that most public libraries might achieve, and obtain local support to achieve, the provision of such services. Many of these services can be produced and provided remotely. External funding might improve the quality of these services and might subsidize local availability. External support that would make a basic networked library service package available to vulnerable local libraries should be considered.

Lack of remote access to library services via a library Web site is a barrier to technology use in rural (and other) areas.

Assistance Needed: Advocate for external support and encouragement for remotely accessed library services.

Databases and digital collections available from school or library should be available from school and library, and at home or office.

Assistance Needed: Action is needed by external agents to encourage state library, consortia, systems and education departments to agree that database contracts should be mutually accessible. At the local school library level, grassroots support for these agreements that may exist among librarians, teachers, and parents must be extended to include principals, superintendents and boards (who may need to be educated about the importance of this issue).

Staff and public training opportunities, two hallmarks of successfully networked public libraries, must be supported. Staff must have the IT training adequate to do their jobs; and public libraries should offer public IT training.

Assistance Needed: External agents can work to make the provision of staff and public training a requirement. Presentation scripts and aids (including videos), capable of local customization, should be created as a useful training tool to help establish a quality standard for training. External agents can assist in establishing a context for the need for staff and public training by asking and answering the following questions: Why do these services matter? Why should I use them? How can I use these services to improve my life? What is the role of the information professional in assisting others to use networked services?

Absence of high-quality, independent-use, library networked services. There are few library-specific networked services. The few services identified with libraries that exist (e.g., databases; virtual reference) are cumbersome to use (requiring local library staff intervention which may not be available), and may be of low quality (e.g., search engines used by databases and ILS) when compared to commercial alternatives (e.g., Google).

Assistance Needed: If possible, stimulate or redirect the library marketplace and aid library vendors with the production of more, higher quality, library specific products

Section III: Findings from Focus Groups and Site Visits

INTRODUCTION

A valuable addition to the overall study is a strong qualitative component to better understand the quantitative responses. Specifically, further qualitative detail is needed to recognize what factors influence the library's ability to meet demands for Internet-based services. It is from these findings that libraries can further influence communities to support the valuable services they provide.

The study employs both site visits and interviews with public library directors and other key stakeholders in selected states to:

- Elucidate trends suggested by the quantitative data;
- Explore quantitative data anomalies;
- Deepen our understanding of certain aspects of U.S. public library advocacy, funding and sustainability; and
- Focus attention on current U.S. public library funding hot topics of interest.

Focus groups were held in four of the 10 states eligible to apply in the first round of the "Opportunity Online" hardware grant program from the Bill & Melinda Gates Foundation. From February to April 2007, the project team heard from 40 participants in leadership positions in rural, urban and suburban library settings in Delaware, Maryland, Nevada and Utah.

The project team also made site visits in each of these four states. In total, the team heard from library staff, patrons, trustees, Friends and community leaders affiliated with 29 libraries.

Questions focused on the libraries' fiscal climate, the Internet services most used and requested by library patrons, the impact of technology on staff, how libraries advocate for technology in libraries and what support would be most helpful to them. The complete script for the focus groups, as well as a series of follow-up questions emailed to each participant, can be found in Appendix C. The questions posed during the site visits are located in Appendix D.

METHODOLOGY

The site visit planning and execution employs a number of methods to achieve the goals of this portion of the larger study. These include:
- Reviewing previous studies and reports and state-level data regarding Internet connectivity, technology-based services provided by libraries, and stability of funding;
    - Internet Studies (FSU, et. al);
    - ALA Public Library Funding study; and
    - National Center for Education Statistics (NCES)-Federal State Cooperative System of Public Library Data (FSCS)

- Engaging in discussions with a range of individuals familiar with library funding, governance and telecommunications issues;

- Conducting state site visits to more fully explore factors influencing public libraries providing stable and sufficient funding, staffing, and technology ; and
    - Meet with state library agencies, public library directors, and other key local stakeholder communities (e.g., library trustees, local government, private local funding groups, etc.); and

- Conducting follow-up phone interviews with selected state and public library staff as required or appropriate.

The use of environmental scan techniques, secondary data analysis, focus groups and telephone follow-up enabled the project team to support the detailed data reported by individual libraries by "grounding" those data in the governance and funding realities of a library community.

Building on "best practice" case studies of successfully networked public libraries reported in the 2006 Internet study, the site visits made it possible to "drill down" to learn more about the challenges public libraries face in providing and sustaining sufficient high quality services and high-speed bandwidth for the range of public access services they provide.

Site Selection
Working from the first-year Bill & Melinda Gates Foundation's "Opportunities Online" grant program, the study team:
- Identified 10 states eligible for grant funding in 2007;

- Reviewed qualitative data collected by Joe Ryan in a survey of Chief Officers of State Library Agencies (COSLA);

- Grouped states around geographic representation and physical proximity to one another to facilitate travel logistics in short time frame;
    - Mid-Atlantic: Delaware, Maryland, New York and Pennsylvania
    - Midwest: Iowa and Kansas
    - West: Colorado, Nevada, Utah and Wyoming

- Reviewed and identified proportional data reported by public libraries in the 2004 and 2006 *Public Libraries and the Internet* study conducted by Bertot, McClure & Jaeger;
    - Marginal and adequate funding to sustain public access services
        - Marginal was defined as fewer than 50 percent of libraries reporting increased or stable operating revenue;
        - Adequate was defined as more than 50 percent of libraries reporting increased operating revenue;
    - Confirmed funding data in the NCES FSCS FY2004 report and the ALA Public Library Funding study (2006) http://www.ala.org/ala/ors/reports/FundingIssuesinUSPLs.pdf ; and
    - Selected libraries with varying ranges of connectivity.

- Coordinated with the ALA Office for Information Technology Policy so as not to overlap with site visits scheduled for related site visits on Internet connectivity; and

- Identified states where the 2006 study team had not scheduled site visits.

Based on these criteria, and supporting regional representation, the following states were selected for site visits:
- Delaware
- Maryland
- Nevada
- Utah

Communication with Selected States

The project team contacted the chief library officers in the selected states. The chief officers were asked to recommend public library directors to participate in focus groups during February, March and April, 2007. The project team requested that these library directors reflect a range of libraries of varying population size, budgets and governance structures. The team also sought representation of libraries that had experienced a high degree of success in creating and sustaining technology access, as well as those more vulnerable.

Four to six public library directors were invited to participate in each small focus group, and two focus groups were scheduled per participating state, except in Nevada where only one focus group was held.

Presentation of Summary Findings

In reporting the site visit and focus group findings, it was important to include external research in order to contextualize state-level findings. These sources present data from 2004 and 2007, and represent the most current research available at the time this report was prepared:

- *Public Libraries in the United States: Fiscal Year 2004* (National Center for Education Statistics) was the most recently published national report of public library data at the time this study was completed. The 2004 report was used to put in context public library service areas (population served), organization structure, legal basis and the average size of library buildings. Further, the NCES report was used to describe levels of library service, revenue and expenditure data, and per capita data where available.
http://www.nces.ed.gov/pubs2006/2006349.pdf

- *2007 State New Economy Index* (Information Technology & Innovation Foundation) was used to understand the overall access by residents to technology and Internet services by state. This study reviewed states on their success in providing high-speed telecommunications access, supporting education, job creation and research.
http://www.itif.org/index.php?id=30

- *Speed Matters: A Report on Internet Speeds in All 50 States* (Communications Workers of America, 2007) was used to further position state-level Internet connectivity.
http://www.speedmatters.org/document-library/sourcematerials/sm_report.pdf

EXECUTIVE SUMMARY

The single most significant theme that emerged from both the focus groups and site visits was the need for increased space and capacity. Deployment and use of public access computing in U.S. public libraries have brought more people to the library (1.3 billion visits in FY2004,[123] up from 821.6 million a decade earlier), many more electronic applications and online services, and a growing capacity to accommodate the MP3 players, USB drives and digital cameras library users carry with them. Yet, many libraries are housed in buildings that predate the Internet – or even TV, in the case of several historic Carnegie buildings. Not only does square footage limit the addition of desktop computers, but old wiring and electrical capacity constrain technology growth.

Capacity constraints also extend to bandwidth and staff. More libraries are reporting significant slowdowns in their Internet connection speeds during the busiest times of day – most often on weekdays after school. Even T1 (or 1.5Mbps) access is not enough for some library systems to provide fast download speeds for the audio and video materials brokered by the library or state library – let alone music or video from such popular Web sites as MySpace and YouTube.

Library staff also are feeling the effects of rapid change in technology offerings and user expectations. The more familiar library patrons become with technology, the more they expect from the library.

Funding

In general, library funding is stable but flat, and library directors are not optimistic about future increases. Libraries have always had to compete for public dollars, but the competition is becoming more intense, particularly in states with population growth and stretched public infrastructure. This was particularly pronounced in Nevada and in Delaware where libraries are not seeing an increase in local funding commensurate with the increases in the populations served. Tax caps further exacerbate this issue, with one library reporting a loss of at least $8 million in capital funding. One city manager stated: *"Libraries compete for the same funds as emergency services. They are on the bottom of the food chain."*

In some of the smaller communities, library directors said their funding was fine, but then described the reality of trying to do more with less. One rural library director described a generous budget and good support, but later mentioned that the Internet service had been down for much of the week. Several libraries depended on part-time or volunteer IT support because they were unable to attract or afford staff with specialized technology skills.

Directors in Maryland and Delaware reported recent funding successes at the state level. Maryland libraries will see annual increases in state funding through 2010, and Delaware has dedicated matching funding for technology replacement in libraries. Most directors in large city and county systems in Utah reported positive funding environments at the state and local level where property tax funding for libraries has grown as their communities have grown.

While many libraries have integrated technology costs into their general operating budgets and have created line items for equipment, electronic collections and telecommunications costs, some

---

[123] National Center for Education Statistics. Public Libraries in the United States: Fiscal Year 2004. (NCES 2006-349). Washington, DC: NCES, 2006. http://www.nces.ed.gov/pubs2006/2006349.pdf

libraries reported that their greatest funding successes were in securing grant funding for new computers – most often from the Library Services and Technology Act (LSTA) and/or the Bill & Melinda Gates Foundation. One director reported: *"We wouldn't have a single computer without LSTA."* Friends groups also are an important fundraising source for general library funding.

Patron Technology Use

Public libraries, particularly in rural communities, continue to be the only sites of free public access computing. But library staff report high technology usage even in communities where home computer and Internet use is quite high. In one county, the library director reported that 85 percent of residents have computers, and 93 percent of these residents have Internet access. *"And we're asking ourselves, how come we're so busy?"* The answer from many patrons interviewed ranged from faster access speeds at the library (broadband versus dial-up), to a need for assistance from library staff, to competition among family members for the home computer. One mother who goes to her library in Nevada with her two teen sons at least twice a week confirmed library computers were much faster than the one at home: *"I can do twice as much in an hour."*

One way libraries are working to expand access and keep up with demand is by providing wireless access. Staff in nearly every library visited either reported high usage of the wireless recently made available (along with an accompanying need for more electrical outlets and capacity) or expressed the desire to add wireless access. In fact, when asking how satisfied he was with his library's computer and technology resources, one library patron said: *"You can never have too many workstations."*

A few libraries also have invested in laptops, but this is still rare, and the laptops are usually secured to furniture rather than mobile to ensure they do not leave the library. In most libraries, patrons must bring their own laptops.

Not surprisingly, library staff and patrons reported uses of library computers as diverse as the Web sites and electronic resources available online. A handful of uses were most frequently mentioned, however:

> **Email:** Most libraries said this was still the most common use of library computers by residents, as well as by travelers from across the nation and the globe. Because many users only need to use the library computers for short periods of time to stay connected, many libraries have dedicated one or more computers as "express" computers for (usually) 15-minute sessions. This practice was reported to reduce friction between residents and tourists competing for limited computers, as well as to enable the library to meet more patrons' needs. It also was reported, though, that more and more younger library users were using chat software – where it was available – instead of email.

> **Job and professional resources:** This broad category encompasses using library computers to search for jobs, run home offices, apply for jobs online and update personal resumes. One single mom in Maryland looking for a job put it this way: *"People need to find jobs, get on their feet."*

One of the most surprising aspects of this use was the dramatic increase in the number of businesses that require applicants to apply online. Staff in several Las Vegas-area libraries reported their libraries were inundated when a new casino opened within the last year and required *all* applicants to apply online. For many job seekers, this was their first time using computers and the Internet. Not only did they need to fill out the online application, they also needed to establish an email account and check back frequently to see if they were a candidate for employment. In addition to low technology skills, many of these new library patrons had low literacy rates and/or spoke English as a second language. Not surprisingly, the impact on staff time was tremendous while helping these users. *"Online job applications are a killer."* Nevada and Delaware also recently put their state government jobs online and are encouraging job applicants to apply online.

Entrepreneurs were almost as common as job seekers. About 10 percent of the library computer users interviewed relied on the library to research grants, stay in touch with professional contacts, update business Web pages, read online business publications, prepare invoices and more.

Homework and education-related resources: The library's complementary role to schools and universities resounded in patron interviews. Parents and students reported coming to the library, often daily or weekly, to do research for school, use word processing and presentation software for class assignments, and even attend classes online. *"When my kids were younger, if it weren't for the library, they wouldn't have had that resource. They were here daily – and were 'A' students,"* said another Nevada library patron. Library staff also reported a sharp rise in test proctoring for high school and college students, though not all libraries offer this service.

E-commerce and "life management" resources: Similar to email, many staff and library patrons reported a high level of use for online banking and bill pay, printing boarding passes for air travel, buying and selling stock and more.

Social networking Web sites like MySpace and YouTube: Not surprisingly, more and more patrons are reporting that MySpace, YouTube and other popular Web sites are part of their routine use of library computers. High school and college-age students were most likely to report that this was a top use for them, but one mother with two children in Maryland also uses MySpace to participate in an online journal with eight of her siblings.

E-government resources: The most common e-government resources reported by library staff were accessing and filing tax forms, seeking and using Department of Motor Vehicle information, and seeking immigration information and making appointments with the Immigration and Naturalization Service.

In addition to wireless access, the most common technology requests or suggestions for improvements were:
- More computers;
- Longer time limits for computer use;
- Faster computer and Internet speeds; and
- More or better peripherals, including scanners, color printers and CD burners.

Almost every library, regardless of size, budget or location, experienced wait times at some point during the day. In the busy after-school hours, queued lines were not uncommon. Most libraries have and enforce time limits on computers ranging from 30 minutes to two hours. Some allow patrons to re-log on as often as they are willing to "take their turn", while other libraries strictly enforce daily time limits – often one or two hours per day.

One of the most striking statements about the impact of time limits came from a Utah librarian, who described the wealth of online resources available through the library and the frustration of limited computer access. *"It's a real contradiction that needs to come through. We're really not allowing people enough time to fill out an application, to do homework.... Thirty minutes is nothing."* Without time limits, however, fewer people would be able to use the library computer resources. One library staff member described trying to find the right balance between serving the most people possible and allowing adequate time online for a meaningful experience. The library has established different time limits for after-school hours and the quieter times in the morning.

Staffing

The impact of technology on library staff is substantial. As library patrons become more and more sophisticated technology users, the demand for faster and better service is growing. Patrons are bringing their iPods, digital cameras and laptops to the library expecting to use them as seamlessly as they might at home or work. Or, they are new users of these technologies who are looking to staff for help configuring their laptop's wireless or help downloading and emailing digital photos. It's a challenge, particularly for staff members who also are new to technology, to feel competent enough to help their patrons.

At the same time, the library technology environment is becoming more complex – from managing the network to updating the library's Web site to troubleshooting new business applications that help libraries track items purchased, cataloged and circulated. Libraries are installing self-check computers and reservation systems to manage time limits on computer sessions. They are providing more downloadable media – from text e-books to audiobooks to videos. They are creating e-newsletters to promote events and services and sending email renewal notices. They are purchasing filtering systems and managing the settings.

High on almost every director's wish list is at least one—or additional— dedicated information technology staff person. Many library staff, particularly in rural libraries, learned computer skills on the job or in training offered at the state or county level. With staffs as small as one or two full-time employees and a handful of part-time employees, many directors struggle to find time for staff training. In these libraries, there are no building-level IT staff at the library. Larger libraries with dedicated staff may still have only one IT employee. *"We have well over 100 computers and just the one guy,"* reported a Maryland library director. Directors at a couple of the larger libraries said they had hired or planned to hire a manager of a "virtual branch" to manage all of the system's online offerings.

Keeping current is an ongoing challenge both in terms of the available training, time and the proclivity of staff members. *"You almost need two levels of IT staff. How do we push to the next level while keeping things running on the floor?"*

While providing technology access can be challenging, most staff also reported it was rewarding. They reported being able to provide better reference services and access to online resources that they never would have had the space or budget for in print. *"Technology is a great leveler between small- and large-sized libraries, but there is a growing sense of unease about there being so much more that I don't know."*

Advocacy

Library directors reflect a wide range of experience and ease in advocating for support of their libraries. Nearly all agreed that library leaders must be "at the table" in local government, and that they must proactively demonstrate the value of library services to local officials and business leaders.

Library directors freely shared examples about how they are creating meaningful relationships at all levels to improve and integrate library services in their communities. Several directors provide an orientation and/or tour of the library to all new city or county elected leaders. Several had commissioned internal audits or surveys of patrons to gauge satisfaction and use of library resources. Many directors talked about building trust with local budget agencies through sound planning and stewardship of resources. At least one library prepares a business case, often discussing the return on investment for each of its technology initiatives. Most libraries used statistics and stories to show the value of the library.

However, many library directors also noted that advocacy was just one more responsibility they struggled to handle with too few staff, little training and limited time. As a result, they were dependent on others' funding decisions, rather than framing the discussion. Since it was often the case that local leaders were not frequent library users, decision-makers often were unaware of the level of use and range of services offered in the library. Several directors described a turnaround in support from the mayor or council member after outreach by library staff brought them to the library for a well-attended event or meeting. Even library supporters need ongoing education about new technology offerings and the value of these to the local community.

Most libraries had Friends groups, and trustees often were advocates for the library when it mobilized support for budget discussions or capital campaigns. One Delaware library Friends' group had mobilized many of its 269 paid members to serve as liaisons to other community groups and "take the library everywhere." One Nevada library board member regularly attends Chamber of Commerce and City Council meetings to provide library updates. It was rare, however, for trustees and members of the Friends groups to be engaged in regular outreach to the community on behalf of the library. Where there was regular communication with community groups – including Lions Clubs, school boards and the Boy Scouts – this was handled by the library director or other library staff.

DELAWARE CASE STUDY

Library technology in Delaware has been well-funded, but the state is now facing an economic downturn. The state funds the statewide library network, a three-year match program for computer replacement, statewide licensed databases and has established and is working toward a statewide Delaware Library Catalog. Public libraries in Sussex and Kent County have integrated their collections in the catalog, and Wilmington Public Libraries and New Castle County Public Library System are considering the move. The state also is investigating how it may be able to offer all libraries wireless access on the statewide network.

Governance and Statistical Information

Delaware has 21 public library systems with 33 physical library locations and two bookmobiles serving more than 4.2 million residents.[124] Delaware's public libraries are organized primarily as library districts (52.4 percent) and county systems (28.6 percent). Another 19.1 percent are organized as municipal government or city/county libraries.

In 2004, Delaware public libraries reported serving more than 3.5 million visitors, answering nearly 500,000 reference questions, and circulating nearly 5 million items (e.g., books, films, sound recordings, audio books, etc.). Delaware public libraries borrowed or loaned another 276,000 items through interlibrary loan on behalf of residents.[125]

Residents are served by 282 library employees, 97 of whom hold Master's degrees in Library and Information Science (MLIS) and another 49 that work as librarians but do not hold a master's degree. Delaware public libraries rank 42nd in overall staffing and 41st in MLIS staffing.

In fiscal year 2004, Delaware public libraries ranked 29th in the number of public-use Internet computers per building (9.39) compared with public libraries in other states.

Funding Summary

Seventy-five percent of Delaware's public library funding comes from local sources (tax dollars), 12.7 percent from state sources, 0.5 percent from federal sources, and 11.9 percent from other sources (e.g., private fund raising, gifts, bequests, etc.).[126]

Delaware ranks 32nd in total operating revenue support ($26.48 compared with $32.21 nationally). Delaware public libraries rank ninth in state support, 35th in local support, and 12th in other support. In 2003, the state increased its investment in upgrading technology access in its libraries. After the Bill & Melinda Gates Foundation and the state provided funds to replace every computer in the state's public libraries, the state created new funding for computer replacement. An incorporation tax provides $300,000 annually for libraries to replace computers on a three-year cycle, plus provides another $100,000 in funding for "innovative library technology." Libraries must provide a 50 percent match for the technology replacement funding. The incorporation tax funding is in addition to roughly $635,000 in state funding for libraries, which is up from $100,000 five years ago.

Fifty-nine point nine (59.9) percent of operating expenditures go toward staff costs (salaries, benefits, retirement), 15.9 percent toward purchasing collections, and 24.1 percent for other things, such as programming, building maintenance and utilities, and computer hardware and software. Regarding other operating expenditures, Delaware's spending is slightly more than the national average of 21 percent. Delaware ranks 33rd in total operating expenditures ($24.83 spent per capita), 37th in staffing and 25th in collections.[127]

---

[124] National Center for Education Statistics. Public Libraries in the United States: Fiscal Year 2004. (NCES 2006-349). Washington, DC: NCES, 2006. http://www.nces.ed.gov/pubs2006/2006349.pdf
[125] ibid
[126] ibid
[127] National Center for Education Statistics. Public Libraries in the United States: Fiscal Year 2004. (NCES 2006-349). Washington, DC: NCES, 2006. http://www.nces.ed.gov/pubs2006/2006349.pdf

In this year's *Public Library Funding & Technology Access Study*, Delaware reported that of those receiving E-rate discounts, telecommunications services (72 percent) and Internet connectivity (28 percent) were the two most commonly funded discount categories. The majority of technology expenses in both fiscal year 2006 and 2007 were paid from local and state revenue sources, and for some libraries, donations and local fund raising were significant contributors to supporting technology purchases.

In fiscal year 2004, Delaware public libraries reported $1.4 million in capital expenditures (building repairs, renovations, or new buildings). Fifty-three-point-six (53.6) percent reported expenditures below $10,000 and 19.1 percent between $10,000 - 99,999. Approximately six libraries, 28.6 percent, reported capital expenditures in excess of $100,000.[128]

This year (2007) the Delaware Committee on Libraries recommended that $10 million for new library construction be included in the Governor's budget. While the Governor usually accepts the recommendation, State Library staff report that competing construction pressures for new schools and roads this year have reduced the anticipated funding to $1 million.

Connectivity Summary

The State Library reports that all of the public libraries have T1 or T3 access. Fifty-one point six (51.6) percent of Delaware's libraries reported access speeds of 6 mbps or higher. Libraries in New Castle County are on the county network. All other public libraries are on the state library network. The major barrier to connectivity in the state is that the capacity for connectivity does not exist in all parts of the state.

Delaware public libraries reported in the *Public Libraries and the Internet 2007* survey that 81.8 percent of its patrons must wait to use public Internet computers at some point in the day. The top three factors influencing the library's ability to add more computers is space (81.8 percent), costs (63.6 percent) and maintaining and upgrading computer equipment. Sufficient staff to support public access computing was ranked fourth.

Wireless connectivity was available in 48.5 percent of Delaware's public libraries, and it was anticipated that another 18.2 percent would add access in the coming year. Speeds of access may be impacted for some libraries that share bandwidth with existing public access computers (30.3 percent) despite the strong connectivity access speeds available in Delaware.

The State of Delaware ranks 27th in the number of Internet users as a share of the population (59.1 percent). In the deployment of computers and Internet use in schools, Delaware ranks 38th nationally.[129]

The Delaware Children's Internet Protection Act (title 29, chapter 66c) requires public libraries to have acceptable use policies, prohibits anonymous use of a library's computers and mandates tiered Internet access for youth under 17 years old. A parent or guardian must accompany the minor to the library to apply for a library card and must designate "no Internet access;" access only to DelAWARE Digital Library databases appropriate for grades K-5; access to all DelAWARE Digital Library databases; or full access to databases and the Internet. Only "full

---

[128] ibid
[129] The Information Technology & Innovation Foundation. 2007 State New Economy Index. http://www.itif.org/index.php?id=30

access" allows youth under 17 years old permission to use the Internet in Delaware public libraries.

Major Challenges
While the state has been supportive of technology infrastructure in libraries, technical support is still an issue. Several libraries do not dedicated IT staff and are dependent on the State Library for assistance. Many of those with support at the county library level still lack trained staff at the building level.

Developing, accessing and maintaining library Web sites also are challenges, particularly for small libraries.

Focus Group Summary
The project team conducted two focus groups at the Sussex County Department of Libraries in Georgetown. In Sussex County, there are three county libraries, plus the bookmobile. There are 11 independent libraries, which also receive funding from the county. In addition, the independent libraries also receive funding from a 1 percent tax for placement of mobile homes and a capitation tax based on a formula devised by library trustees. Some municipalities contribute utilities and other public works. The County Advisory Board also provides guidance on policy issues.

We gratefully acknowledge the assistance of Annie Norman, director and state librarian of Delaware Division of Libraries / State Library, and Carol Fitzgerald, director of the Sussex County Department of Libraries, for their time, thoughts and assistance in organizing our visit. We also would like to thank all of the librarians who participated in our focus groups. A complete list of focus group contributors can be found in Appendix F.

Expenditures and Fiscal Planning
The libraries are braced for a decline in funding, with the amount still to be determined. The mobile home tax has declined recently, and participants expressed concern that state funding may decrease due to a deficit in the transportation budget. While library use and real estate values are increasing, assessments have not changed in years and are unlikely to be increased since low property taxes are part of the area's attraction, especially to retirees. In addition, most libraries must compete with schools, roads, sewers and other growing infrastructure needs.

The amount of private fundraising varies widely. One library received a grant for a projector from a local business. Another received funds for a Little Tyke computer center. Three libraries reported receiving a significant part of their budget from private sources. One library raises about 30 percent of its budget through fundraising efforts. Two libraries conduct an Annual Appeal. Most of the boards and Friends groups are focused on raising money for new buildings.

The State Library Technology Plan calls for the replacement of all library computers every three years, and the new ILS requires up-to-date computers, so libraries must upgrade to take advantage of the statewide catalog in development. The state will fund up to 50 percent of the replacement costs as a matching grant. This year it also provided $3,000 to every library for technology training through a Library Service Technology Act (LSTA) grant for professional development.

The group agreed that county officials' understanding and support for technology has come a long way since the system first made its case for automation in the 1990s. Members of the county library's advisory board have been—and continue to be—active at the local and state levels, writing letters and meeting with legislators.

Participants agreed that getting state money for a new statewide ILS system and for computer replacement was a major achievement. All praised the leadership of the State Library and the Sussex County Department of Libraries director.

"I was in a very rural area in New York State, but we had much more technology than the libraries in Delaware, when I got here... The changes that I have seen in the last five years have been dramatic and it really shows the effort on the part of the state and county and everybody... leadership is really the key. If you have the good leadership, things will happen. But if the leadership isn't there, it can fall apart very quickly."

Meeting Patron Technology Needs for Internet Services

In all but one community (where a community college allows the public to use its facilities), the public library is the only source of free computers and Internet access. All have T-1 lines.

The most frequent computer users cited by the focus group participants are:
- Middle and high school students;
- Young adults: ages 20-30;
- Retirees (in the coastal resort communities);
- Foreign students (in coastal resort communities); and
- Men

What they use most are:
- Email;
- MySpace and online dating;
- e-Bay;
- Online games;
- Job applications (the State of Delaware has put all its job applications online);
- Taxes;
- Classes;
- Genealogy;
- Word processing and PowerPoint; and
- Databases

One library sets aside a special computer with a three-hour time limit to accommodate time-intensive uses. Two libraries proctor tests. Computer classes—everything from basic to preventative maintenance—continue to be popular.

Foreign students who work summers in the resort communities pay for a nonresident card. They use the library mainly to do email with family and friends. Retirees are heavy users in the retirement communities. They learn about databases in Lifelong Learning Classes and some do research for classes they are either taking or teaching. One library director pointed out a success story reported in her library's newsletter.

"His name was Bernie ... He'd never touched a computer in his life. He came and took some of the computer classes. He got so good that he would come in with his oxygen tank, trailing it behind him. It turned out, he had adopted a foster child, a girl in Guam, and he would show us her photos and he was so proud of her, because she graduated from nursing school there. And she would write back to him..."

Another told of a man in his fifties who had retired from the state and needed to supplement his income. He couldn't read, but the library staff helped him fill out job applications online and he ended up with a job as a night watchman that pays more than the staff member earns.

It was noted that libraries today serve both the technology "haves" and "have nots." Lines of five or six people are common. Some people get tired of waiting and leave.

The most frequently requested services:
- More computers;
- Wireless;
- Quiet area;
- Color printers;
- Scanners; and
- CD burners

Impact on Staff

"I keep trying to remind them, you know, nobody's going to die over this. We're not an ER here. But people come in, demanding what they want. And they don't want us to have to figure it out; they don't want us to have to learn it. I find it is very difficult for the staff to cope when things are constantly changing."

The directors expressed concern that customer service suffers when staff are not technologically savvy. The learning curve hasn't been easy, particularly with the speed of change. One director said that many on her staff are still uncomfortable with technology.

Finding time to spend on training can be challenging. One director said she finds it hard even to have staff meetings because so many of her employees work only part-time. (*"Even if I pay them to come in, they have other jobs or other commitments or college or whatever, and it's very hard."*) Staff turnover, especially part-timers, means there is a need for continual training and retraining. Hiring tech-savvy teenagers has been a help for some, although it was noted that Dairy Queen pays $10 an hour—more than the library.

The group had high praise for the technical staff at the county and state levels. But they also said every library should have its own full-time IT person to manage the Web site, train other staff and the public, and do day-to-day troubleshooting. They did not, however, foresee a way of funding such a position—both because of the higher pay scale for IT workers and the required benefits. Only two libraries hire outside help with technology needs on a part-time basis. It is more often the case that one staff person becomes the de facto "technology person" to troubleshoot and coordinate with the county or state library IT staff.

"I don't have to wait. I don't have to go, 'I have no idea when the computers are going to be up' ... That's the plus side. The down side is that it's extremely stressful and I don't get my other work done. So I end up putting in additional hours that I'm not getting paid to do."

Libraries serving resort communities face an additional challenge in terms of traffic, which often doubles during the summer months, and training seasonal visitors to use new systems.

"I think the worst day we had last year, we had 1,500 in one day... Every summer person that comes back this year is going to have to be retrained in how to get on the computer, and also how to release a print job. We're going to invest at least 15 minutes per person . . ."

Stress has a big impact on staff. Participants said their staffs struggle to keep up with constant upgrades, and many feel inadequate. A new integrated library system (ILS) and time management system introduced by the State Library has been greeted with great relief. But the previous system – a source of considerable frustration and stress – left many staff feeling unsure and anxious.

The bottom line is staff like technology when it's working and they feel competent. Several, especially those who work at the circulation desk, said technology has made their work faster and easier. Staff also like the new time management software that times people out automatically and allows staff to monitor behavior without a confrontation.

Advocating Support for IT Services
"So from our point of view, meeting with another person to advocate that we need more computers is simply another thing on our pile."

The directors readily admitted they could use help with advocacy.

"As a small library director, you're doing everything, and your life is consumed by your library. I have done other jobs – this is not one of the hardest, but it's one of the most challenging when it comes to consuming your life. You do everything, and you do it in order to make that library work, because you don't have enough staff to do it all."

One director said her library's best advocate is a board member who volunteers at the circulation desk because she knows what goes on in the library on a daily basis. But it also was noted that many board and Friends members lead busy lives and don't feel they have time to reach out to policymakers. If they do speak out, it is more likely to be for a new building, which has a clear needs assessment, than for technology or other ongoing operating issues. Not surprisingly, library board members who are technology users themselves are more likely to be supportive. But a director, who described her board as technology savvy, noted that they are still surprised at how quickly things change and how much it costs.

The directors said they could use help at several levels:
- Assessing their library's technology needs;
- Assessing their staff's skill levels;
- Assessing job applicant's computer skills;
- A guide to how many computers are needed;
- Facts about computers in libraries, how many people use them and how they use them;
- Training other people to be advocates; and
- Educating their boards and legislators about technology needs and the need to update equipment

One director recalled an ALA intellectual freedom kit that she said was very helpful.

"It had everything in it I needed so that I could create a program taking the least amount of time on my end."

Wrap-Up Discussion: Biggest IT Needs
If money were no object, this is what would be on the directors' list:

- Full-time IT staff
- More computers, including laptops
- Computer lab
- Bigger building to accommodate more computers
- Wireless (that is easy to administer)

Site Visits Summary
The project team visited four libraries, one serving a coastal community and three serving rural areas. All serve small (20,000 or under) but growing and increasingly diverse populations. Three of the four are the only source of free computers and Internet access in their communities. In one town, a community college offers free public access on a limited basis.

Most of the adult computer users observed are men, many of them looking for jobs or doing job-related research. Interviews with computer users found that those at the rural libraries were less likely to have Internet access at home than at the coastal library. They also were a more ethnically diverse group.

At one library, a local author comes to the library daily to work. Other users monitor National Oceanic and Atmospheric Administration weather Web cams throughout the Eastern Shore, check stock quotes and go to online dating sites.

Computer users at the coastal library included a semi-retired NASA scientist who was checking in with a colleague about a project and a young man who runs his online business from the library (*"This is faster. I have to get out of the house. I don't want to become a secluded hermit."*)

Needs
The greatest needs expressed by the rural libraries were for more space, more computers and more staffing. All three libraries are fundraising for an addition or new library building, which would then allow them to double or triple the number of computers. All three libraries have one-hour time limits per session, which can be extended for another hour if no one is waiting.

One library operates in an historic building built in 1866. Previously a church, it has served as the town's library since 1919. Not surprisingly, they've invested thousands of dollars to update electrical and wiring. About a year ago, the library installed new routers, switches and wiring. Before that, Internet access was down on a daily basis. With the recent annexation of 1,300 homes and plans for a new development bringing 2,000 more homes, the town will have grown by about 50 percent. The library currently has about 1,400 square feet and eight public access Internet workstations.

Another library in need of a new building operates out of two small rooms. Its seven computers are divided between two rooms, one of which serves as a meeting/study area. When the room is closed, three of the computers cannot be used. The server is in the staff bathroom. The other library, whose building dates from 1993, has 16 public access computers (two for children), and there are often lines after school. In addition to more space for computers, the addition would double the children's area and create quiet areas and meeting rooms. None of the rural libraries offer wireless access yet, but it is one of the most frequently requested services.

The coastal library, which opened a new building in 2001, has 30 public access computers – including ones dedicated for children's use. There is a half-hour time limit, but there are unlimited extensions if no one is waiting. There are generally only lines during the summer months. The library has wireless and the director is exploring adding laptops. If money were not an object, she would like to have an Internet cafe with all the computers grouped and a separate area for teens.

Staff members at all levels expressed concern that they are not able to help everyone who needs it—either because they don't have the time or lack technology skills. *"Short of closing the doors and not helping the public, where do you find the time to have staff training?"* one director asked. In fact, another director reported that she does close her library occasionally to offer training.

One of the rural libraries, which logs some 2,200 computer sessions a month, has a "mostly dedicated" IT person to handle updates and assist patrons. She estimated that she helps 25 people a day, but that there are more who could use assistance. One director noted, *"It's a constant learning situation. If staff doesn't enjoy it, it can be a problem."*

Part of the challenge in recruiting and retaining staff was the low pay available – as well as a lack of benefits.

In the coastal community, the library's computer use triples during the summer when vacationing families and foreign students employed for the summer come in to email, read their hometown papers and complete course work. Even with the addition of a part-time staff person, the staff is stretched to the limit.

Keeping up
Only one of the libraries has a technology plan, other than the three-year replacement plan put in place by the state. All of them rely heavily on the county or state libraries for planning, technical assistance and training. One staff member described her library's policy as, *"If it ain't broke, don't fix it."*

The coastal library only recently started offering a basic computer class. The rural libraries currently don't offer classes. One stopped when the staff member who was teaching left the library.

Advocacy
All of the library boards and Friends actively campaign in their communities for new buildings, but have not focused on technology per se. One library Friends' group has mobilized many of its 269 members to "take the library everywhere." Friends members' often serve on community event committees and collaborate with organizations ranging from the Chamber of Commerce to

the Hospital Auxiliary to the local garden club. *"It's foolish to stand alone,"* said the Friends president, who also frequently attends library legislative day. *"The more we work together, the better we are."* The library also held a legislative breakfast to raise awareness and gain support for a planned expansion.

Another library director said she believes many directors are hesitant to ask for increases or don't ask for enough—*"We'll ask the Rotary or Jaycees for $1,000, but that's not what pays the salaries."* She also said directors should be out in the community educating people about the library, but that most don't have the time.

MARYLAND CASE STUDY

Maryland public libraries benefited early from Internet access, thanks in large part to the vision of then State Librarian Maurice Travillian and the public library administrators. Building Sailor, the online public information network, residents had dial-in access to the Internet as early as 1995 through each public library in the state. The network also supports state government and K-12 education (http://www.sailor.lib.md.us/sailor/). This network quickly expanded both in number of access points and in bandwidth, and now provides high-speed access to the Internet.

Many of the librarians interviewed in Maryland describe their state as *"Library Heaven."* The network of 24 library systems allows all library directors to *"be in one room,"* and they maintain a proud tradition of working together on cooperative initiatives. The State Library has provided strong leadership, and state funding for libraries also is strong. The library community has worked together effectively on recent funding increases.

Despite strong state funding, local funding continues to be a challenge, but most libraries reported they were "holding their own." Internet services are highly utilized for job searches and applications, social networking and email, homework, e-government, online education and downloadable media.

The libraries' greatest needs are for more dedicated IT staff, increased bandwidth, space for more computers, and videoconferencing to improve staff training. There also is growing interest in research and development to stay ahead of the curve and continue to lead. Even in *"Library Heaven"* there is no room for complacency.

Governance and Statistical Information

Maryland has 24 library systems organized by 23 counties and the city of Baltimore. There also are three regional library systems and a State Library Resource Center that provide support to libraries in the state. There are 179 physical library buildings and 11 bookmobiles serving more than 5.4 million residents in fiscal year 2004.[130]

In 2004, Maryland public libraries reported serving more than 27.7 million visitors, answering nearly 7.3 million reference questions and circulating nearly 50.8 million items (books, films, sound recordings, audio books, etc.). Maryland public libraries borrowed or loaned an additional 280,000 items on behalf of residents, who are served by 3,200 library employees. Of these employees, 634 hold master's degrees in Library and Information Science (MLIS) and another

---

[130] National Center for Education Statistics. Public Libraries in the United States: Fiscal Year 2004. (NCES 2006-349). Washington, DC: NCES, 2006. http://www.nces.ed.gov/pubs2006/2006349.pdf

1,219 have been trained as librarians but do not hold a master's degree. Maryland is unique in offering a Library Associate Training Institute, which is a 12-week training program that also requires 90 hours of in-service training to become certified by the state. Library associates are enrolled by their employers.

Maryland public libraries rank first in the number of public-use Internet computers per building (16.79), as compared with public libraries in other states.[131] The national average is 10.32.

Funding Summary

Sixty-nine point seven percent (69.7 percent) of Maryland's public library funding comes from local sources (tax dollars), 13.3 percent from state sources, 16 percent from other sources (private fundraising, gifts, bequeathals, etc.), and less than 1 percent (.9 percent) from federal sources. Maryland public libraries rank 15th in total operating revenue support – 4th in state revenue support, 22nd in local revenue support, and 7th in other forms of revenue support.

Sixty-nine point seven (69.7 percent) of operating expenditures go toward staff costs (salaries, benefits, retirement), 15 percent toward purchasing collections, and 15.3 percent for other things, such as programming, building maintenance and utilities, and computer hardware and software. Maryland ranks 15th nationally in overall operating expenditures – eighth in collections expenditures, and 13th in staffing expenditures.

Maryland public libraries reported in the *Public Libraries and the Internet 2007* survey that of those receiving E-rate discounts, telecommunications services (100 percent) and Internet connectivity (37.9 percent) were the two most commonly funded discount categories. The majority of technology expenses in both fiscal year 2006 and 2007 were paid from local and state revenue sources, but fees/fines and donations and local fund raising were significant contributors to supporting technology purchases.

In fiscal year 2004, Maryland public libraries spent more than $29.7 million on capital expenditures (building repairs, renovations, or new buildings), ranking 15th nationally.

The Information Technology and Innovation Foundation *2007 State New Economy Index* ranked Maryland third in the United States based on 26 indicators in the following five categories: knowledge jobs, globalization, economic dynamism, transformation to a digital economy, and technological innovation capacity.[2] Driving much of Maryland's high ranking is broadband deployment, availability of high-tech jobs and workforce education, IT professionals, managerial, professional and technical jobs, and scientists and engineers (a result of the expansion of federal research agencies locating in Maryland).

A strong economy and advocacy from the library community has translated into increased state funding for public libraries in recent years. The Maryland Library Association was successful in 2006 in securing a three-year per-capita state aid increase of $1 per year.[132] This legislative change positively impacted the expenditure capacity of Maryland public libraries. Per-capita

---

[131] ibid

[132] Maryland Public Library Survey: Customer Survey of Maryland Residents about Libraries. FINAL REPORT (November 1, 2004). Prepared by Potomac Incorporated for The Southern Maryland Regional Library and the Division of Library Development and Services, Maryland State Department of Education. http://www.maplaonline.org/dlds/adobe/survey03.pdf

expenditures rose from $36.30 in fiscal year 2004 to $37.48 in fiscal year 2005. This incremental increase will continue through fiscal year 2010.

While state funding for libraries was on the rise, most focus group participants expected flat funding for the coming year from county and other local sources. One county library director was asked to submit a flat budget and a budget with a 10 percent reduction, which would mean the loss of a branch library. Another director expected an increase, which has been the case for the past several years.

Connectivity Summary

It's not possible to talk about connectivity in Maryland without talking about Sailor, the statewide network that was conceived in 1989. Working cooperatively and pooling federal grant money, Maryland libraries established themselves as pioneers in providing Internet access in libraries, as well as to government agencies and schools. Planning for what would become the network began in 1989, and it continues to have a lasting impact.

Bertot and McClure reported in their 1996 assessment of the Sailor project that "The goal to provide free, local, and instant access to electronic networked information resources pushed Maryland to the forefront of public librarianship. Through creativity, DLDS (Division of Library Development and Services)-public library collaboration, and an entrepreneurial spirit, Maryland is now in a position that far exceeds the current state of the nation in terms of Internet connectivity. Indeed, while the rest of the nation's public libraries contend with issues of establishing Internet connections, Maryland, through the Sailor network, is entering a new era of electronic content and service development. This will once again place Maryland on the frontier of statewide electronic networking."[133]

Not only did Sailor put librarians in the driver's seat for technology access in Maryland, it also continues to be cost-saver for libraries and their users. *"Without Sailor, we'd be individually out there trying to acquire broadband at God knows what cost,"* according to one library director.

In addition to the Sailor backbone, individual public libraries in Maryland provide high-speed connectivity, with the state library reporting more than 90 percent of its libraries operating with such access. Specifically, 45.9 percent support at T1 levels, and 49 percent at 6 mbps or greater. Further, the state library feels there are few, if any, barriers to high-speed connectivity.

Wireless connectivity was available in 54.7 percent of Maryland's public libraries, and it was anticipated that another 35.2 percent would add access in the coming year. Although high-speed connectivity is prevalent, a number of libraries reported sharing bandwidth to support wireless access (77.8 percent). This has caused some libraries to split connectivity between Sailor connections and locally supported connections.

The state of Maryland ranks 10th in the number of Internet users as a share of total population at 65.1 percent, compared to 58.7 percent nationwide, but is 46th in the deployment of computers and Internet use in schools.[134]

---

[133] Bertot, John Carlo, Charles R. McClure, and Suzanne Eastham. Sailor Network Assessment Final Report: Findings and Future Sailor Network Development (1996), p.3.
http://eric.ed.gov/ERICDocs/data/ericdocs2/content_storage_01/0000000b/80/23/c0/00.pdf
[134] The Information Technology & Innovation Foundation. 2007 State New Economy Index.
http://www.itif.org/index.php?id=30

Major Challenges

The high-speed pipe simply isn't large enough. Concerns expressed by public library administrators, staff and trustees, as well as the public, all point to the need for faster connection speeds. One library, for example, has blocked the annual college basketball "March Madness" playoffs because it crashed the library's network more than once. Perhaps because Maryland libraries are relatively well-funded and provide rich online content, they are the victims of their own success as downloadable and streaming audio and video – often purchased and provided by libraries – gobble up bandwidth.

Some library administrators need guidance on developing compelling talking points with which to approach county government and external funding organizations to fund libraries and provide support for training and outreach. This was especially true in the smaller, less affluent and more rural of Maryland counties.

Focus Group Summary

The project team conducted two focus groups in Maryland, one in person in Howard County on April 4, 2007, and one by conference call on April 17. Staff from five libraries participated on April 4, and staff from four libraries participated on April 17. We gratefully acknowledge the assistance of state librarian Irene Padilla in helping organize our visit, to Brian Auger and Howard County Library staff for hosting us, and to all of the librarians who participated in our focus groups. A complete list of focus group contributors can be found in Appendix G.

Expenditures and Fiscal Planning

All of the focus group participants mentioned the increased state funding, which is available to local jurisdictions through a formula based on the population and wealth of the county. On average, the state contributes about 15 percent to public library budgets – although this can range from libraries receiving about 40 percent from the state to those receiving about 10 percent.

Most of the focus group participants expected flat local funding for the coming fiscal year, although one county director expected an increase, and another said she was asked to submit a flat budget, as well as a budget reflecting a 10 percent cut.

"The county doesn't have a lot of money. So, when it comes to fixing a bridge or funding a library, it's hard to be out there in front," said one director in a mostly rural county.

Because of the Sailor project, no public libraries reported needing to pay for Internet connectivity. If they no longer participated in Sailor, they had worked to create another network system in concert with other government agencies. Most databases also were funded through the state or regional library systems.

Several focus group participants also said that Sailor and the fact that Maryland public libraries were or are Internet service providers (ISPs) means they have more credibility when they request funding for technology initiatives. Librarians have been leaders in providing Internet access not only within their walls, but also for other public agencies, schools and home users.

"The attitude from county managers is: 'If they say they need it, we'd better pay attention.'"

Meeting Patron Technology Needs for Internet Services
The Internet services available and highly utilized ranged widely, but participants reported that the most frequent uses included:
- Searching or applying online for jobs;
- MySpace;
- Homework help, including tutor.com and use of databases;
- Online education;
- Downloadable media (e-books, audio, video); and
- Email

"It (computer use) has grown tremendously, and not only because of MySpace, but we're also finding that more and more people don't want to have to deal with all the spamming, firewall and technical issues required to run a home network."

Also mentioned were: e-government services, chat, online banking and bill payment.

"We're seeing a steep increase in accessing government forms online."

Time limits of 30 or 60 minutes were the norm for most libraries in the focus groups.

"It's not only the space and number of computers – it's the time. We have some people who want to stay on there all day, and right now, we're just saying one hour. We're building all of these expectations."

Most of the focus group participants also offered computer classes for library users. These classes are in high demand, but one library recently discontinued the classes due to staffing limitations. Another library is dealing with class waiting lists by digitally videotaping introductory computer and Internet workshops and putting them online. When classes fill up, people have the option of taking the class online

"We could probably fill three times as many classes as we can afford to offer."

There also was a discussion of how technology has improved traditional library services. *"Our world is revolutionized. Reference is so much easier.... We now provide more services, but books don't give us the same kind of problems."*

The top technology requests also varied widely from library to library, including:
- Videoconferencing to improve staff training;
- Increased bandwidth to accommodate the growing demand for downloadable media;
- More physical space and better configurations for additional computers; and
- Additional support for digitization efforts

Impact on Staff
At the top of most focus group participants' wish list was a desire for more dedicated IT staff. Several county libraries reported they have only one dedicated staff person for all their branches. *"We have well over 100 computers and just the one guy,"* reported a Maryland library director.

Another library director with only one IT staff person was appreciative of the support he received from county IT staff, as well as from the regional library system and Sailor network staff. Other directors also emphasized the vital role played by the regional library systems.

Larger and better funded libraries also were adding IT staff or hoped to add them in the future. One county just received funding for a manager of a "virtual branch." The library also had dedicated IT support staff to help patrons with troubleshooting and technology questions.

"You almost need two levels of IT staff. How do we push to the next level while keeping things running on the floor?"

The difficulty of keeping up with new technology offerings, patron demand and staff training was mentioned by several focus group participants. One library has found success with "just-in-time" staff training via the library's intranet. Trainings are videotaped, and then cut into two-minute segments that can be watched online as needed. The ability and vision to offer cutting-edge services, while minimizing costs and maintenance, was a consistent concern. Other staff impacts included turning Internet filters on and off, and troubleshooting equipment.

Technology like computer reservation software and self-checkout is freeing staff for more one-on-one interaction, but the demands of library patrons continue to grow.

"Technology is a great leveler between small- and large-sized libraries, but there is a growing sense of unease about there being so much more that I don't know."

Advocating Support for IT Services
While most focus group participants felt they didn't need to "sell" technology in libraries, they shared many experiences about how they had successfully built and maintained relationships with elected officials and community leaders.

> A recent TV news story highlighted a library's community database and how it was being used by emergency management staff. The reporter interviewed emergency staff who used the database when they were responding to 911 calls and realized they needed to refer people for support services from other community agencies. The library is now upgrading the services with a $40,000 grant from the county Human Services Council. *"If we try to position the library as a critical agency in the county, I can't think of something that's more critical than the emergency responders out there using your database."* The library also has worked with county IT staff to develop point-to-point wireless access that serves library patrons and local police in their squad cars.

> *"In terms of my budget pitch, the library was always thought of as a 9-to-5 operation, but I can clearly walk in there and give them the calendar of the week and say, 'This is our 24 hour, seven day a week cycle of activity, and you know, we're seeing over 1600 people a day.' And I challenge any county commissioner to find another county agency that serves that many people a day – walk-in, as well as virtual users of all the resources that we have."*

> Another director said she treats other county departments as library customers. *"What are you doing? How can we help? What kind of partnership can we form? We bring them*

over and show them how what we're doing impacts what they're doing. They see the relevancy of our programs and services. We're in their face." Library staff members are involved with other city and county initiatives, such as the Sister City program. The library also involved County Council members in the library's strategic planning process.

Library directors also encouraged library board members to use Internet resources available through the library Web site, including tutor.com and an online story time program. The trustees' positive experiences made them more effective advocates for the library's electronic services. Librarians also shared statewide polls and research with key decision-makers.

The unity of the Maryland library community was largely credited for the unanimous passage of dedicated state funding for library operating budgets.

Wrap-Up Discussion: Biggest IT Needs
Several participants in the Maryland focus groups focused on the future. Topics ranged from disappointment with current integrated library systems (ILS) and the need for a better, library-responsive ILS to expressing the need for library technology research and development (R&D) departments, to envisioning attractive, edutainment software – *"so that we can get a lot more kids using the services, but at the same time, improving their skill sets so there is positive impact when they are in school."* There was strong agreement that it is difficult to balance the daily maintenance of technology with planning for the future.

"You have to be nimble and pay attention."

Site Visits Summary
The project team also met and talked with library staff members and patrons at six libraries. A list of sites visited can be found in Appendix G.

Expenditures and Fiscal Planning
Local funding holds steady: Most libraries visited enjoy good relationships with county funding agencies. Even in an area where home sales were down, the library reported a small funding increase last year – larger than most other local government agencies. Still, though, the library was a relative bargain – comprising less than 1 percent of the overall county budget for most libraries visited.

Meeting Patron Technology Needs for Internet Services
Keeping up is the major challenge: The greatest needs voiced in our interviews were for more computers and faster speeds. For some libraries the greatest limitation was the amount of bandwidth available. One library staff person described waiting several minutes for a Web page to load during peak hours. For another library, it was the age of the computers. *"The county has a beltway (fiber), but we are traveling on bicycles (computers more than five years old)."* Fifty percent of the library's computers are more than six years old.

Another library staff member proudly described the system's six-year-old computers, powered with open-source software ranging from Open Office to Groovix. The library does not have a replacement schedule for its computers now because they are not tied to a particular operating system. On the flip side, another library uses open-source software as a last-resort because its software licenses have expired. Both libraries agreed patrons as a group are not familiar with open-source software and often prefer commercial software similar to what they use at home, work or school.

Libraries tackle time limits: Most libraries reported time limits of 45 minutes or an hour. One library reported that there is some wait time (ranging from 15 to 60 minutes) much of the day. While most libraries had moved to time management systems, one library system was successfully using the "honor system" when its computers reached capacity – usually in the after-school hours and on weekends. A public announcement would be made asking patrons to wrap up what they were doing and relinquish computers if they had been on for a while. The staffer said the system worked well and saved the library the expense of installing time and print management systems. Printing costs also were voluntary – with the library allowing five free pages and then requesting 10 cents per page.

Other library staff reported that the time management software was a boon in relieving staff from the duty to ask patrons to give up their computers at a set time. *"Managing time limits was our staff's biggest complaint,"* one director reported.

Several libraries also worked to ease time pressures with "express" Internet workstations that allowed patrons online access for a limited time – usually 15 minutes – which would allow them to avoid lines for quick tasks like checking email or printing a boarding pass.

Wireless a priority: For libraries not yet offering wireless access, it was the top patron request. Libraries offering wireless reported frequent use – and requests for more power outlets. One student at Georgetown Law School uses the library's wireless access twice a week to write papers and check email. A tutor at another library uses the wireless access daily with his high school and college students. Several libraries noted they segregate the networks for staff and patron wireless access to improve security and bandwidth. One librarian called wireless a "win-win" because it transfers hardware maintenance costs to the users, and it gives users more flexibility.

Top uses: Staff and patrons reported social networking – including MySpace, Flickr and BlackPlanet – is one of the top uses of library computers and Internet access. One mother of two reported that she uses MySpace to participate in an online journal with her siblings – including several living overseas. One of the libraries visited, however, blocks MySpace because it crashes the computers. Other high-volume uses included: email, job searching and applications, gaming, and homework resources.

Of interest and note is a 2005 survey Baltimore County Public Library conducted of its in-library computer users over four days. Email and general Internet browsing were the top uses reported, although popular activities varied significantly by age range. Younger users (under 21) were more likely to play games, do homework or participate in online chat. Users ages 22-39 were the most likely to look for and apply for jobs. Users were more likely to e-mail the older they were.[135]

---

[135] Waxter, Susan. "Baltimore County Public Library Computer Users' Survey." *Public Libraries*, November/December 2006.

Impact on Staff

More tech support, please: Library staff visited echoed the request for more IT support heard from the focus groups. Library staff reported they do not receive tech support from the county IT staff, although staff reported networking with school and community college IT staff formally or informally. One library added two IT staff last year and plans to add a Web content manager this year. Most of the libraries offered classes for their users

Advocating Support for IT Services

Reputation is key: One reported key to sustained funding is the reputation library staff have built with county leaders. *"We have a fabulous reputation. Our budget is distributed as a model. Librarians are ahead of others in planning,"* one director said. The library ties its budget priorities to county goals. One library schedules library orientations for all new county council members while another library highlighted its outreach to schools and the Board of Education.

Overall, library staff also reported trustees are not actively engaged as advocates or community liaisons on behalf of the libraries' technology services. While the boards and Friends groups are supportive and can be mobilized as needed, it was rare to have a sustained outreach effort on the part of board members in the community.

NEVADA CASE STUDY

The population of Nevada has been growing steadily for at least a decade. U.S. Census Bureau data reports a 24.9 percent increase in population between April 2000 and July 2006, as compared to a 6.4 percent increase nationwide. In some communities, the legal service area of the public library has more than doubled in less than five years. However, there has not been a corresponding growth in the number of library capital projects or library funding. Most libraries are reporting that their community use is at or near capacity.

Local economies have not kept pace with the increasing demand for more sophisticated technology. As in Jackson County, Oregon, where the timber industry is gone and has not been replaced by another economy that provides ongoing stability for local government (and libraries), Nevada deals with similar issues where the mining industry is no longer viable. Nevada libraries suffer when markets for cyclical goods or services (minerals, tourism) are weak.

Overall, funding is a problem for county libraries, and even those with independent taxing districts. Tax caps mean population growth doesn't pay for itself. Nevada only taxes on 35 percent of a property's value (if $100,000 home, the tax is only on $35,000 of the home's value). The cap on property taxes does not apply to new properties in the first year. On top of this, the state legislature has capped recurring revenue from assessments so that it can be no more than 3 percent per year for residential property or 8 percent for commercial property. Libraries are hurt disproportionately by tax caps because their services are free (unlike other agencies that may charge fees for services).

The top concerns limiting optimal access to computing and the Internet include:
- Constrained space;
- Limited staffing, especially in rural libraries, where this also impacts the ability to offer computer training and maintain open hours for library use; and

- Lack of dedicated IT staff: Libraries without dedicated IT staff struggle to adequately support aging hardware; and

Rural libraries are the *only* free site of public access computing in their communities, and can also offer higher access speeds, as compared with those available to most residential users. All rural libraries have sign-up sheets, with waiting lists at some point in the day – even with time limits set for as little as 30 minutes.

Waits are common during peak periods in all Nevada public libraries, whether located in urban, suburban or rural areas. Although wireless and high-speed wired access is readily available in urban locations, the demand for these Internet services frequently outpaces supply. Urban libraries offer time limits for public access computers that range from 60 to 90 minutes, with two hour sessions allowed in computer labs.

Although the libraries in Clark County benefit from dedicated property tax funds, they also report difficulties in obtaining needed capital funds for new construction. In addition to the state licensed databases and downloadable audio, the larger libraries provide downloadable video and interactive homework help.

Governance and Statistical Information

Nevada has 22 public library systems with 85 physical library locations and four bookmobiles to serve its more than 2.5 million residents. Nevada's public libraries are organized primarily as county library systems (50 percent), and library districts (40.9 percent).[136] The rest are organized as municipal and multi-jurisdictional libraries (9.1 percent). Public libraries located in remote areas are often in shared facilities with limited space for public access stations.

In fiscal year 2004 (the most recent year for which national statistics are available), Nevada public libraries reported serving more than 9.9 million visitors; answering nearly 1.6 million reference questions; and circulating more than 14.9 million items (e.g., books; films; sound recordings; audiobooks). Nevada public libraries borrowed or loaned an additional 60,000 items through interlibrary loan on behalf of its residents, who are served by 828 library employees. Of these employees, 160 hold a Master's degree in Library and Information Science (MLIS), and 63 work as librarians, but do not hold a master's degree.

Nevada public libraries ranks 18th in the number of public-use Internet computers per building (11.06), as compared with public libraries in other states.[137]

The size of Nevada's public library buildings range considerably in square footage. Interestingly, library service areas of 10,000 to 24,999 residents have larger libraries than do those serving 25,000 to 49,999 residents. A similar pattern is observed with even larger service areas, attributed to the availability of more branch library outlets in larger service areas, whereas smaller communities may have only one main library building. For communities serving fewer than 5,000 residents, square footage ranges from 2,764 to 6,049.

---

[136] National Center for Education Statistics. Public Libraries in the United States: Fiscal Year 2004. (NCES 2006-349). Washington, DC: NCES, 2006. http://www.nces.ed.gov/pubs2006/2006349.pdf
[137] ibid

Funding Summary

Seventy percent of Nevada's public library funding comes from local sources (tax dollars). The balance comes from other sources (25.1 percent), such as private fundraising, gifts, bequests, fines, and fees; state sources (3.2 percent); and federal sources (1.3 percent)

Nationally, Nevada ranks 22nd in total operating revenue support; 26th in state support; 33rd in local support; and 3rd in "other." The fact that Nevada public libraries rely so heavily on non-tax support is important to consider in order to understanding the state's overall capacity to provide services, especially technology-related services. The national average for non-tax support is $2.59 per capita, but in Nevada it is $7.50. Only Rhode Island ($7.65 per capita) and New York ($7.70) have higher per capita non-tax revenue. Nevada libraries rely significantly on grant funds or sponsorships to underwrite library improvements and launch new initiatives.

Nationally, Nevada ranks 28th in total operating expenditures ($27.13 spent per capita); 29th in staffing; and 14th in size of collections. In Nevada, the largest percentage (65.6 percent) of operating expenditures are used for staff costs (salaries, benefits, retirement), with 17.5 percent spent on collections, and the remaining 16.9 percent for other things, such as programming, building maintenance and utilities, computer hardware, and software.

Nevada public libraries reported in the *Public Libraries and the Internet 2007* survey that of those receiving E-rate discounts, telecommunications services (100 percent) and Internet connectivity (35.7 percent) were the two most commonly funded discount categories. The majority of technology expenses in both fiscal year 2006 and 2007 were paid from local revenue sources.

When it comes to capital expenditures, only four states spent less (Hawaii, North and South Dakota, and Wyoming). About 36 percent of Nevada public libraries (roughly 38 branches) benefited from $1,075,000 in capital expenditures (e.g., building repairs; renovations; new buildings). Approximately 11 branch libraries made minor repairs (paint, etc.) costing under $5,000. Only nine of Nevada's public libraries reported spending more than $50,000 on capital improvements (possibly for major repairs and renovations). In 2005, North Las Vegas built a new branch library that cost about $5 million, on donated land.

During the focus groups and site visits used to develop this profile, rural library directors projected flat funding at best for the coming fiscal year; several directors anticipate budget and staffing cuts. Urban library directors, mainly in the Clark County area with tax districts, stated that they expect to see continued funding growth as a result of new construction. Library directors and several library trustees and community members noted what *Governing Magazine* in 2003 called "a deeply rooted anti-tax ethos in the state."

Connectivity Summary

Of Nevada's 22 public library systems, 14 jurisdictions are members of the Cooperative Libraries Automated Network (CLAN), which provides a shared library application system, telecommunications network, and Internet-delivered catalogs, indexes and databases. The remaining 8 public libraries systems (Washoe; Las Vegas-Clark County; Henderson; North Las Vegas; Boulder City; Pahrump; Smoky Valley; and Amargosa) manage their own autonomous internal systems.

The Nevada State Library estimates that the majority of the state's public libraries (90 percent) are on broadband connections (not dial-up), although not necessarily with high-speed or dedicated access. However, of the 85 physical public library locations, six are limited to dial-up access.

Like other states, Nevada supports multiple telecommunication networks, and the infrastructure in some parts of the state is not as robust as it could be. Much of the state is sparsely populated, and the telecommunications infrastructure in Nevada reflects that reality. Unless there is a reason to develop an infrastructure in parts of the state without the population to support it, change will happen slowly.

Forty-two-point-seven (42.7) percent of Nevada's libraries reported access speeds of 6mbps or higher. Another 35.9 percent support public access computing at 768kbps-1.5mbps, and 21.5 percent at speeds below 768kbps.

Wireless connectivity was available in 28.6 percent of Nevada's public libraries, and it was anticipated that another 18 percent would add access in the coming year. Speeds of access may be impacted for some libraries that share bandwidth with existing public access computers (54.7 percent) despite reasonably strong connectivity access speeds available to Nevada's public libraries.

According to the 2007 State New Economy Index, Nevada ranks 40th in the number of Internet users as a share of the population at 55.6 percent, compared to 73 percent nationwide. The state ranks next to last in the deployment of computers and Internet use in schools, followed only by Utah.[138] While Nevada ranks fifth in the nation in the deployment of residential and business broadband lines, public libraries in some parts of the state are not served by commercial providers of broadband services or cannot afford the high implementation costs. The State Library considers six public libraries to be "vulnerable."

Major Challenges
Most of the significant obstacles to increased access to computers and the Internet are rooted in limited local funding. Most rural library buildings are at least 12 years old and predate the need for computer wiring and workstations. Even in libraries willing to be open with only one staff person on duty, directors of small libraries expressed that hours were limited due to staffing shortages. One small library reported dozens waiting in line for the library to open at 10 a.m. on weekdays.

The lack of IT support also was named a consistent issue impacting public computer access. All CLAN libraries are able to use the cooperative's staff resources for help, in addition to their counties' IT staff. However, those seeking help from their county frequently report finding themselves at the bottom of the service priorities – particularly if the county only has one IT person to provide IT service to all departments and agencies. Several libraries devote part of a library staff person's time to supporting and troubleshooting IT; most staff have learned how to manage routine problems while on the job.

---

[138] The Information Technology & Innovation Foundation. 2007 State New Economy Index. http://www.itif.org/index.php?id=30

Focus Group Summary

The project team conducted a focus group among all the attendees of a regularly scheduled CLAN Board meeting in Winnemucca on March 8, 2007. We gratefully acknowledge the assistance of CLAN director Dana Hines and the Nevada State Library & Archives in coordinating our visit and would like to thank the CLAN members for allowing us to take a large part of their board meeting agenda. A complete list of focus group participants can be found in Appendix H.

Expenditures and Fiscal Planning

Overall, participants anticipate flat budgets, at best, for the coming fiscal year. Three participants expected budget cuts in the coming fiscal year. Most county budgets were still in development and due in May 2007. All attending libraries are funded through a sales and/or room tax; none of the participants derive revenue from separate taxing districts.

Participants referred several times to the fact that libraries are not a mandated county service, per Nevada Revised Statutes. In part for this reason, they feel libraries consistently rank at the bottom of priorities for their county/local governments – particularly as compared with public safety agencies.

One director noted that one of her county commissioners didn't support the library and its technology until he was in the library and saw the use—particularly among Hispanic children. She has moved the copy machine to the back of the library to ensure that county commissioners make their way through the entire library. Participants also agree that the perception that libraries provide pornography is a real problem for obtaining funding for technology in libraries.

A single funding success was reported by the group: writing grants for technology, along with carpeting, electric and other capital improvements. One participant stressed the importance of sharing personal stories to make the case for libraries. Her story featured two women with infants who were using the library to complete their degrees online. She used this anecdote in grant applications, a newspaper story, and word of mouth.

Meeting Patron Technology Needs for Internet Services

Participants reported the most frequent uses of library computers are:
- Email;
- Google;
- Printing boarding passes for air travel;
- Online banking;
- E-government (particularly tax forms and immigration documents);
- Downloadable audiobooks; and
- Continuing education.

One participant highlighted the fact that Nevada personnel forms now are available only online. *"This is true for a lot of job application forms now."* People also take job tests online.

The top technology requests are:
- Wireless access;
- Downloadable media; and
- Genealogy databases.

The top priority with any additional funding is for new or expanded buildings, followed by dedicated IT staff at the building level.

One participant said: *"I would do more of everything I'm already doing."* Her priorities are a bigger server and triple the bandwidth.

Other expressed needs included:
- Flash drives;
- Time management software; and
- Dedicated space for computer labs.

Less than half of the libraries offer formal technology training; most is done one-on-one. Several participants reported inadequate staffing levels and too few computers to offer training. At least one library mentioned using volunteers to do public training; another participant commented that demand for training was decreasing at her library.

Impact on Staff

Overall, most participants stated that the biggest impact of technology on library staff was managing time limits. All libraries reported 30-minute or one-hour time limits as the norm, with waits for computers common. One library reported that it had previously used time management software, but stopped because users were losing documents when the time limit was reached. Another said that the time management software was important for the library, as it was often 'ugly' to get people to relinquish the computers they were using.

Most participants reported they are dependent on county IT staff for technical support that is woefully inadequate. *"If we could get away from some of the junk (outdated equipment) we have in the library, the IT person would be less busy."*

Libraries also depend on CLAN for technology support or hired an outside company. A couple of libraries dedicate part of their library staff time to technology support.

Advocating Support for IT Services

"We don't promote the computers. It's just expected."

Most participants mentioned they had done some initial promotion of technology when computers were first introduced, but now it's mostly handled through word of mouth. One participant mentioned that DSL only recently became available residentially. Nearly all reported they were the sole providers of free public access to the Internet, and even home computer users come to the library for faster Internet access. There was overall agreement that more promotion could overwhelm library capacity, which already is stretched thin.

All libraries reported having Friends groups. Most participants reported they do not have strong local government support. *"They want you to have the best and the fastest, but they don't want to pay for it."* Library boards are helpful, but libraries can't compete with public safety concerns at budget meetings. *"The sheriff is threatening that people will die without more funds, while the library can only promote the positive."*

Participants provided some examples of how they are engaging the local community to improve support. One library leverages performance opportunities for other community organizations.

When the library brings in a performance group, the director asks them to add an additional performance at a local nursing home for a small fee. *"The library needs to become the giver, not just with its hand out."*

Another participant mentioned its sponsorship of an oral history project, as well as a photography competition and exhibition that now contributes more than $300,000 to the local economy. Another participant sponsors a high school art show, which help brings people into the library. *"The library is a common ground – a neutral ground."*

Wrap-Up Discussion: Biggest IT Needs
When asked to identify their community's biggest IT needs, requests for more staff, more space, and more hours re-emerged. A specific challenge mentioned is that rural communities need more bandwidth at affordable rates. *"During telecom deregulation, providers made a lot of promises, but Congress has never held them accountable."*

Other challenges include: the need for librarian recruitment, as many of the participants are nearing retirement; and increased support for school librarians and information literacy efforts. Many shared the concern that children are coming to the public library without critical research skills.

Site Visits Summary
The project team visited several libraries, serving populations ranging from roughly 2,000 to 478,000 residents, meeting with library staff members, library patrons, trustees and city leaders representing 14 libraries.

The following findings, summarized by broad themes, emerged during site visits and focus group discussions:

Expenditures and Fiscal Planning
Funding is not keeping pace with increased use: Although library use (visits and computer session) is increasing, there has not been a corresponding growth in funding for county libraries. In fact, library directors in county libraries and community leaders agreed almost verbatim that libraries are at or near the bottom of funding priorities, particularly when competing with public safety and roads/transportation.

"I fear for parks and recreation and for libraries. Sales taxes are down. Libraries are not a mandated service. Libraries compete for the same funds as emergency services. They are on the bottom of the food chain," one city manager said. In fact, the city technology director characterized the library's equipment as "aged and antiquated." The city planned to install a new server, new computers, and new security this year.

The fiscal climate for libraries with dedicated taxing districts is more positive, as funds from property taxes increase with population growth. Many of these directors, however, shared their rural colleagues' experience of anti-tax voters. Ballot measures to support capital funding for new building projects have been largely unsuccessful at the same time that all service indicators are on the rise. Property tax caps also have limited library growth, reducing revenue by $8 million in capital funding, according to one director's estimate.

Despite constraints on consistent and sustainability local funding, library staff continues to fundraise and collaborate to meet increased demands. One public library recently began offering wireless access after receivers were donated by the library's active computer user group. A local computer store owner provided system set-up, and a commercial provider offered free bandwidth. At another library, the board funded wireless access when the city balked in offering the service.

Another library director recently secured corporate sponsorship to underwrite online reference services and live homework help offered by the library. This library also has a Friends group that raises about $70,000 per year, holds an annual fundraising event, and has recently started a foundation to focus more on fundraising and planned giving.

Meeting Patron Technology Needs for Internet Services

Public libraries are the only sites of free public access computing: All have sign-up sheets or electronic reservation systems for computer usage, and all have waits during some point in the day, even with time limits as few as 30 minutes. Library computer usage has grown greatly in the past two years. For example, one library's computer usage grew to 11,999 in 2006 from 9,577 the previous year—this in a town with a population of only 7,700.

Libraries and Internet-use computers are being used at or near capacity on a daily basis: At many locations, staff reported a line of patrons seeking Internet access waiting for the library to open, especially on Mondays. The peak computer usage time for most libraries is after school from 2 p.m. until closing. Weekends also are busy during most times of the day. Library staff members encourage adults to visit the libraries in the morning to ensure the maximum access to computer time.

Impact on Staff

Online job searching; all types of applications increasing: Interviews with library staff and users confirmed that the leading uses of library computers and Internet access are: email; job searching and applications; research; and "life maintenance" (e.g., online banking; printing boarding passes; using social networks like MySpace; and gaming). Las Vegas-area libraries particularly emphasized the growth in online job applications, which require many people to use computers for the first time, establish email accounts and check back frequently on job prospects. Several staff members noted the difficulty of completing this task in one hour and the heavy impact on front-line staff in assisting patrons one-on-one. *"Online job applications are a killer."*

One library staff person reported: *"The biggest change in tech services is that the computers have gone from toy to tool, especially for adults looking for jobs."* The library helps job seekers fax resumes, use job resources and navigate e-government sites. Members of the community are frequently referred to the library from other community agencies. Increase use of e-government services also was cited by several staff members. For example, the Immigration and Naturalization Service (INS) requires that people go online to make an appointment to meet with agency staff.

Libraries offer more than access: While most libraries grouped public access computers together, one library also located two staff computers in the area. Library staff reported they were better able to notice a patron struggling online and library users were more likely to ask for help. Computers are always staffed with at least one person.

Accessing and printing job and government forms (e.g., birth records; death certificates; Department of Motor Vehicle forms; and state income tax forms) is a frequent use. *"People are overwhelmed. Computers aren't just in libraries for people to find information on their own. Having staff nearby is critical."* The library's T1 access also was cited as a draw for library users – including those with Internet access at home. One branch manager noted, *"People don't have IT staffs at home."* The leading requests for technology were for wireless, more computers and faster access speeds.

Advocating Support for IT Services

Relationships are key: One library trustee regularly attends Chamber of Commerce and City Council meetings to update them on library activities. He began networking with a new business that had moved into the library's service area, inviting them to conduct job interviews in a library meeting room installed with free wireless access. The company is now a library donor.

One director commented, "I can only do so much. I need the Chamber (of Commerce) to be advocates. Libraries shouldn't be positioned as charity – then you're treated like a second-class citizen. What we do is important – it's not trivial or entertainment, it's lifelong learning." The library has actively participated in true partnerships, those in which the library is able to contribute to its strengths – such as community programming, meeting space or online homework help – in return for community support and funding.

In addition to collaborations with community businesses, several libraries are looking to develop relationships with school districts. *"School administrators now have a greater stake in kids passing – which is an opportunity for libraries. Homework help needs to actively support curriculum, not just term paper support."* The library is buying textbooks and creating homework help centers for students.

Another key advocacy relationship is the collaborative way in which the libraries relate to one another. The rural library branches in the Las Vegas Clark County District, despite small building sizes, are able to rotate their collections and benefit from the IT staff expertise of system staff. This relationship allows the library to be more responsive to the local community, and provides far greater offerings than the local economy could otherwise support. Several members of CLAN also highlighted the importance of this cooperative relationship in providing technology connectivity and a shared catalog.

UTAH CASE STUDY

The public libraries in Utah range from the beautiful and bustling new Salt Lake City Public Library to the also bustling rural library with a "No Internet Today" sign posted on the door of its historic Carnegie building. With huge population growth in many areas, the state is doing well financially, so most libraries also are doing well. Yet, although libraries in small communities tend to say funding is good, they then go on to describe the challenge of doing more with limited resources.

About 80 percent of the state's population is located in the "Wasatch Front" – which is about 100 miles long, 30 miles wide and includes Salt Lake City, the major urban center of the state and the center of the Church of Jesus Christ of Latter-Day Saints (Mormons). Home to resorts and tourist destinations like Park City and Moab, Utah public libraries serve users from around the world. Many library directors reported they are renovating or building new library buildings to accommodate increased demand – or that they need more space and currently lack funding.

New technology is seen as positive change, but also is a challenge to all public libraries. There is a need for more computers and more space – new buildings – more bandwidth, and wireless, if they don't have it already. Many directors and staff noted that technology has improved library operations, from better and faster reference service to emailed pre-due and hold notices etc. Maintaining and servicing equipment also is challenging. Most small libraries don't have dedicated IT staff and depend on service from their city or county, where they may not have much clout.

Email, e-government, homework, genealogy databases and personal business (e.g., boarding passes, paying bills) were cited as the most used Internet services. Time limits on computers range from 30 minutes to two hours, and many libraries are using time management software to manage these sessions. In small libraries, it was noted that staff often don't have time to help people use computers. While training provided by the State Library is appreciated, keeping staff up-to-date is a widespread challenge.

There was agreement that more technology planning is needed in individual libraries and that establishing strong relationships with local government, schools, business and other partners will help increase support for new technology and for libraries in general.

Governance and Statistical Information

Utah has 72 public library systems with 113 physical library locations and 23 bookmobiles serving more than 2.3 million residents in fiscal year 2004.[139] Seventy percent of Utah's public libraries are single building systems, and nearly 28 percent have branch libraries. Utah's public libraries are organized primarily as municipal or city libraries (61 percent), and county library systems (39 percent).

In 2004, Utah public libraries reported serving more than 15.8 million visitors, answering more than 3.7 million reference questions, and circulating more than 29.5 million items (books, films, sound recordings, audio books, etc.). Utah public libraries borrowed or loaned another 33,000 items on behalf of residents, who are served by 1,082 library employees. Of these employees, 162 hold Master's degrees in Library and Information Science (MLIS) and another 302 that have been trained as librarians but do not hold a master's degree.

Utah public libraries rank 10th in the number of public-use Internet computers per building (11.96), as compared with other states. The national average is 10.32.[140]

Funding Summary

Ninety-three percent of Utah's public library funding comes from local sources (tax dollars), 1 percent from state sources, and 5.4 percent from other sources (private fundraising, gifts,

---

[139] National Center for Education Statistics. Public Libraries in the United States: Fiscal Year 2004. (NCES 2006-349). Washington, DC: NCES, 2006. http://www.nces.ed.gov/pubs2006/2006349.pdf
[140] Ibid

bequeathals, etc.). Utah ranks 26th in total operating revenue – 38th in state, 21st in local, and 34th in other.

Sixty-six percent of operating expenditures go toward staff costs (salaries, benefits, retirement), 16.7 percent toward purchasing collections, and 17.2 percent for other things, such as programming, building maintenance and utilities, and computer hardware and software. Utah ranks 24th nationally in total operating expenditures ($27.90 spent per capita) – 24th in staffing, 15th in collections, and 30th in other.

Utah public libraries reported in the *Public Libraries and the Internet 2007* survey that of those receiving E-rate discounts, Internet connectivity (77.3 percent) and telecommunications services (56 percent) were the two most commonly funded discount categories. The majority of technology expenses in both fiscal year 2006 and 2007 were paid from local and state revenue sources, and for some libraries grants were significant contributors to supporting technology purchases.

In 2004, Utah public libraries spent more than $7 million on capital expenditures (building repair, renovations, or new buildings), ranking 38th nationally.

Connectivity Summary
The Utah State Library estimates that the majority of the state's public libraries (90 percent) are on broadband connections (not dial-up), although not necessarily with high-speed or dedicated access. All Utah libraries have access to the Utah Education Network (UEN), but each library must pay a local telecom provider to be able to connect to the UEN backbone. The major connectivity issues relate to cost variation (especially in areas where smaller telecommunications providers are located) and IT staffing challenges.

As reported in the *Public Libraries and the Internet 2007* survey, 23 percent of Utah libraries have access speeds below 768kbps, 46.1 percent supported access between 769kbps-5mbps, and another 26 percent supported access at speeds greater than 6mbps.

The State Library estimated that 29 percent of Utah public libraries are vulnerable – those at greatest risk of being unable to support certain basic infrastructure, internal network services and external network services. Approximately 10 libraries are in areas with smaller telecommunications providers whose prices for connectivity are much higher than mainstream carriers. One large system and about 14 smaller public libraries do not have adequate sustained IT support.

Utah ranks third in the number of Internet users as a share of total population at 69.6 percent, compared to 58.7 percent nationwide. The state ranks last, however, in the deployment of computers and Internet use in school.[141]

In 2004, the Utah State Legislature passed a state version of the Children's Internet Protection Act. Amending Utah Code 9-7-215 and 9-7-216, in order to receive state funds, Utah public libraries must have an Internet policy regarding use of the Internet by minors and an Internet filter on all computers available to the public. This filter must be set up to block images of child

---
[141] The Information Technology & Innovation Foundation. 2007 State New Economy Index. http://www.itif.org/index.php?id=30

pornography and obscenity to all users, and items harmful to minors to users under 18. Library staff may disable the filters for adults for "research or other lawful purpose."[142]

Summary of Major Challenges
The two major challenges identified by State Library staff are:
- Need for new information technology (IT) – upgrades or replacement. Budgeting and planning for regular technology upgrades is emphasized.

- IT staff support: Rural libraries are unable to find, hire or keep IT staff. Staff expertise in smaller libraries does not systematically include IT.

A third challenge identified by nearly every library director interviewed is for additional space to better accommodate demand for public Internet access and other library resources. *"Our operating and technology budget has been adequate. Our facilities have not."*

Focus Group Summary
The project team conducted two focus groups in Utah, one at the State Library on February 20, 2007, and one at the Manti Public Library on February 21. Staff from six libraries participated on February 20, and staff from five libraries participated on February 21. We gratefully acknowledge the assistance of State Librarian Donna Jones Morris, Library Development Program Manager Douglas Adams, State Data Coordinator Juan Tomás Lee and other state library staff for hosting us, sharing their time and thoughts, and organizing the focus groups and site visits for us. We also would like to thank all of the librarians who participated in our focus groups. A complete list of focus group contributors can be found in Appendix I.

Expenditures and Fiscal Planning
The larger city and county library systems reported being in good condition fiscally. As their communities have grown, there has usually been a corresponding growth in library services and resources. All are funded primarily with property taxes, and most have dedicated tax districts. A few of the libraries reported they had built reserve funds for capital and technology projects.

Libraries in smaller communities were more likely to report that funding is OK, but then would go on to describe the reality of trying to do more with less. One director noted there was no budget growth, and she was struggling to keep enough people on staff to stay certified in the state. Another said her library has a generous budget and good support, but later mentioned that the Internet service had been down for most of a week. And another director of a very small library said, *"We have no problems…passed a bond issue last year and are doing a renovation, but would like to be open longer. People would appreciate it. If they see a light on, people show up."* Only one of the rural libraries had a dedicated tax district.

The larger libraries have separate line items for technology, most reported good relationships with their city or county IT departments, have replacement schedules for equipment, and have dedicated IT staff. One library director mentioned that the county IT department does all of the bidding for new equipment and provides telecom networking at no charge to the library.

---
[142] Utah State Library. UCIPA Frequently Asked Questions. Http://library.utah.gov/librarian_resources/laws/ucipa_faq.htm

"Our IT department has been very willing to experiment with us on things. So contrary to their instinct, they let us use some laptops that were scheduled for discard. They hate doing that sort of thing, but they put them out at the branches and made them work for wireless, so that we could expand the number of PCs we had for the public by using anchored laptops. We're now buying laptops and putting them in places where we otherwise would not be able to provide access very easily."

Even well-supported libraries face the challenge of keeping up with new technology and public demand for services. There are ever-present technology maintenance and replacement costs. Many reported they've run out of space for new technology, although demand continues to grow.

"Maintenance charges seem to just keep stacking up for each new implementation of technology. There's service, there's support, there are upgrades, and there is everything that comes along with it."

The support for technology in the small libraries is more varied, with some getting equipment and service from their city governments, and others working with local phone companies. One library receives free Internet service from its local phone company, which also has donated three computers to the library. The library has placed small sponsorship cards at each of the computers. Another of the small library directors said, *"We wouldn't have a single computer without LSTA."* Two of the directors of small libraries mentioned they had frequent problems maintaining Internet access.

Meeting Patron Technology Needs for Internet Services
The Internet services used most include:
- Email;
- E-government (e.g., tax forms, Department of Motor Vehicles forms);
- Databases (e.g., homework, genealogy, Kelly's Blue Book);
- Downloadable audiobooks; and
- Personal business (e.g., boarding passes, paying bills)

Most libraries that offer free wireless access reported significant growth in its use in the past two years. Two libraries had added electrical outlets or a "laptop lane" to accommodate the growing demand. *"As we design new buildings, that's going to more of an issue to power them (laptops) all over the library."*

One of the libraries reported remote use of the library's online resources, including that the use of the online catalog, databases and downloadable audiobooks, is "growing by leaps and bounds." The library reported 2,500 to 3,000 unique uses outside the library, with genealogy databases the most frequently used. All libraries expressed appreciation for the premier databases funded by the state and provided through the State Library, which save individual libraries as much as $200,000 a year.

Several libraries reported a growth in non-English speakers in the library. One has had great success with a locally developed software program to help teach English as a Second Language (ESL) and reports classes are "packed constantly." Staff frequently are called upon to help navigate patrons through the "maze" of getting a driver's license. *"Government e-business is a struggle for them."*

E-government can be challenging for any patron. Several library directors mentioned the prevalence of filing divorce papers online. *"That is very demanding on staff time, if you get even one. It can be very staff-intensive with people who are under unusual pressure."* The librarian reported that the courts often direct people to the library and the free public computer access they offer.

All of the libraries in the focus groups have time limits on computer use, ranging from 30 minutes to two hours. Most do not allow online chat. The larger libraries offer wireless and most report it is heavily used. The smaller libraries receive many requests for wireless but few have managed to add it to their services. Three of the large libraries are involved in digitization projects with their local newspapers.

There also was discussion regarding how technology has improved library operations and efficiency with self-check, automated sorting equipment, email newsletters, and "pre-due" notifications etc.

"Our email notices, overdue notices, courtesy notices, and hold notices are all email. That been a huge change in the way that some of our workflow happens in our circulation departments. And on a very positive side of that, also we've seen our postage drop by about $20,000 a year."

The top technology requests shared by the smaller libraries are for wireless and downloadable audiobooks. In larger libraries, the requests are for scanners, color printing (one offers color printing), and the ability to download media to iPods.

"The demand is always for the next service that can be delivered via the Web or email."

This demand also is taking a toll on available bandwidth. One focus group participant with two T1 lines at his library said they are nearly at 90 percent utilization from 4 p.m. to closing time every day.

If money were no object, the libraries would want more space – new buildings – more bandwidth, workstations, and/or laptops, plus downloadable video and more downloadable music (instead of CDs). If they don't have it already, wireless is high on their list. Two of the smaller libraries need new online catalogs.

Impact on Staff
There was agreement that technology has greatly changed staff work, and older staff members find it more difficult to adjust. Library patrons are becoming more and more sophisticated users of technology, and expect the library and library staff to be able to accommodate the full range of devices they carry to the library. All agreed Internet search tools are much better and greatly aid with reference requests. Staff now spends a lot of time managing computer use and helping people with new technology.

"As soon as we got time management software, then my staff started thinking they were librarians again. But they never – I don't think they're ever going to be librarians like they were. The questions are different. The questions are sometimes more difficult. The expectations are much higher."

Troubleshooting wireless access is taking a toll on library staff. More and more patrons are bringing their own hardware – from laptops to PDAs – to the library and asking for staff help in configuring and using the devices on the library's network. There also is a learning curve for downloading new media. *"We're in an on-demand society."*

In the smaller libraries, staff reported difficulty providing training or computer assistance for patrons due to limited staffing and available time. There also is a continuing need for staff training both to help users and to manage and use new systems for circulation. Focus group participants acknowledged that the State Library provides training, but most prefer to handle this in-house to save travel time and meet specific local needs and schedules.

Another staff impact is complying with the state Children's Internet Protection Act, both by monitoring computer use and turning filters on and off when requested by adult patrons.

Advocating Support for IT Services
The questions about increasing support for new technology – and for libraries in general – inspired spirited discussions about getting to know the local political environment and building relationships with local officials. Personal library tours and presentations to new City Council members were mentioned as ways to build knowledge and trust. *"We give a thorough tour of the library, along with a PowerPoint presentation with fun and interesting statistics. I can tell you that is one of the most worthwhile things that I do in the year. One gentleman had never been to the library before, and now he's a big library supporter."*

Another library used its development fund to pay for an outside management audit. The focus group participant credited the audit's positive findings with providing the support and background needed for the county commission to approve a tax base increase.

Another participant shared her experience advocating for library services and technology: *"It was a big surprise to a number of county officials that we're doing the volume of computer use and support that we do, and that so many people come to us. They live in this bubble that people have home computing. And now that government services have moved online, how do people get online to access those government services?"*

Good advance planning also is key to gaining respect, along with visibility and participation in the community. By planning five years in advance and following the plan, the county IT department *"trusts us more, and they become part of our success."* At least one library prepares a business case, often discussing return on investment, for each of its technology initiatives.

The smaller libraries focused even more on local partnerships with schools, other libraries, businesses and individuals. One director mentioned that her board members help with grant writing, and another has a board member who also serves on City Council. One library has a literary club that does story hour programs and fundraising, another receives regular donations for audiobooks from a trucking company, and one even has two donated cows (the library will receive funds from a local rancher after the cows are sold). This focus group also said the State Library does a good job with training and support for libraries, and the Gates grants were a turning point.

"What Gates has done is amazing...It was the first training we received, and we got help from the technicians. Having requirements made a difference..."

"Our communities can't afford to hire staff with an MLS (Master's degree in Library Science), but we know our communities, and we can get help from other places. The only free access to the Internet is through our libraries."

One director noted that some elected officials *"look at libraries as a drain. They don't bring in money."* Another shared her positive experience bringing the mayor to her library to do a storytime for kids. He was surprised by the turnout. The discussion concluded with one of the directors noting that her library is the single resource for learning that serves the whole community, and that in a recent survey, the library had the highest ranking among public services.

Site Visits Summary

The project team also visited five libraries serving populations from about 3,000 to 19,000, based on 2000 Census. One was a county library, and the others were municipal libraries. The team met and talked with library staff members, trustees and patrons. A complete list of sites visited can be found in Appendix I.

Expenditures and Fiscal Planning

Space is at a premium: Most of the communities visited have experienced growth since the decennial census. Two libraries reported that population growth has translated into new and larger library buildings within that same time period. Another library sought voter approval for a bond issue and lost. One library is completely landlocked and needs a new plot of land, as well as funding for a new building in order to expand services.

The Utah site visits included a library in a dramatic new building shared with a senior center, a rural library temporarily housed in basement of city hall while its Carnegie building is being renovated, and a bustling suburban library in what the staff described as one of the fastest-growing cities in the country. Its population was 13,000 in 2000 and is 40,000 in 2007.

Meeting Patron Technology Needs for Internet Services

The top uses reported include email, genealogy, business, e-government, schoolwork, shopping, and My Space. Most libraries visited do not allow gaming. *"The board feels like the computers should be used for more serious purposes."* Interestingly, an adult patron that uses that library about four times a week said he would like a gaming space and related teen programs for community youth – along with more computers overall. Another library that allows gaming reported that this was a major reason for time limits. *"Otherwise people would be in all day, every day."*

A surprising service that came up several times during focus group conversations and site visits was the frequency of library staff helping people get divorces online.

Many people still have dial-up access at home, so the libraries' high-speed connections are popular. Where wireless is available, it also is heavily used.

At one library, staff give an orientation and tour to the library's Web site with each new library card issued (five or 10 per day). As a result, remote use of the library Web site has quadrupled.

Time limits range from 30 minutes to two hours, and most of the libraries are acquiring time management software. Staff at one library with four public Internet workstations reported waits are frequent throughout the summer months. Patrons interviewed said they usually don't have to wait a long time, and are generally satisfied with the services they receive.

Impact on Staff

Technology is a challenge for all of the libraries visited, but most see it as providing a positive change in both service and operations. Each library has a different arrangement for keeping their tech services up-to-speed. In one small library, the city had provided tech help, but the library wasn't a priority, so found it more effective to contract with a *"geek with a sense of humor."* Another library has a building-based staffer who works for the county but 'lives' at the library.

A common issue for libraries that depend on city or county IT is the difficulty in balancing the unique needs of libraries serving the public with the local government concerns about network security. Some examples of this include: new security software installed across one county that required library workarounds to allow patrons to print and to access email accounts; whether or not to allow online chat features *("Some people are all email, others only use chat for communicating.")*; filtering; and differences in bandwidth needs between government staff and library users, particularly during the high-volume after-school hours.

A small town library had a "no Internet today" sign on the front door. Due to a problem with the state network's filtering, they had eliminated all Internet access on their five public access workstations for the previous four days. Over the course of an hour, several people came to the library hoping to get online.

In addition to keeping equipment in operation, all of the staff interviewed mentioned the challenge of keeping up with new technology trends. The speed of change and demands of increasingly savvy patrons can be intimidating for staff – particularly for those who are not regular technology users themselves. One library director in a small community said her patrons tend to be slow adaptors, and haven't made much use of online services. Most others are racing to meet the demands. Not all of the libraries have technology plans, but there is growing awareness at the board and director-level that there is a need for this. One board member is working to make regular technology planning part of the library's by-laws.

Technology has greatly changed staff work. *"Some people you have to help every single time they come in. It's a small town, so people know you and expect help."* There was the usual consensus that some staff have adapted more quickly than others, especially the younger ones. The State Library has provided training and counsel, and networking at county library meetings was also mentioned as helpful.

Advocating Support for IT Services

Several library staff and one trustee interviewed said they don't need to promote the technology services available at the library. *"People already understand it."*

A library trustee and staff at one library outlined the various factors necessary to pass a library bond issue and increased levy after a previous attempt had failed. *"We drew a picture for voters with a poll that presented concrete, hard facts"* – including community needs like space for a separate children's program space and auditorium. They also reached out to senior citizens to create a joint library building and senior citizen center for exercise space, Meals on Wheels, and public auditorium. The final deciding factor for the County Commission was the donation of two acres of land, which was matched by the county. The bond passed by 80 votes; the library square footage and operating budget have subsequently tripled.

Important community partners included: schools and community colleges, Wal-Mart (which has supplied many libraries with small grants that have supported technology and other library services) and Friends groups. Most libraries had not established relationships with the local Chambers of Commerce or community service organizations (e.g. Lions, Kiwanis).

Requests for advocacy support included: more and better statistics about library and library technology use; radio and TV public service announcements to promote library use; and workshops and materials for trustees to build advocacy skills.

APPENDIX A

2006 National Survey of Public Library Computer and Internet Access

The American Library Association and the Information Use Management and Policy Institute in the College of Information at Florida State University, with support from the Bill & Melinda Gates Foundation, are surveying a national sample of public libraries regarding their Internet connectivity and computing resources. Dr. John Carlo Bertot, Dr. Charles R. McClure, and Ms. Denise M. Davis are the study managers. You may access the survey at **http://www.plinternetsurvey.org**.

This survey provides, and has provided since 1994, valuable data regarding public library public computing resources; Internet connectivity; bandwidth; Internet service/resource funding and sources; and challenges associated with connectivity and public computing. Such data enable practitioners, policymakers, and researchers to understand the nature, extent, and changes of public library public computing and Internet connectivity. To facilitate the development advocacy strategies for public access computer and Internet services, the 2006 survey focuses on the impacts, benefits, and challenges of public computing and Internet access services in public libraries. More information regarding the overall study is available at http://www.ala.org/plinternetfunding. Data and reports from previous surveys are available at http://www.ii.fsu.edu/plinternet/.

> **Complete the survey, and enter to win one of three Apple iPod nano MP3 players!**

On the survey website, specific instructions are provided for completing the web survey. The survey contains questions about specific library system branches as well as system-wide questions. If your library system does not have branches, you essentially will be completing the questionnaire for the same library. If your library system does have branches, you may be asked to complete questions regarding *some* of your branches prior to answering questions about your entire system. Your library and the branches selected to participate (if applicable) were selected randomly. If you wish to complete the survey for the additional branches in your system (again, if applicable), you will be given the opportunity to do so – and we would certainly appreciate your additional efforts and time.

IMPORTANT: To facilitate completion of the web-based survey, the branch and system questions are presented separately. PLEASE COMPLETE BOTH PORTIONS OF THE SURVEY.

To participate in the 2006 study, please go to **http://www.plinternetsurvey.org** and follow the "Complete Survey" button. You will need to enter your library's survey ID number (see the affixed label below for that number). The survey ID number has a total of two letters followed by four numbers, and is your FSCS library number as assigned by the state library. If you cannot remember and/or locate your library's survey ID number, the survey website provides a link to locate your library ID by state and city. If you prefer, you may complete this print version of the survey and mail/fax your responses back (the contact information is located at the end of they survey).

The survey is not timed. You may complete part of it, save your answers, and return to it at a later time. You may also answer part of the survey and have other members of your library staff answer other parts, if appropriate. Please be sure to complete the survey by **February 1, 2007**. Once completed, you will be able to print or save the answers you provided and keep a copy for your own records.
If you have any questions or issues regarding the survey, please call (850) 645-5683 or e-mail pl2006@ci.fsu.edu.

A. LIBRARY BRANCH LEVEL QUESTIONS

A.1: Connectivity and Access

1a. How many **total average hours per typical week** is this library branch **open to the public**? (ENTER THE APPROPRIATE NUMBER IN THE BLANK ROUNDING TO THE NEAREST HOUR) [Note: if the branch closed within the last year, please skip to question 2)

_____ average hours/week (e.g., 30, 35)

1b. In the last year, the **total average hours per typical week** that this library branch is **open to the public has**: (MARK ONE ● ONLY AND ENTER THE APPROPRIATE NUMBER IN THE BLANK) (Please continue to Question 3)

○	Increased since last fiscal year	_____ # hours increased (round to nearest hour)
○	Decreased since last fiscal year	_____ # hours decreased (round to nearest hour)
○	Stayed the same as last fiscal year	

2. If this library branch **closed within the last year**, please indicate the **reason for the branch's closure**: (MARK ONE ● ONLY)

○	Closed temporarily due to renovations
○	Closed temporarily due to storm or other damage
○	Closed temporarily due to budgetary reasons
○	Closed permanently due to budgetary reasons
○	Closed for other reason (please specify):

3. Is this library branch currently **connected to the Internet in any way**? (MARK ONE ● ONLY)

○	No (If 'no' please skip to question 12)
○	Yes, staff access only (If 'yes' please skip to question 12)
○	Yes, public and staff access (if 'yes' please go to question 4)

4. **During a typical day**, does this library branch **have people waiting to use its public Internet workstations**? (MARK ONE ● ONLY)

○	Yes, there are consistently fewer public Internet workstations than patrons who wish to use them throughout a typical day
○	There are fewer public Internet workstations than patrons who wish to use them at different times throughout a typical day (e.g., during the morning, during lunch time, or evenings)
○	No, there are always sufficient public Internet workstations available for patrons who wish to use them during a typical day

5a. Please indicate **the number and age of the public Internet workstations** provided by this library branch (include in the count library-provided laptops and multi-purpose workstations that allow access to the Internet. Exclude workstations that only access the library's Web-based Online Public Access Catalogs). **Even if you cannot estimate the ages of the workstations, please provide the total number of workstations.** (ENTER THE APPROPRIATE NUMBERS IN THE BLANKS)

Number of Public Internet Workstations	Average Public Internet Workstation Age
_____ workstations	_____ workstations less than 1 year old
	_____ workstations 1-2 years old
	_____ workstations 2-3 years old
	_____ workstations 3-4 years old
	_____ workstations greater than 4 years old

5b. Please indicate **the total number of OTHER public workstations** not connected to the Internet provided by this library branch for patron use (e.g., multi-purpose workstations for word processing, presentation development, Online Public Access Catalog access only).

_____ other workstations

5c. Are there plans to **add additional public Internet workstations or laptops** at this library branch **during the next year**? (MARK ONE ● ONLY. IF APPLICABLE, INCLUDE THE APPROPRIATE NUMBER OF WORKSTATIONS OR LAPTOPS)

○	The library plans to add _____ workstations within the next year
○	The library plans to add _____ laptops within the next year
○	The library is considering adding more workstations or laptops within the next year, but does not know how many at this time
○	The library has no plans to add workstations or laptops within the next year
○	The library has plans to **REDUCE** the number of workstations or laptops to a total of _____ workstations and laptops within the next year

5d. Are there plans to **replace or upgrade existing public Internet workstations or laptops** at this library branch **during the next year**? (MARK ONE ● ONLY IN EACH COLUMN)

	Workstation Replacement (MARK ONE ● ONLY)		Workstation Upgrades (MARK ONE ● ONLY)
O	The library plans to replace _____ workstations within the next year	O	The library plans to upgrade _____ workstations within the next year (e.g. add memory, upgrade graphics card, etc.)
O	The library plans to replace _____ laptops within the next year	O	The library plans to upgrade _____ laptops within the next year (e.g. add memory, upgrade graphics card, etc.)
O	The library plans to replace some workstations/laptops within the next year, but does not know how many at this time	O	The library plans to upgrade some workstations/laptops within the next year, but does not know how many at this time
O	The library has no plans to replace workstations/laptops within the next year	O	The library has no plans to upgrade workstations/laptops within the next year

5e. Is the library branch able **to maintain its workstation/laptop replacement, addition, or upgrade schedule**? (MARK ONE ● ONLY)

O	Yes
O	No
O	The library has no workstation replacement, addition, or upgrade schedule
O	Not applicable

5f. Please identify **up to three factors** that affect the library branch's ability or plans to **add or replace more public Internet workstations**. (MARK ● UP TO THREE FOR EACH FACTOR)

	Factors Affecting Adding Workstations (MARK UP TO ● THREE)		Factors Affecting Replacing Workstations (MARK UP TO ● THREE)
O	Availability of space	O	Cost factors
O	Cost factors	O	Maintenance, upgrade, and general upkeep
O	Maintenance, upgrade, and general upkeep	O	Availability of staff
O	Availability of staff	O	Other (please specify):
O	Availability of bandwidth to support additional workstations		
O	Availability of electrical outlets, cabling, or other infrastructure		
O	The current number of workstations meets the needs of our patrons		
O	Other (please specify):		

6. Is **wireless Internet access available for public use** (e.g., with patron laptops, PDAs, or other wireless devices) within the library branch? (MARK ONE ● ONLY)

O	Yes, wireless access is currently available within the library branch
O	No, it is not currently available within the library branch, but there are plans to make it available within the next year
O	No, it is not currently available within the library branch and there are no plans to make it available within the next year

7. As part of the library branch's **wireless Internet access strategy**, the library branch is: (MARK ALL ● THAT APPLY)

O	Purchasing laptops for in-library patron use instead of Internet workstations
O	Not adding more Internet workstations or laptops, but is providing (or about to provide) wireless access for patrons with laptops to help to meet public demand

8. Does the library offer **wireless access for public use outside the library building** as wi-fi hotspots (e.g., in public places, buildings, or other locations) (MARK ALL ● THAT APPLY)

O	Yes, the library currently provides wireless access outside the library building and in locations within the community as a library initiative
O	Yes, the library currently provides wireless access outside the library building and in locations within the community in partnership with others (e.g., county/city government, telecommunications provider, other)
O	Yes, it is currently available outside the library building through a bookmobile with wireless access
O	No, it is not currently available outside the library building and in the community, but there are plans to make it available within the next year
O	No, it is not currently available outside the library building and in the community and there are no plans to make it available within the next year
O	Other (please specify):

9a. Please indicate the **type AND maximum speed** of this library branch's **PUBLIC Internet service connection**. (MARK APPROPRIATELY ● IN EACH COLUMN)

Type of Connection (MARK ALL ● THAT APPLY)		Maximum Speed of Connection (MARK ONE ● ONLY)	
O	DSL	O	Less than 56 Kbps (kilobits/second)
O	Cable	O	56 Kbps – 128 Kbps
O	Leased Line	O	129 Kbps – 256 Kbps
O	Municipal Networks (wireless or other)	O	257 Kbps – 768 Kbps
O	Satellite	O	769 Kbps – 1.5 Mbps (megabits/second)
O	Fiber	O	1.6Mbps – 5.0Mbps
O	Other (please specify):	O	6.0Mbps – 10Mbps
O	Don't know (If you do not know your library's connection speed, please contact an individual or group who may know before checking "Don't know")	O	Greater than 10Mbps
		O	Don't know (If you do not know your library's connection speed, please contact an individual or group who may know before checking "Don't know")

9b. If applicable, does the **library branch's wireless connection share the same bandwidth/connection** as the library's public Internet workstations? (MARK ONE ● ONLY)

○	Yes, both the wireless connection and public access workstations share the same bandwidth/connection
○	No, the wireless connection is separate from the public access workstation bandwidth/connection
○	Don't know (If you do not know if the connection is shared, please contact an individual or group who may know before checking "Don't know")

9c. Given the uses of the library branch's public Internet access services by patrons, does the library branch's **public Internet service connection speed meet patron needs**? (MARK ONE ● ONLY)

○	The connection speed is insufficient to meet patron needs
○	The connection speed is sufficient to meet patron needs at some times
○	The connection speed is sufficient to meet patron needs at all times
○	Don't know

9d. If desired, would the library branch be able to increase the **maximum speed** of its **public Internet service connection** now or in the future? (MARK ONE ● ONLY)

○	No, there is no interest in increasing the speed of the library's public access Internet connection
○	No, this is the maximum speed available to the library branch
○	Yes, but we cannot afford the cost of increasing the branch's bandwidth
○	Yes, and we have plans to increase the bandwidth within the next year
○	Yes, but we have no plans to increase the bandwidth within the next year
○	Yes, but we do not have the technical knowledge to increase the bandwidth in the library
○	Other (please specify):

A.2: Impact of Computer and Internet Access

10. Please identify **up to three public Internet services** that are critical to the **role of the library branch in its local community**? (MARK ● UP TO THREE)

○	Provide education resources and databases for K-12 students
○	Provide education resources and databases for students in higher education
○	Provide education resources and databases for home schooling
○	Provide education resources and databases for adult/continuing education students
○	Provide information for local economic development
○	Provide information about state and local business opportunities
○	Provide information for college applicants
○	Provide information for local business marketing
○	Provide information about the library's community
○	Provide information or databases regarding investments
○	Provide access to local public and local government documents
○	Provide access to federal government documents
○	Provide computer and Internet skills training
○	Provide services for job seekers
○	Provide services to new citizens and residents
○	Other (please specify):

11. Please identify the three most significant impacts **of the library's** patron information technology training **on the community that the library serves:** (MARK ● UP TO THREE)

○	The library does not offer patron information technology training
○	Facilitates local economic development
○	Offers technology training to those who would otherwise not have any
○	Helps students with their school assignments and school work
○	Helps business owners understand and use technology and/or information resources
○	Helps patrons complete job applications
○	Provides general technology skills
○	Provides information literacy skills (i.e., how to access and use Internet-based resources)
○	Helps users access and use electronic government services and resources (e.g., license applications, tax filing, other)
○	Other (please specify):

For libraries not connected to the Internet or that only provide staff access

12. Please indicate the **three most important factors** that affect **your library branch's ability to provide public Internet services**: (MARK ● UP TO THREE)

O	The library does not have space for workstations and/or necessary equipment
O	The library building cannot support the necessary infrastructure (e.g., power, cabling, other)
O	The library cannot afford the necessary equipment (i.e., workstations, routers, etc.)
O	The library does not have access to adequate telecommunications services (e.g., phone lines, leased lines, cable, other)
O	The library cannot afford the recurring telecommunications costs
O	The library does not have the staff necessary to install, maintain, and/or upgrade the necessary technology
O	The library does not control its access to Internet services (i.e., local/county government provides access)
O	There is no interest among library staff or management in connecting the library to the Internet
O	There is no interest within the local community in connecting the library to the Internet
O	Other (please specify):

B. LIBRARY SYSTEM LEVEL QUESTIONS

B.1: Public Computer and Internet Services and Community Impact

13. Please identify the **Internet-based services the library makes available to users** either in the library or remotely (i.e., website). Include services that the library may not provide directly (i.e., statewide databases, digital reference): (MARK ● ALL THAT APPLY)

Service/Resource	Service Available to Users
Digital reference/Virtual reference	O
Licensed databases	O
E-books	O
Video conferencing	O
Online instructional courses/tutorials	O
Homework Resources	O
Audio content (e.g., pod casts, audio books, other)	O
Video content	O
Digitized special collections (e.g., letters, postcards, documents, other)	O
Other (please specify):	O

14. Please indicate the **roles and services the public library provides to its community on a regular basis and/or during emergency/disaster situations**: (MARK APPROPRIATELY ● IN EACH COLUMN)

	Disaster/Emergency Services (MARK ALL ● THAT APPLY)		**E-Government Services** (MARK ALL ● THAT APPLY)
○	The library building(s) serve(s) as emergency shelters during storms, hurricanes, or other disasters	○	The library staff provide assistance to patrons applying for or accessing e-government services (e.g., completing Medicare Part D forms; applying for licenses; accessing tax forms)
○	The library staff provide emergency responder services during times of need (e.g., manage emergency call centers; assist first responders; provide relief services)	○	The library staff provide as-needed assistance to patrons for understanding how to access and use government websites, programs, and services (e.g., assistance navigating the website, helping users understand the programs)
○	The library's equipment (e.g., bookmobiles with wireless Internet access; public access workstations; laptops) is used by first responders during times of disaster	○	The library offers training classes regarding the use of government websites, understanding government programs, and completing electronic forms
○	The library's public computing and Internet access services are used by the public to access emergency relief services and benefits (i.e., FEMA) during times of disaster	○	The library is partnering with government agencies, non-profit organizations, and others to provide e-government services
○	Other (please specify):	○	Other (please specify):

15. Please indicate the following **regarding the library's disaster/emergency plan**: (MARK ● ALL THAT APPLY)

○	The library has no current written disaster preparedness plan, and is not in the process of developing such a plan
○	The library has no current written disaster preparedness plan, but is in the process of developing an emergency/disaster plan
○	The library has a current written disaster preparedness plan that provides instruction and guidance for library staff in the event of an emergency/disaster situation (note: current is defined as reviewed, revised, and/or written within the last year)
○	The library has a written disaster preparedness plan that provides instruction and guidance for library staff in the event of an emergency/disaster situation, **but it is more than one year old**
○	The library is involved in disaster and emergency planning activities at the local level (e.g., town, city, county)
○	The library's existing or plan which is underdevelopment, was developed in conjunction with local or other emergency services organizations (e.g., fire, police, disaster relief)
○	Don't Know
○	Other (please specify below):

16. Is the library the only **free of charge public computer and Internet access center** in the library's service area? (MARK ONE ● ONLY)

○	Yes, the library is the only place in the community that provides **free** public computer and Internet access services
○	No, there are other places in the community that provide **free** public computer and Internet access services (i.e., community technology centers)
○	Don't Know
○	Other (please specify):

B.2: Funding and Public Computer and Internet Services

17a. **Did the library apply for E-rate discounts** during the July 1, 2006 E-rate funding year? (MARK ONE ● ONLY)

○	Yes (If yes, please go to question 17b)
○	Yes, another organization applied on the library's behalf (If yes, please go to question 17b)
○	No (If no, skip to question 17c)
○	Unsure (If unsure, skip to question 18)

17b. If this library is, or will be, **receiving E-rate discounts during the July 1, 2006 E-rate funding year**, please indicate for which services the library receives E-rate funds: (MARK ● ALL THAT APPLY)

○	Internet connectivity
○	Telecommunications service
○	Internal connection costs

17c. If this library **did not apply for E-rate discounts in 2006**, it was because: (MARK ● ALL THAT APPLY)

○	The E-rate application process is too complicated
○	The library staff did not feel that the library would qualify
○	Our total E-rate discount is fairly low and not worth the time needed to participate in the program
○	The library receives it as part of a consortium, so therefore does not apply individually
○	The library was denied funding in the past
○	The library did not apply because of the need to comply with CIPA's (Children's Internet Protection Act) filtering requirements
○	The library has applied for E-rate in the past, but no longer finds it necessary
○	Other (please specify):

18. Did your **state library, state legislature, or other state agency/office** pay directly for any of the following on your library's behalf: (MARK ● ALL THAT APPLY)

Expenditure Category	State Funding Sources Fiscal Year FY2006	FY2007
Staff only hardware	___	___
Staff only software	___	___
Public computing hardware	___	___
Public computing software	___	___
Telecommunications services (including Internet connectivity)	___	___
Wireless access (hardware, software)	___	___
Instructional technology (video conferencing hardware and software, projection equipment)	___	___
Licensed resources (databases, e-books, audio books, etc.)	___	___

19. Please indicate in **whole dollars your library's total operating expenditures** from all funding sources for **fiscal years 2006 and 2007**:

	Fiscal Year 2006 Expense Category		
Source of Funding	Salaries (**including benefits**)	Collections	Other Expenditures
Local/county	$	$	$
State (including state aid to public libraries, or state-supported tax programs)	$	$	$
Federal	$	$	$
Fees/fines	$	$	$
Donations/local fund raising	$	$	$
Grants (local, state or national grant programs)	$	$	$

	Fiscal Year 2007 Expense Category		
Source of Funding	Salaries (**including benefits**)	Collections	Other Expenditures
Local/county	$	$	$
State	$	$	$
Federal	$	$	$
Fees/fines	$	$	$
Donations/local fund raising	$	$	$
Grants (local, state or national grant programs)	$	$	$

20. Please indicate in **whole dollars your library's total technology-related operating expenditures** from the below funding sources for **fiscal years 2006 and 2007**:

	Fiscal Year 2006 Expense Category			
Source of Funding	Salaries (**including benefits**)	Hardware	Software	Telecommunications
Local/county	$	$	$	$
State (including state aid to public libraries, or state-supported tax programs)	$	$	$	$
Federal	$	$	$	$
Fees/fines	$	$	$	$
Donations/local fund raising	$	$	$	$
Grants (local, state or national grant programs)	$	$	$	$

	Fiscal Year 2007 Expense Category			
Source of Funding	Salaries (**including benefits**)	Hardware	Software	Telecommunications
Local/county	$	$	$	$
State (including state aid to public libraries, or state-supported tax programs)	$	$	$	$
Federal	$	$	$	$
Fees/fines	$	$	$	$
Donations/local fund raising	$	$	$	$
Grants (local, state or national grant programs)	$	$	$	$

21. Please **estimate to the nearest whole dollar** how much your library **spent on the following technology-related expenditures** (including staffing):

	Fiscal Year FY2006	Fiscal Year FY2007
Expenditure Category		
Staff only hardware	$	$
Staff only software	$	$
Public use computing hardware	$	$
Public use computing software	$	$
Telecommunications services (including Internet connectivity, and may include e-rate discount if applicable)	$	$
Wireless access (hardware, software)	$	$
Instructional technology (video conferencing hardware and software, projection equipment)	$	$
Licensed resources (databases, e-books, audio books, etc.)	$	$
Staff in technology support positions in the library or under contract to the library for such support	$	$
Staff providing technology-related training to library staff or the public (other than those reported above)	$	$

THANK YOU FOR YOUR PARTICIPATION

For questions concerning the survey, please contact:

John Carlo Bertot <pl2006@ci.fsu.edu>
Professor and Associate Director
Information Use Management and Policy Institute
College of Information
Florida State University
244 Shores Building
Tallahassee, FL 32306
(850) 645-5683 phone
(850) 644-4522 fax

GLOSSARY OF SURVEY ABBREVIATIONS/KEY TERMS

CIPA (Children's Internet Protection Act)	A Federal law requiring the use of filters on public access Internet workstations (see below) when the library receives either LSTA or E-rate (see below) funds.
Digital Reference/ Virtual Reference	The provision of interactive reference services for patrons via email, chat, or other electronic means.
E-books	Digital documents, licensed or not, where searchable text is prevalent, and which can be seen as analogous to a printed text. (Based on NISO Standard Z39.7 definition, see http://www.niso.org/emetrics)
E-rate Funds	Funding provided by the federal government through the Universal Service Fund to libraries to cover expenses associated with Internet access.
Fiscal Year	A financial 12-month period as reckoned for reporting, accounting, and/or taxation purposes (i.e., the date range that a library uses in reporting to local government agencies).
Funding Sources	**Local/county government** - Includes all tax and non-tax receipts designated by the community, district, or region and available for expenditure by the library. The value of any contributed or in-kind services or the value of any gifts and donations are excluded. **State** - All funds distributed to the library by State government for expenditure by the library, except for federal money distributed by the State. This includes funds from such sources as penal fines, license fees, and mineral rights. **Federal** - All federal government funds distributed to the library for expenditure by the library, including federal money distributed by the State. **Other** - All income other than that included under local, state and federal. Includes grants from non-profit organizations or corporations, donations from Friends as well as other donations, gifts, interest, fines, and fees. The value of any contributed services or the value of in-kind gifts and donations are excluded.
Hours Open in a Typical Week	Report an unduplicated count of hours a library facility or facilities are open in a typical week, including the main library and branches, using the following method. If a library is open from 9 a.m. to 5 p.m., Monday through Friday, it should report 40 hours per week. If several of its branches are also open during those hours, the figure remains 40 hours per week. Should Branch A also be open one evening from 7:00 to 9:00, the total hours during which users can find service becomes 42. If Branch B is open the same hours on the same evening, the total remains 42, but if it is open two hours on another evening, or from 5:00 to 7:00 on the evening when Branch A is open later, the total becomes 44 hours during which users can find service. Collect service hours separately from hours a library facility is open.
Information Technology Budget	Funds allocated specifically the costs associated with information technology.
Information Technology Training	Formal or informal training sessions that cover specific topics (e.g., Web browser basics, Internet searching, basic computing skills).
Kbps	Kilobits per second.

GLOSSARY OF SURVEY ABBREVIATIONS/KEY TERMS

Library Branch	A library facility. In the case of some public libraries, there is only one facility. Other public libraries have several facilities, which are sometimes referred to as branches.
Licensed Databases	Collection of electronically stored data or unit records (facts, bibliographic data, and texts) with a common user interface and software for the retrieval and manipulation of the data. Licensed databases are those typically contracted through a vendor by the library for patron access (e.g., Gale, Ebsco, ProQuest). (Based on NISO Standard Z39.7 definition, see http://www.niso.org/emetrics)
Mbps	Megabits per second.
Online Public Access Catalogs (OPACs)	An electronic catalog of library materials and/or services that patrons can access.
Operating Expenses	Current and recurrent costs necessary for the provision of library services, such as personnel, library materials, binding, supplies, repair or replacement of existing furnishings and equipment, and costs incurred in the operation and maintenance of the physical facility. Operating expense categories include: **Salaries/benefits -** All monies paid before deductions to all library staff paid from library's budget (reporting unit's budget) for work performed. This definition INCLUDES employee fringe benefits. Professional staff are staff members doing work that requires professional education (the master's degree or its equivalent) in the theoretical and scientific aspects of librarianship; also, in some libraries, staff performing professional level tasks who, though not librarians, have equivalent education and training in related fields (e.g., archives, computer sciences, business administration, education). Also include paid support staff and paid student workers. **Collections -** All expenditures for materials purchased or leased for use by the public, such as print materials (including microforms), machine-readable materials, audio-visual materials, etc. **Other expenditures -** Operating expenditures not included in any other expenditure subcategory. (Also called Miscellaneous Expenditures).
Public Internet Workstations	Those workstations (see below) within the library outlet that provide public access to the Internet, including those that provide access to a limited set of Internet-based services such as online databases. This includes circulating laptops.
Public library single outlet system or library system headquarters	A library system may be a single main or central library, or may be the operational center of a multiple-outlet library. Usually all processing is centralized here and the principal collections are housed here.
Public library branch	A branch library is an auxiliary unit of an administrative entity which has at least all of the following: 1) Separate quarters; 2) An organized collection of library materials; 3) Paid staff; and 4) Regularly scheduled hours for being open to the public.

	GLOSSARY OF SURVEY ABBREVIATIONS/KEY TERMS
Technology-Related Expenditures	Include Computer Hardware, Software, Supplies and Maintenance expenditures, and Electronic Access Expenditures. Computer Hardware, Software, Supplies and Maintenance expenditures are defined as expenditures from the library budget for computer hardware and software used to support library operations, whether purchased or leased, mainframe or microcomputer. Includes expenditures for maintenance and for equipment used to run information service products when that expenditure can be separated from the price of the product. Electronic Access Expenditures are defined as all operating expenditures from the library budget associated with access to electronic materials and services. Include computer hardware and software used to support library operations, whether purchased or leased, mainframe and microcomputer. Includes expenditures for maintenance. Includes expenditures for services provided by national, regional, and local bibliographic utilities, networks, consortia and commercial services. Includes all fees and usage costs associated with such services as OCLC FirstSearch or electronic document delivery. Excludes capital expenditures.
Typical Week	A "typical week" is a time that is neither unusually busy nor unusually slow. Avoid holidays, vacation periods, days when unusual events are taking place in the community or in the library. Choose a week in which the library is open regular hours.
Wireless Internet Access	Internet access that does not require a direct connection (typically Ethernet) for access. Most typically, wireless access adheres to the IEEE 802.11 standard for interoperability and compatibility.
Workstation	A computer and related components (including a monitor, keyboard, hard drive, and software) that are capable of displaying graphical images, pictorial representations, and/or other multi-media formats.

APPENDIX B
2006-07 Chief Officers Of State Library Agencies Questionnaire

1. State: _____ 2. Contact(s):_____
3. E-mail: _____ 4. Phone: _____
   Please consult with your State Data Coordinators, technology staff or other units as needed.

A. Broadband connectivity
Broadband connectivity is defined as a connection that is direct, "always on," not a dial up connection.

5. What percentage of public libraries in your state would you say have broadband connectivity?

O	under 25%
O	between 26 and 50%
O	between 51 and 75%
O	between 76% and 90%
O	over 90%

Comments (e.g., if you are basing your estimate on recent internal survey data can you identify and supply?):

6. How do public libraries in your state achieve broadband connectivity? Check all that apply:

O	directly through a local telecommunications company
O	through the local school district
O	through the local city/county government
O	through a regional telecommunications network
O	through a regional **library** telecommunications network
O	through a state telecommunications network (education, research, etc.)
O	though a state telecommunications **library** network
O	Other (Describe):

Comments:

7. What are major barriers to state's public library broadband connectivity? Check all that apply:

O	Few or no barriers
O	Capacity for connectivity does not exist in all parts of the state
O	Too many telecommunication companies for any statewide coordination
O	Cost for broadband connectivity is too high
O	State telecommunication policy (be specific below)
O	No expertise by library staff at the local level to implement or sustain broadband connectivity
O	Other (Describe):

Comments:

B. Vulnerably Networked Public Libraries

The definition for a vulnerably networked public library is a work in progress and one we would like your help to better define (see question 9). But begin with the following definition. A vulnerably networked public library is at risk of being unable to offer, in whole or in part:

- Access to electronic services within the library (e.g., offers public access Internet capable workstations, an OPAC or ILS); or,
- Network services external to the library (e.g., offers a library web site with content easily updated and controlled by the local library); or,
- Infrastructure to support internal or external networked services (e.g., library has sufficient broadband connectivity; ability to maintain or replace IT; or, has access to or employs locally available, library dedicated, IT staff).

8. Estimate how many "vulnerably networked public libraries" there are in your state that might accept and derive long term benefit from external assistance in any form? _____
Comment: (If it helps, please mention specific public libraries in your state)

9. Are there measurable criteria you could suggest which would better specify and help you more accurately identify "vulnerably networked public libraries" in your state?

Criteria Defining a Vulnerably Networked Public Library	
Criterion/Measure used	**Rationale for using criterion**
e.g., Library does not have broadband connectivity	e.g., Library cannot effectively offer internal or external network services without broadband connectivity.

Comments: (If it helps, please mention specific public libraries in your state)

10. What connectivity, IT, economic, political, staff and other challenges will vulnerably networked public libraries in your state, or a region of the state, face during the next three years?

Challenges faced by the State's Vulnerably Networked Public Libraries	
Challenge	**Description and Discussion**
Connectivity/Telecom.	e.g., 10 public libraries do not have a broadband connection, state library has offered to fully fund connection but local provider says area connections are not profitable and has refused so far. State Library has not had time or expertise to investigate other alternatives.
Challenge	**Description and Discussion**
IT	
Challenge	**Description and Discussion**
Economic	
Challenge	**Description and Discussion**
Political	
Challenge	**Description and Discussion**
Staff	
Challenge	**Description and Discussion**
Other	

Comments: (If it helps, please mention specific public libraries in your state)

C. Successfully networked public libraries with a limited local economic or population base

This definition is a work in progress as well. A successfully networked public library or library system with a limited local economic or population base has maintained broadband connectivity, IT and has developed networked services even though its' population served, or economic, or political or community circumstances suggest it would be unlikely to do so.

11. Can you identify and briefly describe 3-4 successfully networked public libraries with a limited local economic or population base in your state that might supply clues to enable other public libraries to succeed or suggest ways external partners might assist? Behind the question: The study team might wish to contact these libraries or conduct a site visit to the libraries.

Unexpectedly successfully networked public libraries				
A.) **Library Name**	Contact	E-mail	Phone
Brief description/What we might learn:			
B.) **Library Name**	Contact	E-mail	Phone
Brief description/What we might learn:			
C.) **Library Name**	Contact	E-mail	Phone
Brief description/What we might learn:			
D.) **Library Name**	Contact	E-mail	Phone
Brief description/What we might learn:			

Comments:

D. External Partner Assistance Needed by Vulnerably Networked Public Libraries

12. What types of assistance might external partners (including the state library, ALA, external funders and others) provide to your state's vulnerably networked public libraries to demonstrably improve (within a 3-5 year timeframe) and sustain their networked resources and services?

Recommended Assistance to Improve & Sustain Funding & Technology Access in Public Libraries	
Assistance Needed	**Demonstrable impact**

Comments:

APPENDIX C
Focus group questions/script

Introduction
Thank you all for being here and helping us better understand the local economic and political environment for supporting technology access and funding in your libraries. We expect today's session will take about two hours, and we will be asking a few questions in four major areas: expenditures and fiscal planning, Internet services, staffing for technology and local support for technology efforts. All the information you provide here will be confidential, unless you give us permission to quote you.

Expenditures and Fiscal Planning
One of the difficult questions we're trying to answer has to do with ways libraries fund technology access. We know that many libraries don't break out technology expenses, but we're hoping you can help us better understand how you fund and sustain technology access.

1. Tell us about your fiscal climate. Has the funding environment for your library improved, declined or stayed the same in the last few years? [[For instance, has a tax cap or supermajority requirement been put in place? Has your tax base changed?]]

2. How do you currently pay for the various aspects of IT? By this, I mean do you fund these items with grants, private fundraising, general operating budget, line item, etc. – local, state, federal or private funding
    i. New, replacement or upgrades of hardware
    ii. Software
    iii. Telecom/connectivity
    iv. Wireless
    v. Licensed resources
    vi. IT staff – tech support and/or tech trainers

3. Now, can you tell us what obstacles you face to securing and sustaining dedicated local funding for IT – public and private?

    PROBE: If you're the only provider of free computing in your community, is this a benefit or a burden in your efforts to maintain and upgrade your infrastructure?

4. On the flip side, please describe successes you've had in identifying, securing and sustaining local funds (such as empowerment or community development funds) for technology.

    PROBE: Was there a "tipping point" or a key factor or player that made the difference?

Meeting Patron Technology Needs for Internet Services

Technology-based services are both active and passive. By active, we mean the library plans and supports various services (training, collection development, downloadable audio, going to wireless access, etc.). By passive, we mean those services the patron requests through a discovery process (they hear about a Web site that supports a hobby or business activity they are engaged in). As you think about such services:

5. What are the Internet-based services or resources most frequently used by patrons?

   PROBE: Does your library support online collaboration utilities - software or sites – such as chat services, online sharing utilities like YouTube, Facebook, etc.

   PROBE: Does your library offer downloadable audiobooks or other media? How about gaming?

   PROBE: Does your library offer wireless access? Do you check out laptops for in-library use? Can people send documents to print while using wireless access?

   PROBE: Does your library support e-government services (such as completing IRS forms or registering for Medicare or local services)? Have you seen an increase in this use?

   PROBE: Does your library support online continuing education or training resources via the Internet?

   PROBE: How does your library spot the next "new and hottest" thing and work on offering and adapting it into your services?

   PROBE: How often is it the case (rare/once a month/once a week/more often) that you have one or more computers unavailable to the public because it's broken or the network is down? What is the process for getting the computer back in working order – how long does that usually take?

   PROBE: Can you tell us a little about who the most frequent users of these services are – children, teens, seniors?

6. Do you receive requests for Internet-based services the library doesn't provide? For what? How do you manage these requests?

7. If resources were not an issue, what is the single most important improvement that could be made in your public access computing services at this time?

Impact on Staff
Knowing all of the different impacts technology can have in a community, we'd like to focus now on the impacts technology access has on your staff.

8. What have been the two or three biggest impact of technology on your staff in the last 12 months? (For example, enforcing time limits, troubleshooting hardware, gaming, managing a large network, etc.)

9. What are the two or three biggest challenges you face in staffing technology? For instance:
    o Providing training to library patrons
    o Troubleshooting hardware/software/network issues
    o Managing the network and network equipment
    o Getting staff training on new Internet content and resources
    o Fundraising or advocacy for new technology
    o Marketing or outreach around technology offerings
    o Not enough staff overall
    o Not enough computers to meet needs
    o Other

    PROBE: Are you using more non-MLS staff (either IT or paraprofessional) for these needs?

    PROBE: Do you have dedicated IT staff? If so, how many? Do you outsource IT support or planning? Does your state library agency or county/local government provide this?

    PROBE: If you rely on an outside entity for your IT, can you tell us a little about the pros and cons of this arrangement? How is funding for library technology determined/affected?

Advocating Support for IT Services
From information libraries provided in the 2006 ALA public library funding study and the FSU Internet connectivity study, we know that many libraries have been flat funded for several years – which ultimately means less money for the library over time. We also know libraries continue to be asked to do more with the same flat funds. We'd like to get a better understanding of what your local "climate" is like, and what opportunities or partnerships you may have found to increase the library's capacity.

10. What types of support – both monetary and non-monetary (such as contributed services, IT support) – does the library receive from local government and others within the community for technology?

11. What other types of support would you find helpful?

PROBE: Do your library trustees/Friends speak out/advocate in support of funding for library IT, Internet connectivity, and other Internet-based resources and services?

PROBE: Have others in the community spoken out? If so, who and how?

12. How do you best show or illustrate the value of the library and its technology access to decisionmakers?

PROBE: Do you collect feedback/stories about how technology-based services make a difference for people in your community? Do you quantify the value of the technology services offered by your library? If so, how?

PROBE: Are there new library users as a result of new technology and services? Have they generated new support for the library and its services?

13. Have you successfully mobilized library users to support the library? If so, how did you do it (strategies)?

PROBE: Would you use resources from a national advocacy campaign in your local community? What would be most helpful to you?

Conclusion
14. Bottom line: What are your library's/community's biggest needs in terms of IT?
15. Do you have any other thoughts/comments about your library's needs, public libraries in general and what would be needed to meet them? If not, what are the challenges?

APPENDIX D
Follow-up questions emailed to focus group participants

Technology planning
- Is your planning for library technology integrated in any way with community (city/county) technology planning? If so, how?

Technology staffing
- How much staff time would you estimate is used addressing patron needs related to technology and related services? Would you say:
  - 10 percent of time
  - 25 percent of time
  - More than 50 percent of their time?

- Can you give us an approximate idea of how much more staff time is going to technology concerns now versus a few years ago?
  - Less time
  - No change
  - 10 percent increase
  - 25 percent increase
  - More than 50 percent increase

Funding
- How would you raise local matching funds for a library technology grant?

- Have you asked voters for increased library funding? When? Were you successful? What factor(s) most influenced the vote, do you think?

Advocacy
- Are there statewide advocacy training initiatives or campaigns that have been implemented from the state library?

- Did you/or your library participate?

- Was the training/campaign beneficial? Why or why not?

- Have you received other advocacy training? From whom? Was this useful?

- What kind of advocacy training would be helpful to you?

YOUR NAME & LIBRARY _____

Thanks!!!

APPENDIX E
Site visit questions

(Library staff)
- When is your busiest time of day? Are there waits to use the computers? Do patrons sign up to use computers?

- What are the Internet-based services or resources most frequently used by patrons?
    - Do you receive requests for Internet-based services the library doesn't provide? For what? How do you manage these requests?

- Has the technology changed the way you serve your users? How?
    - What is the biggest impact of the technology on your time during the workday (helping people find information online, e-government, online job forms, enforcing time limits, troubleshooting hardware, gaming, providing training)?

- Are your technology users different or the same as users of other library services (more teens, for instance)?
    - Who are your most frequent users of the computers and technology (children, HS students, adults, senior citizens, tourists)?

- If resources were not an issue, what is the single most important improvement that could be made in your public access computing services at this time?

(Library trustee/other influentials)
- How do you see your role in supporting the library and its technology services?

- Who do you see as the library's key partners and advocates in the community (Friends, City Council, community service organization, school administrators)?

- What has the library board done to increase support (financial or non-monetary) for the library? Did the Board work with library staff or other groups/organizations to improve support?

- How do you best show or illustrate the value of the library and its technology access to your community?

- What do you see are the most important Internet-based services or resources the library provides your community?

- How would you describe the fiscal climate in your community?

- If resources were not an issue, what is the single most important improvement that could be made in your public access computing services at this time?

(Library users)
- Why is it important for the library to offer computers and technology (even if you don't use them)?

- For people using the library computers - What do you use them for (gaming, research, e-mail, learning new software)?

- How could the library best improve its technology (more computers, more software, training, wireless access, gaming)?

- Do you have a computer at home? At work? At school?

APPENDIX F
Delaware focus group and site visit participants

Focus group participants
- Bridgeville Public Library
- Delmar Public Library
- Georgetown Public Library
- Lewes Public Library
- Milton Library
- South Coastal Library
- Seaford Public Library

Delaware site visit locations
- Bridgeville Public Library
- Georgetown Public Library
- Milford Public Library
- Rehoboth Beach Public Library

APPENDIX G

Maryland focus group and site visit participants

<u>Focus group participants</u>
April 4, 2007
- Allegany County Library System
- Baltimore County Public Library
- Caroline County Public Library
- Carroll County Public Library
- Montgomery County Public Libraries

April 17, 2007
- Anne Arundel County Public Library
- Dorchester County Public Library
- Ruth Enlow Library of Garrett County
- Worcester County Library

<u>Maryland site visit locations</u>
- Catonsville Library (Baltimore County Public Library)
- East Columbia Branch Library (Howard County Library)
- Elkridge Branch Library (Howard County Library)
- Hyattsville Branch (Prince George's County Memorial Library System)
- La Plata Branch (Charles County Public Library)
- Woodlawn Library (Baltimore County Public Library)

APPENDIX H
Nevada focus group and site visit participants

Focus group participants
- Lyon County Public Library
- Nevada State Library & Archives
- Storey County Public Library
- Mineral County Public Library
- Douglas County Public Library
- Carson City Library
- Pershing County Library
- Carson City Library
- Elko-Lander-Eureka County Library System
- Churchill County Library

Nevada site visit locations
- Boulder City Public Library, Boulder City
- Carson City Public Library, Carson City
- Fernley Branch Library, (Lyon County Library System)
- Humboldt County Library, Winnemucca
- Indian Springs Library (Las Vegas-Clark County Library District)
- Las Vegas Library (Las Vegas-Clark County Library District)
- North Las Vegas Public Library Main Branch
- Pahrump Community Library, Pahrump
- Paseo Verde Library (Henderson District Public Libraries)
- Pershing County Library, Lovelock
- Rainbow Library (Las Vegas-Clark County Library District)
- Silver-Stage Branch Library (Lyon County Library System)
- Storey County Public Library, Virginia City
- Winnemucca Public Library, Winnemucca (in Humboldt County)

APPENDIX I
Utah focus group and site visit participants

Focus group participants
- Davis County Library
- Ephraim Public Library
- Gunnison Civic Library
- Logan Library
- Manti Public Library
- Mount Pleasant Public Library
- Park City Library
- Salt Lake County Library System
- Salina Public Library
- Springville Public Library
- Weber County Library System

Utah site visit locations
- Brigham City Library
- Wasatch County Library
- Ephraim Public Library
- Mount Pleasant Public Library
- Lehi City Public Library

Printed in the United States
98085LV00003B/1-130/A